Join the Recomme
Travelers' C

MW01166362

The Recommended Country Inns® guides are the preeminent guidebooks to the finest country inns in the United States. Authors personally visit and recommend each establishment listed in the guides, and **no fees are solicited or accepted for inclusion in the books.**

Now the Recommended Country Inns® guides offer a special new way for travelers to enjoy extra savings: through the Recommended Country Inns® Travelers' Club. Member benefits include savings such as:

- Discounts on accommodations
- Discounts on food
- Discounts on local attractions

How to Save: Read the profile for each inn to see if it offers an incentive to members. For participating establishments, look for information at the end of the inn's profile or in the index at the end of the book. Simply mention that you are a member of the Recommended Country Inns® Travelers' Club when making reservations, and show your membership card when you check in. All offers are subject to availability.

How to Join: If you wish to become a member of the Recommended Country Inns® Travelers' Club, simply fill out the attached form and send it by mail to:

Recommended Country Inns® Travelers' Club
c/o The Globe Pequot Press
P.O. Box 833
Old Saybrook, CT 06475
Or fax to: 860–395–2855

A membership card will be mailed to you upon receipt of the form. Please allow 4-6 weeks for delivery.

Sign up today and start saving as a Recommended Country Inns® Travelers' Club member!

(All offers from participating inns expire November 30, 1998, unless otherwise mentioned.)

Recommended Country Inns® Travelers' Club

Membership Form

Name: ____

Address: ____

City ______________________________ State ________ Zip __________

Phone ________________ Fax ________________ E-mail ______________________

Age: 18–35 _____; 36–50______; over 50________

Sex: Male ____ Female ____ Marital Status: Single _____ Married______

Annual Household Income:

under $35,000 _________; $35,000–$75,0000 _________; over $75,000_________

Credit cards: Mastercard_____; Visa ______; Amex _______; Discover _____; Other ________

Book purchased at: Store Name: ________________; City __________________, State ______

Mail completed form to:

Recommended Country Inns® Travelers' Club
c/o The Globe Pequot Press
P.O. Box 833
Old Saybrook, CT 06475
Or fax to: 860–395–2855

RO

RECOMMENDED COUNTRY INNS SERIES

Recommended Romantic Inns™ of America

Third Edition

by
Julianne Belote ❧ Brenda Boelts Chapin
Doris Kennedy ❧ Eleanor S. Morris ❧ Sara Pitzer
Bob Puhala ❧ Elizabeth Squier
(the Authors of the Recommended Country Inns® Series)

A Voyager Book

Old Saybrook, Connecticut

Copyright © 1992, 1994, 1997 by The Globe Pequot Press, Inc.
Illustrations copyright © 1992, 1994, 1997 by The Globe Pequot Press, Inc.

All rights reserved. No part of this book may be reproduced or transmitted in any form by any means, electronic or mechanical, including photocopying and recording, or by any information storage and retrieval system, except as may be expressly permitted by the 1976 Copyright Act or by the publisher. Requests for permission should be made in writing to The Globe Pequot Press, P.O. Box 833, Old Saybrook, Connecticut 06475.

Cover design: Mullen & Katz
Map design: Nancy Freeborn
Text design: Saralyn D'Amato-Twomey

Recommended Romantic Inns is a trademark of The Globe Pequot Press, Inc.

ISBN 0-7627-0007-6
ISSN 1078-554X

Manufactured in the United States of America
Third Edition/First Printing

Contents

Romantic Inn-Sights ... vi
How to Use This Inn Guide ... vii
New England ... 1
Mid-Atlantic and Chesapeake Region ... 49
The South ... 97
The Midwest ... 145
The Southwest ... 193
Rocky Mountain Region ... 241
West Coast ... 289

Indexes

Alphabetical Index to Inns ... 336
Inns on or near Lakes or Rivers ... 338
Inns at or near the Seashore ... 339
Inns with, or with Access to, a Swimming Pool ... 339
Inns with Downhill or Cross-Country Skiing Nearby ... 340
Inns with, or with Access to, Golf or Tennis Facilities ... 341
Inns with a Sauna, Whirlpool, or Hot Tub ... 341
Inns with a Full-Service Dining Room or Dinners Available by Special Arrangement ... 342
Inn with Bicycles, Canoes, or Other Sports Equipment ... 343
Inns Offering Travelers' Club Benefits ... 343

Romantic Inn-Sights

When the mind and body have been kept too long to the tasks and worries of the workplace and, yes, even to those of the old homestead, the spirit rebels and begs for attention. "Ah, but for a little romance," your inner voice may sigh. This book is for you.

Describe romance in any terms you like, and you're likely to find an inn in these pages to satisfy your yearnings. Take your partner's hand and prepare to soak up delight after delicious delight at one of these most soul-soothing hostelries.

Researched and selected by seven incurable romantics, the inns profiled here define romance. If you are looking for starlight and moonglow, soft rain and sea breezes, shimmering sunsets and breathtaking vistas, Mother Nature will provide them. If you need candlelight, bubble baths, champagne, porch swings, fabulous food, breakfast in bed, carriage rides, secluded picnics, and turret bedchambers, the inns will provide them. And if you need whispered promises, urgent kisses, and passion of any sort these inns inspire you to kindle, *you* will provide them. True romance, after all, is what you bring with you.

Among these romantic establishments are inns at the seashore and inns in the mountains; inns miles (but not too many miles) from nowhere and inns close to hubs of culture and entertainment; inns with room for scores of travelers and inns with room for just a few (or even only two). The authors have chosen island inns, city inns, inns that provide gourmet meals and inns that will guide you to fine restaurants. Many of the inns are in historic structures; some are new or nearly new; but all share the ambience that harkens back to quieter times.

As in other volumes of the Recommended Country Inns® series, every inn in this book has been personally visited. Their inclusion depends on meeting the highest standards of atmosphere, service, comfort, hospitality, hist-ory, and location: the elements that make inn travel unique. Where but at an inn can you relax near a crackling fire, sipping wine or feeding each other strawberries? Where else can you stroll through glorious gardens to secluded benches and arbors specially placed so that none but the roses will hear your murmurs?

These innkeepers have endeavored to ensure your pleasure, delight your senses, renew your spirit, and relight your passion. Our authors have endeavored to share their experience that, for any excuse at all, you can rendezvous most romantically at each and every one of these memorable inns.

How to Use This Inn Guide

This in guide contains descriptions of 140 inns in seven regions of the United States. These inns were selected by the authors of The Globe Pequot Press's seven regional *Recommended Country Inns®* guides as the most romantic inns in their regions. *All inns were personally visited by the authors. There is no charge of any kind for an inn to be included in this or any other Globe Pequot Press inn guide.*

The guide is arranged geographically by region, beginning along the Atlantic Ocean. These regions, in order, are: New England; Mid-Atlantic and Chesapeake Region; the South; the Midwest; the Southwest; Rocky Mountain Region; and the West Coast. Within each region, the states are listed alphabetically; within each state, the towns are arranged alphabetically.

Preceding each region's listings is a regional map and a numbered legend of the twenty romantic inns found in that region. The map is marked with corresponding numbers to show where the inns are located.

Indexes: At the back of the book are various special-category indexes to help you find inns located on a lake or at the seashore, inns with golf or tennis, inns with skiing, inns with swimming pools, and more. There is also an alphabetical index of all the inns in this book.

Rates: The guidebook quotes current low and high rates to give you an indication of the price ranges you can expect. They are more than likely to change slightly with time. Be sure to call ahead and inquire about the rates as well as the taxes and service charges. The following abbreviations are used throughout the book to let you know exactly what, if any, meals are included in the room price.

EP: European Plan. Room without meals.
EPB: Room with full breakfast. (No abbreviation is used when continental breakfast is included.)
MAP: Modified American Plan. Room with breakfast and dinner.
AP: American Plan. Room with breakfast, lunch, and dinner.

Credit cards: MasterCard and Visa are accepted unless the description says "No credit cards." Many inns also accept additional credit cards.

Reservations and deposits: These are so often required that they are not mentioned in any description. Assume that you'll generally have to pay a deposit to reserve a room, using a personal check or a credit card. Be sure to inquire about refund policies.

Pets: No pets are allowed unless otherwise stated in the description. Always let innkeepers know in advance if you are planning to bring a pet.

Wheelchair access: Some descriptions mention wheelchair access, but other inns may be feasible for the handicapped. Therefore, if you're interested in an inn, call to check if there is a room suitable for a handicapped person.

Air conditioning: The description will indicate if an inn has rooms with air conditioning. Keep in mind, however, that there are areas of the country where air conditioning is totally unnecessary. For example, in the Rocky Mountain region, where the inn is at a high elevation (stated in the description), you will be comfortable without air conditioning.

Television: Some inns offer televisions and VCRs in guest rooms; the room description will mention if the rooms are so equipped. Sometimes there's a television or VCR in a common room. *Note:* Most innkeepers say there is so much to do at the inn or in the area that guests generally don't watch television. In addition, most inns inspire true romantics to engage in pleasures the television can't enhance.

Telephone: Assuming that when you yearn for romance you want to get away from it all, the descriptions generally do not state if you will find a telephone in your room.

Smoking: More than 60 percent of these inns forbid or restrict smoking. See the *Rooms* entry of each profile for specific information.

BYOB: It is often acceptable to bring your own bottle, especially if an inn has no bar service. If you see no mention of BYOB or a bar in the description, you may want to check in advance.

Meals: Most of the inns profiled offer dinner as well as breakfast. Those that do not are more than happy to make reservations for you at fine, nearby restaurants. Some inns also offer brunches, lunches, hors d'oeuvres, or afternoon tea. The authors often indicate some favorite foods they enjoyed at an inn, but you should not expect the menu to remain the same forever. Menus usually change seasonally or monthly. The description of the inn's food should give you a general idea of the meals served; with notice, innkeepers and chefs are happy to fill special dietary requests or create celebration cakes or the like.

Recommended Country Inns® Travelers' Club: Please observe the discount, free night's stay, or other value offered by inns welcoming club members. Note that all discounts listed refer to room rates only, not to meals, and that most offers are subject to availability.

A final word: The authors have convinced the editors that these innkeepers are themselves the soul of romance. Drink deeply of their sweet ministerings and renew the promises romance makes so easy to whisper.

New England

by Elizabeth Squier

New England is a very special place, and you the visitor are in for a special treat whatever season you decide to come. Spring is so romantic; the trees bud and flowers poke up from sometimes-lingering snow. The birds do their mating dances; beautiful swans sit on their nests. Oh, yes—romance is all around. Country inns are a special part of the romance of New England—after all, this is the region where they started.

For this book I have selected some of the most romantic country inns I have visited. Each has been chosen for one romantic reason or another—a quiet corner, wonderful dinners, breakfast in bed, a walk in the snow. Just remember they are off the beaten track, and romance is everywhere. Winter brings its own magic—the snow, the glow of a fire. I know of nothing more romantic than sitting by a fire, a glass of wine and someone very special by your side.

Many of the inns have common areas with magazines and newspapers for guests to read—even whole libraries to browse in. There are puzzles to put together, games to play, televisions, and VCRs for movies. Special touches in the rooms are also important criteria for romance—fluffy pillows, good mattresses, extra blankets, good lighting, and chairs for reading. For bed readers like me, good bed lamps are a must.

In the fall, when the leaves are turning glorious colors, what a romantic feeling it is to turn up the driveway of a beautiful inn, meet a welcoming innkeeper, relax near a crackling fire, and enjoy a lovely, romantic interlude.

I can remember a few occasions when my husband and I were caught in one of these lovely inns either by rain or snow. We sat by the fire, played some gin rummy, and sipped some fine concoction to warm the tummy. Oh, what romantic times we had.

Well, by now you know it—I am a romantic, and I love my inns and their innkeepers. All inns in their own way are romantic. Come on up to New England and enjoy.

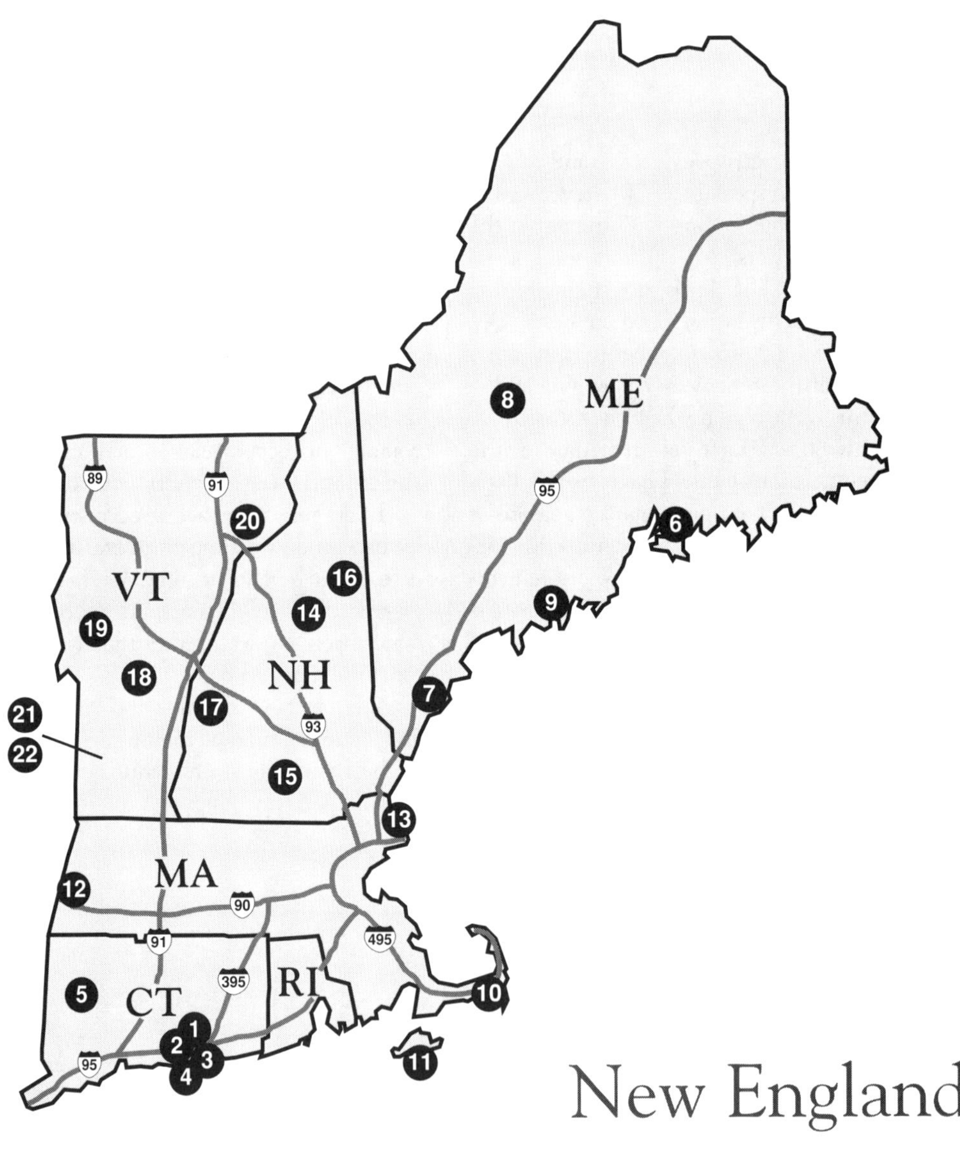
ME
VT
NH
MA
CT
RI
89
91
95
93
90
495
395
1
2
3
4
5
6
7
8
9
10
11
12
13
14
15
16
17
18
19
20
21
22
New England

New England

Numbers on map refer to towns numbered below.

Connecticut

1. Chester, The Inn at Chester 4
2. Ivoryton, Copper Beech Inn 6
3. Old Lyme, Bee and Thistle Inn 8
4. Old Saybrook, Saybrook Point Inn & Spa . . 10
5. Washington, The Mayflower Inn 12

Maine

6. Castine, The Pentagöet Inn 14
7. Kennebunkport, White Barn Inn 16
8. Kingfield, The Inn on Winter's Hill 18
9. New Harbor, The Bradley Inn at Pemaquid Point 20

Massachusetts

10. Chatham, Wequassett Inn 22
11. Edgartown, The Charlotte Inn 24
12. Lenox, Wheatleigh 26
13. Rockport, Yankee Clipper Inn 28

New Hampshire

14. Bartlett, The Notchland Inn 30
15. Hancock, The John Hancock Inn 32
16. Jackson, The Inn at Thorn Hill 34
17. Plainfield, Home Hill Inn 36

Vermont

18. Barnard, Twin Farms 38
19. Brandon, The Lilac Inn 40
20. Lower Waterford, Rabbit Hill Inn 42
21. Manchester Center, The Inn at Ormsby Hill 44
22. Manchester Village, The Village Country Inn 46

The Inn at Chester

CHESTER CONNECTICUT 06412

John D. Parmelee, the original owner of this inn built from 1776 to 1778, would not know the place today, but he'd probably enjoy it. The old house now serves as a private dining room and has a private suite. An L-shaped bar now graces the tavern, called Dunks Landing (after the boat landing of the same name in the yesteryear shipbuilding heyday of the town of Chester on the Connecticut River). The tavern serves light dinners and daily specials, plus lunch. Try the spare ribs grilled with an oriental barbecue sauce, chicken wings cajun-style, or crabcakes and more, while you listen to live music and enjoy your favorite cocktail.

There is much to do in the inn. Downstairs is the Billiard Room, where you can play billiards, backgammon, or cards. The library is filled with books—a nice place to have nearby. There is an exercise room with weights, stationary bikes, a treadmill, and a Nordic ski machine. Get a massage here or use the sauna. On the grounds are tennis, boccie, and croquet courts, and bicycles for your riding pleasure.

Each of the inn's rooms is individually appointed with Eldred Wheeler reproductions. They really are lovely and include telephone, television, and air conditioning.

The chef of the inn's Post and Beam restaurant is very talented. Try Mediterranean fish soup, warm duck salad, or entrees such as fillet of beef, pork loin, lamb stew (so nice to have this on the menu), and lots of other wonderful dishes. The breast of duck sautéed in port wine with peaches, blueberries, and nutty wild rice sounds scrumptious. This is a lovely inn in a beautiful part of Connecticut. Schedar is the inn cat—do ask about her beginnings. And ask Deborah about her seafaring days.

How to get there: Take exit 6 off Route 9 and turn west on Route 148. Go 3⅖10 miles to the inn. By private plane, fly to the Chester airport.

Innkeeper: Deborah Lieberman Moore
Address/Telephone: 318 West Main Street, (860) 526–9541
Rooms: 42, plus 2 suites; all with private bath and air conditioning, some specially equipped for handicapped.
Rates: $98 to $175, double occupancy; $205 to $425, suites; continental breakfast.
Open: All year.
Facilities and activities: Lunch, dinner, Sunday brunch. Bar and tavern, elevator, sauna, exercise room, tennis court, conference room, gift shop.
Recommended Country Inns® Travelers' Club Benefit: 10 percent discount, Monday–Thursday.

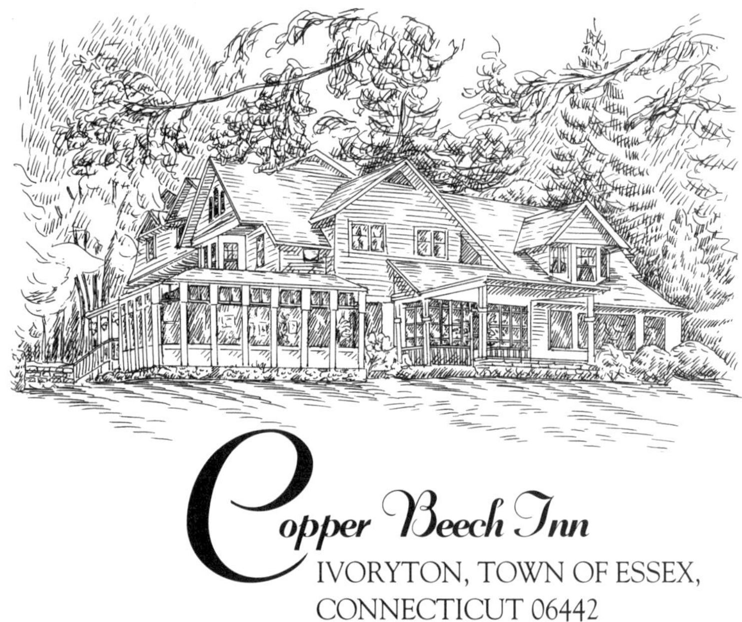

Copper Beech Inn

IVORYTON, TOWN OF ESSEX,
CONNECTICUT 06442

One of the most beautiful copper beech trees in Connecticut shades the lawn of this lovely old inn and is the reason for the inn's name.

The grounds are beautiful. Eldon, who really is a gardener, has done wonders with the property. There is an authentic English garden, many bulbs are in bloom at different times of the year, and everything is just breathtaking.

Sally is an interior designer, and her expertise really shows in this inn. There is a lovely parlor on the first floor with bookcases and a table for playing cards or writing or whatever. Very warm and comfortable.

Accommodations at the Copper Beech are wonderful. There are four rooms in the inn itself, and they have unbelievable old-fashioned bathrooms. The towels are soft and fluffy. Nine more guest rooms are in the carriage house, and each one has a Jacuzzi tub, so wonderful after a day of exploring the lovely towns of Essex, Mystic, and other area attractions. The carriage house has an elegant country atmosphere. The halls have very nice early nineteenth-century botanical prints. In fact, there is nineteenth-century art all over the inn and a wonderful collection of fine oriental porcelain.

The four dining rooms have comfortable Chippendale and Queen Anne chairs. The Garden Porch, which is a favorite place for me, features white wicker and nice Audubon prints on the walls. The spacious tables are set far apart for gracious dining. Fresh flowers are everywhere and the waiters are friendly and courteous.

The hors d'oeuvres menu is a beauty. One hors d'oeuvre is made of layers of delicate puff pastry, with smoked salmon and mousse of smoked salmon, garnished with crème fraîche, diced onions, and capers. Another is a salad of chilled poached lobster and fresh orange with an orange-truffle vinaigrette. The lobster bisque is always spectacular, and there are about eight more appetizers to choose from. Good fresh fish is used for entrees. The lobster is always easy to eat; no struggling with it here. My companion and I ordered different veal dishes. The veal was so tender, we didn't need to use a knife. Beef Wellington and roast rack of lamb are always winners here, and so are the fresh sweetbreads and a very different breast of chicken—a little French and a little oriental. Desserts are super. I love chocolate and raspberries, so I had some in the form of a cake and mousse and berries. No matter what you order, it is good at the Copper Beech and always exquisitely presented.

The Victorian conservatory is a wonderful addition to this fine inn. It's so nice for an aperitif before dinner or coffee and cognac after.

How to get there: The inn is located 1 mile west of Connecticut Route 9, from exit 3 or 4. Follow the signs to Ivoryton. The inn is on Ivoryton's Main Street, on the left side.

Innkeepers: Eldon and Sally Senner
Address/Telephone: 46 Main Street; (860) 767–0330
Rooms: 4 in inn, 9 in carriage house; all with private bath, carriage house rooms with whirlpool tub, deck, and TV.
Rates: $105 to $160, double occupancy, continental breakfast.
Open: All year.
Facilities and activities: Restaurant closed on Mondays; Tuesdays in winter; Christmas Eve, Christmas Day, and New Year's Day. Dinner, full license. Victorian-style conservatory.
Recommended Country Inns® Travelers' Club Benefit: Stay two nights, get third night free, Monday–Thursday, excluding holidays.

Bee and Thistle Inn

OLD LYME, CONNECTICUT 06371

This lovely old inn, built in 1756, sits on five and one-half acres bordering the Lieutenant River in historic Old Lyme, Connecticut. During summer the abundant flower gardens keep the inn filled to overflowing with color.

The guest rooms are all tastefully decorated. Your bed, maybe a four-poster or canopy, is covered with a lovely old quilt or afghan. The bath towels are big and thirsty. How I love them. The cottage is air-conditioned and has a reading room, bedroom with queen-sized bed, kitchen, bath, and a large TV room. A deck goes around the outside. There is also a fireplace and a private dock on the river.

There are six fireplaces in the inn. The one in the parlor is most inviting—a nice place for a cocktail or just good conversation. On weekends there is music by A Wrinkle in Time, a wonderful husband-and-wife duo who make magic with their music. There is also a harpist on Saturday nights.

The innkeepers are very romance-minded, and they will help in any way they can—even as far as proposing. Ask them for details; it's pretty funny.

Be sure to say hello to Callebaut (Bo), the Nelsons' large chocolate Lab, and to Jack, a real inn dog.

Breakfast in bed is an especially nice feature of the inn. Freshly squeezed orange juice is a refreshing way to start any day. Muffins are made fresh each day, buttery crepes are folded with strawberry or raspberry preserves, and there's much more. Lunch is interesting and inventive. Try the wild mushroom lasagne, Maryland-style crabcakes, or the Bee and Thistle shepherd's pie. Sunday brunch is really gourmet. Fresh rainbow trout, chicken hash, three different omelets—I could eat the menu.

Dinners here are magnificent. The inn just keeps winning awards. *Connecticut* magazine's readers voted the inn Connecticut's best restaurant and most romantic place to dine. They sure do deserve it. Here's some of what you'll enjoy here: candlelit dining rooms, a good selection of appetizers and soups, entrees such as spiced breast of chicken, pork medallions, shrimp, scallops, veal, and rack of lamb, and wonderful desserts. The menu changes seasonally, each time bringing new delights.

Afternoon tea is served from November 1 to May 1 on Monday, Wednesday, and Thursday from 3:30 to 5:00 P.M. The tea service is beautiful; coffee and aperitifs are also available.

This is a fine inn in a most interesting part of New England. You are in the heart of art, antiques, gourmet restaurants, and endless activities. Plan to spend a few days when you come.

How to get there: Traveling north on I–95, take exit 70 immediately on the east side of the Baldwin Bridge. At the bottom of the ramp, turn left. Take the first right at the traffic light, and turn left at the end of the road. The inn is the third house on your left. Traveling south on I–95, take exit 70; turn right at the bottom of the ramp. The inn is the third house on your left.

Innkeepers: Bob and Penny Nelson, Jeff and Lori Nelson
Address/Telephone: 100 Lyme Street; (860) 434–1667 or (800) 622–4946, fax (860) 434–3402
Rooms: 11, plus 1 cottage; 10 with private bath, all with telephone.
Rates: $69 to $140, double occupancy; $195, cottage; EP.
Open: All year except Christmas Eve, Christmas Day, and first two weeks of January.
Facilities and activities: Breakfast; lunch and dinner every day except Tuesday; Sunday brunch; afternoon tea, November 1 to May 1. Bar, lounge, library.

Saybrook Point Inn & Spa

OLD SAYBROOK, CONNECTICUT 06475

"Experience the magic at Saybrook Point Inn & Spa." These are the inn's words, and they're so true. The panoramic views of the Connecticut River and Long Island Sound are magnificent. From the moment you walk into the lobby, the Italian marble floors, beautiful furniture, and glorious fabrics let you know this is a special inn. Even the carpet is hand loomed.

All the guest rooms and suites have a water view, and most have a balcony. They are lavishly decorated with eighteenth-century–style furniture, and Italian marble is used in the bathroom with whirlpool bath. Also in the rooms are a miniature wet bar and refrigerator; an unbelievable telephone that turns on lights; double, queen-, or king-sized bed; and hair dryer.

This is a full spa, with indoor and outdoor pools, steamroom, sauna, and whirlpool. The licensed staff will pamper you with a therapeutic massage, European facial, manicure, pedicure, even a quality makeup application. There's also an exercise room with life bikes.

Breakfast, lunch, and dinner are served in an exquisite room that overlooks the inn's marina, the river, and the Long Island Sound. There was a full moon the evening I dined here. What a beautiful sight to enhance the memorable food. Such appetizers as smoked Norwegian salmon, escargots, smoked pheasant, and Beluga caviar are an elegant way to begin your dinner. Pastas are cannelloni, linguine, or wild mushroom. I had one of the best racks of lamb I have ever had. There is always a fresh seafood special. My friend had shrimp Provençale—shrimp sautéed with garlic, shallots, and scallions. A flower may be a garnish on your plate; you can eat it.

Do try to save room for dessert. I had chocolate–chocolate chip cake, which was dark and beautiful and delicious. The service is also superb.

Sunday brunch is a winner. Too much to list, but believe me, you will not go away hungry.

How to get there: From I–95 northbound take exit 67 (southbound, take Exit 68) and follow Route 154 and signs to Saybrook Point.

Innkeeper: Stephen Tagliatela; John Lombardo, general manager
Address/Telephone: 2 Bridge Street; (860) 395–2000, or (800) 243–0212 (outside Connecticut), fax (860) 388–1504
Rooms: 63, including 6 suites; all with private bath, phone, TV, air conditioning, and refrigerator, 40 with working fireplace.
Rates: $135 to $275, double occupancy; $275 to $495, suites; EP. Package plans available.
Open: All year.
Facilities and activities: Breakfast, lunch, dinner, Sunday brunch. Banquet and meeting facilities; health club with whirlpool, sauna, and steam; spa; indoor and outdoor pools; marina with 120 slips and floating docks. Nearby: charter boats, theater.

The Mayflower Inn

WASHINGTON, CONNECTICUT 06793

The Mayflower Inn is glorious. The entrance hall is huge and well appointed with antiques, Persian rugs, and many works of art. Much of it has been collected by the Mnuchins over the years during their travels. There is a cherry-paneled library off this, and the other side has a large gameroom full of beautiful things.

The Shop at Mayflower, watched over by Jeffrey, has unusual vintage jewelry, cashmere gloves, sweaters, and silks; it is just grand.

There are rooms in three buildings: the Mayflower, the Standish, and the Speedwell. Facilities are sumptuous and include feather beds and down comforters and pillows. Quality linens are on the beds, which are either queens, kings, or a pair of twins. Some rooms have a balcony, and others have a fireplace. There is also nightly turndown service.

You can dine in one of three dining rooms or, if the weather is nice, outside on the dining terrace that overlooks the grounds and woods. The English pub-style lounge, which has a piano, leads out to the porch, where there is wicker furniture in the summer. It is called the "drinking porch."

The tea house is an executive retreat; what a wonderful place for conferences. The spa, with a very strong emphasis on massage, is an added plus.

Dining here is grand. I had a nice thick veal chop and salad. The inn has special Mayflower mashed potatoes, and boy, are they good. The menu changes not only seasonally, but frequently. Foods from the local farms are used. There is not enough room to elaborate on breakfast, or the luncheon specials, or even dinner. But wow, save room for the desserts.

Everyone who works here has a smile, and they are more than willing to make your stay a pleasant one.

Orchids are everywhere, the *New York Times* is brought to your door, and a minibar is in your room. One night was not enough for this inn creeper, so I stayed for two.

How to get there: From Hartford, take I–84 west to exit 15, Southbury. Follow Route 6 north through Southbury to Woodbury. It is exactly 5 miles from I–84 to "Canfield Corners" (an 1890s building on your right). Go left here on Route 47 to Washington. It is 8 2/10 miles to the inn.

Innkeepers: John Trevenen; Adriana and Robert Mnuchin, owners
Address/Telephone: 118 Woodbury Road (mailing address: P.O. Box 1288); (860) 868–9466, fax (860) 868–1497
Rooms: 18, plus 7 suites; all with private bath, some with balcony, some with fireplace.
Rates: $230 to $375, double occupancy; $395 to $535, suites; EP.
Open: All year.
Facilities and activities: Breakfast, lunch, dinner. Bar and lounge, gift shop, spa, heated pool, tennis.

The Pentagöet Inn

CASTINE, MAINE 04421

The Pentagöet is a lovely inn located on the unspoiled coast of beautiful Penobscot Bay. Built in 1894, this Victorian inn offers the traveler warmth and a very friendly atmosphere.

Part of the inn is Ten Perkins Street, the building next door, which is more than 200 years old. The suite is here. My husband and I stayed in it, and it's a gem. It has a working fireplace, and wood is supplied so that you can light yourself a fire some cold evening. It's a very romantic spot.

All the rest of the rooms in both buildings are lovely, too. Some have little alcoves with views of the town and harbor. Some are small and have odd shapes, but this goes well with a country inn. Seven rooms have a queen-sized bed.

There is a library to the right as you come in the door of the main inn. Lots of books, a piano, soft stereo music, and very restful couches give this room the perfect atmosphere. The sitting room is to the left with a wood-burning stove and a beautiful picture window.

The wraparound porch is a delight. Good food is served in the dining room. Breakfast when we were here included Maine strawberries, which arrived early in the morning, freshly picked at a local farm. Homemade granola, sourdough blueberry pancakes, homemade jellies, and lots more add up to a good breakfast. All baking is done right here. Good dinner appetizers include shrimp piccata—prepared with little Maine shrimp—lobster crepes, and Maine crabmeat crepes. Pork tenderloin, peppered ribeye steak, and lobster thermidor are some of the entrees. I had lobster pie, a lazy and delicious way to have lobster.

The Maine Maritime Academy is located here, and its training ship, *State of Maine,* is docked at the town wharf. The local professional theater group, Cold Comfort Productions, performs four nights a week.

The innkeepers and Bilbo Baggins, the inn cat, will really make your stay here a pleasant one. There is also Tara, a very nice German shepherd.

How to get there: Take I–95 to Augusta, take Route 3 East to coast. Connect with Route 1 at Belfast, and follow Route 1 north to Bucksport. Two miles beyond turn right onto Route 175. Take Route 175 to Route 166, which takes you into Castine.

Innkeepers: Virginia and Lindsey Miller
Address/Telephone: P.O. Box 4; (207) 326–8616 or (800) 845–1701
Rooms: 15, plus 1 suite; all with private bath, suite with fireplace. No smoking inn.
Rates: $159 to $179, double occupancy, MAP.
Open: May through October.
Facilities and activities: Bar, extensive wine list. Nearby: fishing, sailing, golf.

White Barn Inn

KENNEBUNKPORT, MAINE 04046

A pre–Civil War farmhouse and its signature white barn have been transformed into this lovely inn, which is just a short walk from the beach and the charming village of Kennebunkport with its colorful shops, galleries, and boutiques. When you consider the inn's exquisite food and its warmth and graciousness, it comes as no surprise that it is the only Maine member inn of *Relais et Châteaux* and one of just twenty in the United States.

A feeling of hospitality is evident throughout the inn. When you enter your room, you find a basket of fruit, flowers, luxurious toiletries, and a robe for you to wear. At night your bed is turned down and a pillow treat is left.

The rooms in the inn itself are attractively decorated with antiques, armoires, and brass and iron beds in a variety of sizes. The Gate House's rooms are large, with cathedral ceilings, ceiling fans, dressing areas, queen-sized beds, and wing chairs. May's Annex has six suites with king-sized four-poster beds and large sitting areas with fireplaces. There are oversized marble baths with whirlpool baths and separate showers. The towels are large and lush.

The sunroom is the boardroom, seating up to fourteen people; it's a perfect, sunny spot for small meetings, retreats, and reunions. The breakfast room is large and cheerfully decorated with flower arrangements. The main dining room is the barn; a lovely lounge and piano bar are here, too. Candlelight, linen, and soft music are nice touches. The menu changes weekly.

When I think about the food, I want to go back for more. The restaurant has received five diamonds and an AAA listing; these are prestigious awards and well deserved. The menu changes weekly in order to offer the freshest and finest of ingredients. I know the greens are fresh—I watched them being picked. Soups are amazing: A light cream soup of potato, leek, and watercress is scented with thyme; lobster minestrone comes with black beans, roasted tomatoes, olive-oil croutons, and a bacon *pistou*.

The appetizer of homemade ravioli is glorious. Dinner choices the week I was here included pan-seared striped bass with sautéed eggplant, Niçoise olives, and basil oil in a roasted tomato broth. The veal rib chop came grilled with glazed baby turnips, Swiss chard, garlic-roasted Parisienne potatoes, and a herb sauce. You can guess there are lots of seafood offerings from this Maine inn—lobster, halibut, and salmon were also on the menu.

No matter what size your party—two or eight—when your dinner is ready, that number of waiters arrives to stand behind each diner's chair and on cue serves everyone simultaneously. What a sight.

The little bar is copper, with eight upholstered chairs. The piano bar has a huge flower arrangement in its center.

After dinner, go relax in the living room with a glass of port or brandy, a book from the inn's well-filled bookshelves, or one of the many current magazines. Or you could be ambitious and go for a ride along the beach on one of the inn's bicycles. Just go and enjoy.

How to get there: From the Maine Turnpike, take exit 3 to Kennebunk. Follow Route 35 south 6 miles to Kennebunkport, then continue through the fourth traffic light onto Beach Street. The inn is in ¼ mile on the right.

Innkeepers: Laurie J. Bongiorno and Laurie Cameron
Address/Telephone: Beach Street (mailing address: P.O. Box 560-C); (207) 967–2321
Rooms: 18, plus 7 suites; all with private bath, some with phone, TV, and Jacuzzi, 11 with fireplace.
Rates: $150 to $350, double occupancy, continental breakfast and tea. Packages available.
Open: All year.
Facilities and activities: Dinner, full license. Meeting room, bicycles. Nearby: beach, shops, galleries, golf, tennis.

The Inn on Winter's Hill

KINGFIELD, MAINE 04947

The Inn on Winter's Hill, located in the midst of western Maine's Bigelow, Sugarloaf, and Saddleback mountains, sits on top of a six-acre hill on the edge of town. This Neo-Georgian manor house was designed by the Stanley (steam car) brothers and built at the turn of the century for Amos Greene Winter as a present for his wife, Julia. It is listed on the National Register of Historic Places. Today it is owned by a brother and sister who are doing a great job as innkeepers, following a longtime tradition of casual elegance and warm hospitality.

Accommodations are varied and range from the turn-of-the-century luxury rooms in the inn to the modern rooms in the restored barn. Every one is very comfortable, with nice bathrooms, wonderful views, cable television, and telephone.

Julia's Restaurant is elegant and the food served here is excellent. The night we were here, I had crackers and garlic cheese spread and pineapple wrapped in bacon for appetizers. My garden salad with house dressing was followed by a light sorbet and then Sole Baskets, which were superb. The other entrees were Drunken Duck, chicken Cordon Bleu, and beef Wellington. Salmon in phyllo—Atlantic salmon fillet baked in phyllo with a parmesan-cheese cream sauce—is superb; I had this on my last trip. Desserts are grand. Oh, it's all so good, it's hard to choose.

In the lounge area is an old piano, which came by oxcart from Boston for Julia Winter. It took two and a half months to arrive.

Spring, summer, fall, or winter, there is so much to do up here. Winter brings cross-country skiing from the door and ice skating on the lighted outdoor rink. And remember, downhill skiing at Sugarloaf is minutes away. Hunting, fishing, canoeing, and hiking along the Appalachian Trail welcome outdoors people in the other seasons.

Isn't it romantic (must be a song)? The Maine woods smell so good, and this inn is so romantic. Do come and try it on for size.

How to get there: Kingfield is halfway between Boston and Quebec City, and the Great Lakes area and the Maritimes. Take the Maine Turnpike to the Belgrade Lakes exit in Augusta. Follow Highway 27 through Farmington to Kingfield. The inn is on a small hill near the center of town.

Innkeepers: Richard and Diane Winnick and Carolyn Rainaud
Address/Telephone: RR 1, Box 1272; (207) 265–5421, (800) 233–9687
Rooms: 20, in 2 buildings; all with private bath, phone, and cable TV, 1 specially equipped for handicapped.
Rates: $75 to $150, double occupancy, EP. Golf and fly-fishing packages available.
Open: All year.
Facilities and activities: Full breakfast, dinner for public daily, by reservation. Wheelchair access to dining room. Bar, lounge, meeting and banquet facilities, hot tub, swimming pool, croquet court, tennis, cross-country skiing, ice skating. Nearby: downhill skiing, hunting, fishing, hiking, golf, canoeing, Stanley Steamer Museum, dog-sled rides, white-water rafting.

The Bradley Inn at Pemaquid Point

NEW HARBOR, MAINE 04554

Pemaquid, an Indian word meaning "long finger," is an appropriate name for the point of land that extends farther into the Atlantic Ocean than any other on the rugged Maine coast. This information is from the inn's brochure. What a wonderful ride it is out here! And once you arrive, the terrain is breathtaking. You're just a short walk from the Pemaquid Lighthouse or the beach with its lovely white sand. In the nearby seaside village of New Harbor, you can watch the working boats. Fort William Henry is close by. I drove around the point, parked my car, and watched the surf beating on the rocks below. It was quite a sight.

On this visit I scrambled down to the water's edge and back up. It was a bit scary but well worth it.

The inn is more than eighty years old. There's an attractive living room with a fireplace and a baby grand piano. On Fridays and Saturdays, the piano is played by John Mantica, who has entertained here for years. The taproom has a long, custom-made bar of Portland granite with a mahogany rail. A three-piece band and singer were here when I visited.

"Ships" is the name of the restaurant. It is decorated with some beautiful ship models and a huge ship's wheel. Some of the appetizers are fried calamari and potato and leek tart. Soups are good; I especially liked the shellfish stew. The pastas, such as the seafood Alfredo and roast vegetable and herb oil fusilli, are different.

All these good foods lead into even better entrees. You'll find fresh catch of the day, grilled sirloin strip steak, fresh haddock, and fresh New Harbor lobster. There's also lazy man's or woman's lobster—guess which one I had? The wine list is impressive, and the dessert that won my vote was Chocolate Decadence Cake.

The rooms are charming and very comfortable. The view from some of the second- and third-floor rooms is of Johns Bay or the gardens. The cottage sleeps four people—a good spot for a family. There's a nice yard with lounge chairs. Barney, the inn's golden retriever, is a love.

There's much to do and see out here, so come on up.

How to get there: Take the Maine Turnpike to exit 9, Falmouth–Route 1 interchange. Take I–95 21 miles to Brunswick. Continue on Route 1 to Damariscotta, 27 miles, and from there follow Route 130, 14 miles to the inn.

Innkeepers: Merry and Chuck Robinson
Address/Telephone: 361 Pemaquid Point (mailing address: Route 130 HC 61); (207) 677–2105, fax (207) 677–3367
Rooms: 12, plus 1 cottage, 1 carriage house; all with private bath, rooms with phone and TV.
Rates: $95 to $175, double occupancy, continental breakfast. Special packages available.
Open: April through December.
Facilities and activities: Dinner. Bicycles and helmets, wedding facilities. Nearby: ocean, tennis, golf.
Business travel: Phone with private line in room, conference facilities.

Wequasset Inn
CHATHAM, MASSACHUSETTS 02633

Taking its name from the American Indian word meaning "Crescent on the Water," Wequasset is a country inn resort that includes eighteen separate buildings and is worth a trip from anywhere. Tucked between a secluded ocean cove and a twenty-two-acre pine forest, the lands around Wequasset were once used by native peoples as a summer campground.

A nineteenth-century sea captain's home now houses the inn's main dining room, the Square Top, named for the building's unusual roof line. There is a spectacular view of Pleasant Bay from here, a nice complement to the inn's glorious food, which has been awarded *Mobil Travel Guide*'s four-star rating and AAA's four-diamond rating. The breakfast menu offers so many choices that you could eat all day. At lunch there are six different salads, great burgers, and a deli board. One sandwich I liked was the Yorkshire—thinly sliced roast beef, creamy horseradish, and lettuce and tomato piled high on a kaiser roll. Way to go, Elizabeth—right to the fat farm. Of course, they do have a fitness platter. Well, maybe next time. There's also a lovely selection of really different drinks on the lunch menu.

The dinners? Well, you can imagine. Four cold appetizers and six hot. I can taste the lump-meat crabcakes now. Soups, salads, and fresh pastas—one I tasted was spicy pepper fettucine and blackened shrimp. Oh my! The seafood is wonderful, as are the meat and poultry. It's nice to have half a rack of lamb on the menu. Desserts—are you ready? Wequasset Inn's chocolate truffle cake. I do not know where I put it, but it was all gone. There are eleven coffees along with the regular ones.

The accommodations are unique. Each room has its own bath and entrance, simply styled pine furniture, traditional fabrics, and lots of charm. There are heating and cooling units, color television, and patios and decks. Suites feature fresh flowers, minibar, and VCR.

It would be hard to beat the serenity of sitting on the porch overlooking the bay at any time of the day, but oh, the early-morning calm! What a wonderful place for a honeymoon or anniversary . . . or just because it's a dream spot.

How to get there: Wequasset Inn is on Pleasant Bay midway between Chatham and Orleans on Route 28. If you are driving from the north, take Route 6 East to exit 11. Turn left at end of exit ramp; go 25 yards to Pleasant Bay Road (your first left). Go straight through the first stop sign, and when you reach the second stop sign, you have arrived at Wequasset Inn.

Innkeeper: Mark Novata
Address/Telephone: Route 28, Pleasant Bay, Cape Cod; (508) 432–5400, (800) 352–7169 (in Massachusetts), or (800) 225–7125; fax (508) 432–5032
Rooms: 97, including 7 suites; all with private bath, some with private patio or deck.
Rates: $170 to $480, single or double occupancy, EP.
Open: May to late October.
Facilities and activities: Breakfast, lunch, dinner. Croquet court, 5 all-weather PlexiPave tennis courts plus pro shop and lessons, fitness center, conference center, heated swimming pool, fishing. In 1997 there will be an 18-hole golf course.

The Charlotte Inn

EDGARTOWN, MASSACHUSETTS 02539

The start of your vacation is a forty-five-minute ferry ride to Martha's Vineyard. It's wise to make early reservations for your automobile on the ferry. There also are cabs if you prefer not to take your car.

When you open the door to the inn, you are in the Edgartown Art Gallery, with interesting artifacts and paintings, both watercolor and oil. This is a well-appointed gallery featuring such artists as Ray Ellis, who has a fine talent in both media. The inn also has an unusual gift shop, now located next to the Garden House.

Four of us had dinner in the inn's lovely French restaurant named L'Etoile. The food was exquisite. Capon breast stuffed with duxelles, spinach, and sun-dried tomatoes with coriander mayonnaise was the best I have had. I tasted everyone's food—nice occupation I have. Rack of lamb, served rare, with red wine and rosemary sauce and accompanied by potato and yam gratin was excellent. They also have a special or two, but then everything is so special, the word does not fit. At brunch, the cold cucumber soup was served with chives and followed by entrees like blueberry soufflé pancakes with crème fraîche. For breakfast I had a strawberry crepe that I can still remember vividly. Freshly squeezed juices and fruit muffins. . . Heaven!

The rooms are authentic. There are Early American four-poster beds and fireplaces. The carriage house is sumptuous. The second-floor suite with fireplace I could live in. Paula has a touch with rooms—comfortable furniture, down pillows, down comforters, and all the amenities. As an example, the shower curtains are of eyelet and so pretty. As a finishing touch, there are plenty of large towels.

Across the street is the Garden House, and it is Edgartown at its best. The living room is unique and beautifully furnished, and its fireplace is always set for you. The rooms over here are just so handsome. The Coach House is magnificent, furnished with fine old English antiques, a marble fireplace, and a pair of exquisite chaise longues in the bedroom. It is air conditioned.

Paula, by the way, has green hands, and all about are gardens that just outdo one another.

Gery and Paula are special innkeepers, but they do need the help of Andrew and Morgan, the dogs, and Oscar and Princess, the cats.

How to get there: Reservations are a must if you take your car on the ferry from Woods Hole, Massachusetts. Forty-five minutes later you are in Vineyard Haven. After a fifteen-minute ride, you are in Edgartown, and on South Summer Street is the inn.

Innkeepers: Gery and Paula Conover
Address/Telephone: South Summer Street; (508) 627–4751
Rooms: 21, plus 3 suites; all with private bath, some with fireplace, air conditioning, and phone.
Rates: In-season, $250 to $450; interim-season, $165 to $395; off-season, $125 to $395; suites, $550 to $650; double occupancy, continental breakfast.
Open: All year.
Facilities and activities: In-season, dinner daily. Off-season, dinner on weekends. Reservations a must. Gift shop and gallery. Nearby: sailing, swimming, fishing, golf, tennis.

Wheatleigh

LENOX, MASSACHUSETTS 01240

In the heart of the beautiful Berkshires, overlooking a lake, amid lawns and gardens on twenty-two self-contained acres stands the estate of Wheatleigh, former home of the Countess de Heredia. The centerpiece of this property is an elegant private palace fashioned after an Italian palazzo. The cream-colored manse re-creates the architecture of sixteenth-century Florence. You must read the brochure of Wheatleigh, for it says it all so well.

Patios, pergolas, porticos, and terraces surround this lovely old mansion. The carvings over the fireplaces, cupids entwined in garlands, are exquisite. In charming contrast, the inn also has the largest collection of contemporary ceramics in the New England area. There are many lovely porcelain pieces on the walls. In the dining room are tile paintings weighing more than 500 pounds. They are Doultons from 1830; this was before it became Royal Doulton. They are just beautiful.

The grill room, which is open in-season, provides an à la carte menu of light fare prepared to the same high standards of the dining room. Its casual ambience features an elegant black-and-white color scheme—the plates are beautiful.

There is a service bar in a lovely lounge, and boy, you sure can relax in the furniture in here. It has a wonderful fireplace, and the views from here are glorious. And imagine a great hall with a grand staircase right out of a castle in Europe. There are also exquisite stained-glass windows in pale pastels, plus gorgeous, comfortable furniture. From the great hall you can hear the tinkle of the fountain out in the garden.

The whole inn was done over very recently and, wow, the rooms are smashing. Do you long for your own balcony overlooking a lovely lake? No problem. Reserve one here.

At the entrance to the dining room, the homemade desserts are beautifully displayed along with French champagne in six sizes from a jeroboam to a small bottle for one. This is very nice indeed. I chose grilled quail on young lettuce leaves and raspberries for a dinner appetizer; it was superb. Tartare of fresh tuna was so beautifully presented, just like a Japanese picture, and delicious. I also had chilled fresh pea soup with curry and sorrel, followed by monkfish coated with pistachios, sautéed, with red wine sauce. Homemade sorbets are very good, but then, so is everything here.

Susan's description of the inn is "elegance without arrogance," and Lin's is "the ultimate urban amenity." Mine is "a perfect country inn."

There are very special weekend packages. Do call and ask. Two that come to mind are a Burgundy weekend with Louis Jadot and a chocloate lovers' weekend—that sure sounds romantic—wish I loved closer.

How to get there: From Stockbridge at the Red Lion Inn where Route 7 turns right, go straight on Prospect Hill Road, bearing left. Go past the Stockbridge Bowl and up a hill to Wheatleigh.

From the Massachusetts Turnpike, take exit 2, and follow signs to Lenox. In the center of Lenox, take Route 183, pass the main gate of Tanglewood, and then take the first left on West Hawthorne. Go 1 mile to Wheatleigh.

Innkeepers: Susan and Linfield Simon
Address/Telephone: West Hawthorne; (413) 637–0610, fax (413) 637–4507
Rooms: 17; all with private bath, air conditioning, and phone, 9 with working fireplace.
Rates: $155 to $525, double occupancy, EP.
Open: All year.
Facilities and activities: Lunch for houseguests, dinner, Sunday brunch, in season. Grill room, lounge. Swimming, tennis, cross-country skiing.

Yankee Clipper Inn

ROCKPORT, MASSACHUSETTS 01966

When you are lucky enough to be here and see a sunset, you will be overwhelmed. It's a golden sea and sky, with the town of Rockport in the distance. No camera could truly capture this scene. Wait a while longer, and the moonlight on the sea is an awesome sight.

Three buildings make up the Yankee Clipper. The inn is an oceanfront mansion. Here the rooms have antique furniture, oriental rugs, and some canopied beds. Some rooms have porches. You're sure to enjoy the television lounge with cable television and a really big screen. All meals are served in this building.

The Quarterdeck has large picture windows providing a panoramic view of the ocean. Upholstered chairs are placed in front of the windows. Sit back and relax; it's almost like being on a ship that does not move. All of the rooms in this building are beautifully furnished. Some of the rooms in the Bullfinch House have water views. If you stay here you are on the EPB plan; the other buildings are MAP.

There is a function room, with a wonderful water view and just lovely for small weddings or executive meetings.

The Glass Veranda dining room has marvelous views that are matched by the marvelous food. David Pierson is a chef with imagination. I started my dinner with a taste of one appetizer—lobster polenta, which was a baked blend of cornmeal and native lobster, served with Boursin cheese sauce—and the soup of the day—cold zucchini soup.

I went on to the seafood au gratin, which was shrimp, scallops, and haddock, baked in cream and herbs, and topped with cheddar cheese and bread crumbs. Vegetarian Wellington was new to me; a medley of fresh vegetables was baked in puff pastry with Boursin cheese. Delicious.

To work off some of the calories, you might want to swim in the heated saltwater pool at the inn. In the area there are whale-watching trips, fishing, and in the town of Rockport, fantastic shopping. It really is fun to walk around here.

How to get there: Take Route 128 north and east to Cape Ann. Route 128 ends at traffic lights. Turn left onto Route 127. Drive 3 miles to where Route 127 turns left into Pigeon Cove. Continue on Route 127 for 1⅕ miles to Yankee Clipper in Pigeon Cove.

Innkeepers: Bob and Barbara Wemyss Ellis
Address/Telephone: 96 Granite Street; (508) 546–3407 or (800) 545–3699
Rooms: 27, including 6 suites, in 3 buildings; all with private bath, air conditioning, and phone.
Rates: \$99 to \$239, double occupancy, EPB; \$58 more for MAP.
Open: February 15 to December 20.
Facilities and activities: Dinner. Small function room, heated saltwater pool. Nearby: fishing, boating, shopping, whale watching.
Recommended Country Inns® Travelers' Club Benefit: 10 percent discount, Sunday–Thursday, excluding holiday Sundays, exclusive of other special offers and travel agent bookings.

The Notchland Inn

BARTLETT, NEW HAMPSHIRE 03812

The inn was built in 1862 by a wealthy Boston dentist, Samuel Bemis. He used native granite and timber, and you can bet that the construction of this building was some job.

Seventeen fireplaces are in the inn, and all of the rooms have a working fireplace. Some of the suites have a two-person spa bath. One suite has an exquisite Japanese wedding kimono posted on a wall, and a few suites are in the carriage house and schoolhouse.

There are high ceilings and beautiful mountain views. The front parlor was designed by Gustav Stickley, a founder of the Arts and Crafts movement. The music room is inviting with its piano and stereo, and the sunroom is full of beautiful plants and a fountain. The dining room dates back to 1795, has a raised hearth fireplace, and looks out onto the pond and gazebo.

This is a nice setting for chef Marcia Ackerman's inventive cooking. Every evening dinner is served at 7:00, and patrons are offered a choice of two soups, two appetizers, three entrees, and three desserts. To give you an idea of the varied menu, soup might be lightly curried sweet potato and butternut squash, orange-scented tomato with a fresh herbed yogurt, or Szechwan carrot. Appetizers might be crabcakes or three-tier vegetable pâté with a red pepper coulis. Entrees might be filet mignon with béarnaise sauce, chicken champagne, poached catfish, or poached salmon stuffed with scallops and herbs. And dessert might be very lemon pie, apricot cheesecake, or chocolate walnut tart.

If you can even think about breakfast after such a dinner, you'll delight in the full country breakfast that will start your day right.

There's so much to do in this area that you may have a hard time deciding where to start. Hiking is by far the nicest you'll find almost anywhere. There are beautiful waterfalls and granite cliffs to scale. The Saco River is the place for swimming, fishing, or canoeing, and two swimming holes are on the inn's property. White-water Class III and IV are here in the spring, so come on up with your canoe. Or bring your bicycle, as biking is fun here. Skiing of all kinds is very close by (there are 45 miles of ski trails)—or do you want to try snowshoeing? This is the place for it, or you can go ice skating on the inn's pond. If more sedentary activities suit your fancy, rocking chairs on the porch are ideal for reading and needlework.

The innkeepers love animals as much as I do. Coco, their Bernese mountain dog, is a love and even has "Coco Loco" cookies to give to guests—boy, are those good! Mork and Mindy are the miniature horses, and Dolly is a Belgian draft horse. DC and Sid are the llamas.

When you come in the door of the inn and turn left, there is a living room with a puzzle going at all times; it's always fun to work on it. By the fireplace is a slate marker about Nancy Barton—be sure to read it—it's a riot.

Romance is even in the air you breathe up here. At any time of year, the area activities will keep couple discovering new adventures together. Even the scenic roads are lovely—there's no better place to take a drive and enjoy the magic in the air.

How to get there: Follow Route 302 from North Conway to the inn. It is 20 miles north of North Conway.

Innkeepers: Les School and Ed Butler
Address/Telephone: Route 302; (603) 374–6131 or (800) 866–6131, fax (603) 374–6168
Rooms: 7, plus 8 suites; all with private bath and fireplace, 1 specially equipped for handicapped.
Rates: $80 to $120, per person, double occupancy, MAP.
Open: All year.
Facilities and activities: Full liquor license. Hot tub. Hiking, canoeing, swimming, fishing, bicycling, cross-country skiing, sleigh rides, snowshoeing, and ice skating. Nearby: downhill skiing.

The John Hancock Inn

HANCOCK, NEW HAMPSHIRE 03449

Operated as an inn since 1789, the John Hancock has recently changed hands. Old friends and good innkeepers, Joe and Linda are now in charge.

This is a nice old inn. Its name stems from the fact that John Hancock, the founding father, once owned most of the land that comprises the present town of Hancock. Set among twisting hills with a weathered clapboard facade, graceful white pillars, and a warm red door, the inn represents all that is good about old inns.

The dining rooms are lovely, and the food is superb. They have been awarded the best of the best award: four diamonds, designating this to be one of the top 100 restaurants in the country in the category of American food. Appetizers like cranberry shrub, Maryland crab cake, baked Brie are followed by good soups and an excellent house salad. Their famous Shaker cranberry pot roast is worth the trip alone, but perhaps you'd like to try the roasted maple duck, rainbow lake trout, or summer garden linguine.

At the end of the day, you will retire to the comfort of a four-poster bed, where the sound of the Paul Revere bell from a nearby steeple will gently lull you to sleep. This is a town that hasn't changed much in the past two centuries.

Carefully preserved is The Mural Room, believed to date back to the early years of the inn. The recently remodeled Carriage Lounge is a comfortable and very unusual common room and bar.

Swim in summer in Norway Pond, within walking distance of the inn. Climb mountains, or just sit and listen to the church chimes during foliage time. Alpine and cross-country skiing are nearby in winter. Or browse in the antiques shops on a cool spring morn.

The inn dog is Duffy, a springer spaniel.

How to get there: From Boston take Route 128, then Route 3 to 101 west. Hancock is located just off Route 202, 9 miles above Peterborough.

Innkeepers: Joe and Linda Johnston
Address/Telephone: Main Street; (603) 525–3318, (800) 525–1789 (outside New Hampshire), fax (603) 525–9301
Rooms: 11; all with private bath, air conditioning, and phone. No smoking inn.
Rates: $98 to $150, double occupancy, EPB.
Open: All year.
Facilities and activities: Dinner, lounge. Wheelchair ramp into the inn. Parking. Nearby: swimming, hiking, antiquing, summer theater, skiing, tennis.

The Inn at Thorn Hill

JACKSON, NEW HAMPSHIRE 03846

Over the Honeymoon Bridge to The Inn at Thorn Hill you go, and when you get there you will find a Victorian beauty. Mountains are everywhere you look from this inn. Relax on the porch in a New England rocking chair and enjoy the view. Even on a bad day it is spectacular.

I loved the Victorian parlor, with its baby grand piano, and the spacious drawing room with its wood stove and unbelievable view. A pair of Victorian mannequins in their finery stand at the windows next to the lovely old Victrola. There are board games, cards, and books for you to enjoy. A cozy pub with a fireplace and five bar stools has lots of cheer.

Elegant country dining by candlelight is what you get, and the food is good. The menu is revised seasonally to offer variety and popular seasonal dishes. A seafood sausage of scallops, shrimp, and lobster served with lemon caper butter is an example of their good appetizers. The soups and salads are interesting. And the entrees are grand. Lobster Pie Thorn Hill, served with brandy Newburg sauce in a puff pastry shell. Crisp roast duckling, served with Cointreau sauce and sautéed orange slices. Lamb chops stuffed with tomato, feta cheese, and fresh mint. The list goes on. The desserts that follow are excellent. There are more than 100 different wines. There is an impressive list.

There is a Victorian flair to all the inn rooms. A variety of beds is available—canopies, singles, doubles, kings, and queens—and all rooms have wonderful views of the mountains. The carriage house next door has a 20-by-40-foot great room with a fireplace and seven guest rooms, so bring several couples. This is the place to be. The cottages are very nice and just great for those who want more privacy. Beautifully refurbished, each of the three cottages has a Jacuzzi, front porch, wet bar, television, gas fireplace, and air conditioning. Some have a deck with a view.

There is much to do here. The inn has its own swimming pool; hiking and downhill skiing are close at hand; and cross-country skiing begins at the doorstep and joins the 146-kilometer Jackson touring network.

No wonder the inn was one of ten winners of Uncle Ben's Best Country Inn awards.

How to get there: Go north from Portsmouth, New Hampshire, on the Spaulding Turnpike (Route 16) all the way to Jackson, which is just above North Conway. At Jackson is a covered bridge on your right. Take the bridge, and two roads up from the bridge on the right is Thorn Hill Road, which you take up the hill. The inn is on your right.

Innkeepers: Jim and Ibby Cooper
Address/Telephone: Thorn Hill Road; (603) 383–4242 or (800) 289–8990, fax (603) 383–8062
Rooms: 19, in 2 buildings, plus 3 cottage suites, all with private bath. No smoking inn.
Rates: $70 to $140, per person, double occupancy, MAP.
Open: All year.
Facilities and activities: Bar, swimming pool, hot tub, cross-country skiing. Nearby: downhill skiing, golf club, tennis, horseback riding, canoeing, ice skating, sleigh rides.

Home Hill Inn

PLAINFIELD, NEW HAMPSHIRE 03781

Roger's brochure said Home Hill Country Inn and French Restaurant, and we could hardly wait to get there.

Roger was born in Brittany in northwest France, and he speaks with a pleasant accent. He has an authentic French restaurant here. The food presentation is picture perfect, and the taste is elegant. No gravies, only sauces, and no flour, cornstarch, or fillers are allowed. Roger believes in innovative French cooking.

The menu changes every day. You might try the cream of onion soup, then veal slices, very thin and young with French mushrooms. You may have the salad before, with, or after dinner, and the house dressing is gorgeous. Roger joined us at dinner and had duck prepared with white plums. I tasted it; it was very moist and delicious. Another dish served occasionally is veal with fresh wild mushrooms. Grilled New England sea scallops with red-pepper coulis sounds great. Desserts, as would be expected, are superb. The wine list features both French and California wines.

In the kitchen is a lovely, long pine table where breakfast is served. What a homey spot at which to enjoy the continental breakfast of juice, croissants, butter, jams, and coffee.

The rooms are charming. The cottage is large enough for eight persons. There are French and American antiques, reproductions, and comfort.

The lounge-library is lovely; in fact, you will find it hard to find any fault with this inn.

The carriage house, also on the property, has three bedrooms, each with a bath. This is a nice addition to the inn. We stayed in one of these rooms—a wonderfully romantic spot.

Roger's Great Dane is Bacchus. The inn is on twenty-five acres, only 500 yards from the Connecticut River. There are a swimming pool (a bar is out here), tennis courts, and cross-country skiing. Any season, any reason, head for Home Hill.

How to get there: Take I–89 to exit 20. Follow Route 12A south 3 miles to River Road and turn right. In 3½ miles you'll find the inn on the left.

Innkeeper: Roger Nicolas
Address/Telephone: River Road; (603) 675–6165
Rooms: 6, plus 3 suites; all with private bath.
Rates: $95 to $175, double occupancy, continental breakfast. Fall season and holidays slightly higher.
Open: All year except Sundays and Mondays, two weeks in March, and two weeks in November.
Facilities and activities: Dinner, bar, lounge. Swimming pool, tennis court, cross-country skiing, fishing in Connecticut River, walking trails.

Twin Farms

BARNARD, VERMONT 05031

Twin Farms is a 235-acre hideaway estate that was owned by novelist Sinclair Lewis and given to his wife, Dorothy Thompson, as a wedding present. During the 1930s and '40s, they came here to rest and entertain many literary figures of the time.

You arrive at the entry gate and dial a number indicating who you are. Then you enter an unbelievably unique property. Drive down the lane and along a circular drive to the main house.

The game room, with a beautiful fireplace, has many games and Stave wood puzzles. Off this is the Washington Suite, where we stayed. It has beautiful quilts and down-filled beds, two televisions, a CD player, and a bathroom with a large skirted antique tub and a huge shower. The sitting room has a bay window with a nice view, good couches, and a beautiful fireplace. There's a fireplace in the bedroom, too.

Dorothy's Room, on the second floor, is where she preferred to read and write. Red's Room, the original master suite, is glorious, with a view of Mount Ascutney. Red was Sinclair's nickname.

The guest room's walls and curtains are covered in a green-and-ivory French linen that tells a story. It's just beautiful.

The cottages have fireplaces, sumptuous baths, very private screened porches, and lots of comfort. They all have names. The studio is splendid and has a huge copper soaking tub and front and back porches; a porch overlooks a stream, and a lot of fish-related items decorate the interior. The Treehouse is a wow, with Chinese fretwork in the bedroom. Orchard Cottage is set amid the old apple orchard and features two handcarved granite fireplaces. The two-story Barn Cottage offers grand views, and the Meadow, with its Moroccan interior reminiscent of a desert king's traveling palace, is stunning; the tent ceiling is something you'll just have to see. Wood Cottage has an Italian oak writing table and much charm. And the Log Cabin is an authentic old Tennessee log cabin refurbished the Twin farms way. It's very hard to choose here, so come a lot of times—you won't be disappointed.

A covered bridge takes you to the pub. Here are a self-service bar, pool table, fireplace, and television. Below this is a fully equipped fitness center. In-room massages are available. Up the road is a Japanese Furo. There are separate tubs for men and women, separated by fragrant pine walls, and one larger one for both men and women.

The main dining room is rustic; however, you may dine wherever you choose. We were in the original dining room, and both the food and service are incredible. Cocktails are at 7:00 P.M. There are two bars for you to help yourself from, anytime day or night. Lunch may take any form, and you may have it anywhere. Tea is glorious.

There is much to do here, whatever the season. Tennis and croquet; a lake for swimming, canoeing, or fishing; walking; biking. You can use the inn's mountain bikes. The inn also has its own ski slopes, ski trails, snowshoes, toboggans, and ice skating.

This is an experience few may be able to afford, but what a wonderful trip. This inn was definately made for romance. Say hello to Maple, the golden inn dog.

How to get there: Take I–91 north to I–89 north. Take the first exit off I–89 (exit 1). Turn left onto Route 4 to Woodstock, then Route 12 to Barnard. At the general store, go right and follow this road for about 1½ miles. As the road changes from blacktop to dirt, you will see two stone pillars and a wrought-iron gate on your right, marking the driveway entrance.

Innkeepers: Shaun and Beverly Matthews; Thurston Twigg-Smith, owner
Address/Telephone: Barnard; (802) 234–9999 or (800) 894–6327, fax (802) 234–9990
Rooms: 8 cottages, 1 lodge, 2 suites in the lodge; all with private bath, phone, TV, minirefrigerator, air conditioning, and CD player.
Rates: $700 to $1500, double occupancy, all inclusive.
Open: All year except April.
Facilities and activities: Full license, spa, all winter sports, mountain bikes, tennis, croquet, swimming, canoeing, fitness center.

The Lilac Inn

BRANDON, VERMONT 05733–1121

Wow! This is a beauty. It's a 10,000-square-foot Georgian Revival mansion that was built in 1909 as a summer cottage. Adorned with yellow and white paint, it is a lovely country inn today. Michael and Melanie have recaptured the charm of the era in which it was built.

To the left of the coach entrance is the library, which has a nice fireplace, books galore, chess, and a ton of comfort and charm. On the right is a stupendous butler's pantry hall leading to the tavern. Here is a beautiful copper-topped bar with six leather chairs with backs. Boy, are they comfortable!

The tavern has its own menu, full of glorious food. How about a Loaf of Soup—a freshly baked mini-boule, filled with the soup of the day?

The dining room menu changes weekly. Usually there are four appetizers and soup du jour. A few of the choices when I visited were grilled Angus sirloin, baked cheddar scrod, raspberry lamb, and baked stuffed salmon. Two of the desserts take thirty minutes to prepare. I won't tell you what they are. Come up and find out; they are wonderful.

The staircase is grand. In 1991 a time capsule was inserted into its newel post. At the top of the stairs is an ornate Chinese chest from the 1850s.

The rooms are spacious and well appointed.

The bridal suite has a two-person whirlpool tub and wedding dolls on the fireplace mantel. Televisions are in armoires, and there also are VCRs. Melanie makes the dolls. There is one of her in her wedding dress when you first enter the inn.

What a talented pair of innkeepers we have here! They're assisted by three inn cats—Brown Nose, White, and Sebastian, which is a wonderful Himalayan. The inn dogs are pugs called Dr. Watson and Bella.

How to get there: Follow Route 7 to Brandon. Turn right on Route 73 east (Park Street). The inn is about the fourth building on the right.

Innkeepers: Melanie and Michael Shane
Address/Telephone: 53 Park Street; (802) 247–5463 or (800) 221–0720, fax (802) 247–5499
E-mail: lilacinn@sover.net
Rooms: 9; all with private bath, 1 with whirlpool tub, 3 with fireplace. Phone available. One cottage with bedroom, living room, kitchen, loft.
Rates: $100 to $200, double occupancy, EPB. MAP rates available.
Open: All year. Restaurant closed to public between Easter and Mother's Day.
Facilities and activities: Sunday brunch, lunch summer through fall, dinner Wednesday through Saturday. Catering and room service. Winter Arts Festival on Friday and Saturday nights in February and March. Jazz and classical concerts in summer.
Business travel: Ballroom for meetings. Function planning, secretarial services, telephone, computer, fax, and modem available.
Recommended Country Inns® Travelers' Club Benefit: 10 percent discount, Monday–Thursday.

Rabbit Hill Inn

LOWER WATERFORD, VERMONT 05848

In 1795 Rabbit Hill became an inn. It has had a few owners over the years; however, this pair of innkeepers has really done justice to this lovely old inn.

Each of the inn's rooms is done according to a theme. Some are the Doll Chamber, the Toy Chamber, and Carolyn's Room (which has a blue-and-white canopy bed). One has a cranky rabbit sitting on a bed. I have never seen so many stuffed rabbits, dolls, and such, all so tastefully arranged. I was in Victoria's Chamber, which has a king-sized bed and wonderful Victorian touches.

The Magees have come up with a beauty of an idea. Each room has a cassette player and a tape that explains what you would have seen from your window more than a century ago. The hats that Maureen has had made are worth the trip alone. A diary is in each room for people to write in during their stay. They are fun to read. The suites are in the tavern building. One of the suites has wheelchair access, a special bathroom equipped for the handicapped, and features designed for blind or deaf guests.

The porch on the second floor faces the Presidential Range. It's a special place to just sit and rock with Jake, the inn dog, or Zeke, the cat.

The Snooty Fox Pub, modeled after the eighteenth-century Irish pubs, has an old crane in the fireplace for doing hearth cooking. The doors of the two intimate dining rooms remain closed until 6:00 P.M. They are then opened to reveal highly polished 1850s Windsor chairs and pine tables set with silver and lit by candlelight.

It takes two hours to dine here; it is all done right. The menu changes seasonally, and no processed foods are used in any of the meals. Try the pork and venison pâté or the smoked salmon and seafood sausage to start. Then sample the Vermont turkey and okra chili, the grilled twelve-spice duck breast, rack of lamb, swordfish, vegetarian plate, or beef tenderloin. Be sure to savor the homemade sauces, mustards, and salsas prepared from the vegetables, herbs, and edible flowers from the inn's garden. Save room for dessert. Whiskey toddy cake sounds divine. So does white chocolate tart. These are only a sampling of what you might find at this AAA four-diamond restaurant.

In the evening while you're dining, your bed is turned down, your radio is turned on to soft music, your candle is lit, and a fabric heart is placed on your pillow. You are invited to use it as your do-not-disturb sign and then to take it home with you. Now if this touch isn't romantic, I do not know what is.

The inn is glorious. So is the whole area. You will not be disappointed with this one.

How to get there: Take Route 2 east from St. Johnsbury and turn right onto Route 18. Or coming from Route 5, take Route 135 east to Lower Waterford.

Innkeepers: John and Maureen Magee
Address/Telephone: Route 18, Box 55; (802) 748–5168 or (800) 76–BUNNY (800–762–8669), fax (802) 748–8342
Rooms: 15, plus 5 suites; all with private bath, radio, and cassette player, 1 specially equipped for handicapped. No smoking inn.
Rates: $169 to $249, double occupancy, MAP. EPB rates available.
Open: All year except April and first two weeks in November.
Facilities and activities: Bar, library, wheelchair access to dining rooms, snowshoeing, tobogganing, cross-country skiing, trout fishing, lawn games. Nearby: ice skating, golf.

The Inn at Ormsby Hill

MANCHESTER CENTER, VERMONT 05255

It's nice to have good innkeepers back in business. Chris and Ted had a beauty in Maine, but this inn far surpasses that one. Most important, the whole place is romantic.

When you enter the inn, the first room on the left is a beautifully furnished formal living room. Go on into the gathering room, which has a huge fireplace, games, and books. Continue into the conservatory–dining room. It's a wow. When the inn is full, three tables are in use. There's a really different-looking fireplace in here. The mantel came from either Europe or Newport. It's a beauty. The glass windows at the end of the room remind me of a ship, and Chris has nice plants all around.

The view of the mountains is awesome. There's an apple checkerboard at the ready.

The inn was built around 1760 and added onto in the 1800s. The new wing was constructed in 1996. You cannot tell where the old and new meet. Innkeepers are clever people. The rooms are just beautiful. Almost all have two-person whirlpool baths—now *that's* romantic—and fireplaces, either gas or wood. The beds are kings and queens and so comfortable. There are four-posters and canopies in every guest room. Everything is restful, and the colors are muted. The towels are big and fluffy. The inn reminds me of a gracious manor house in the English countryside, and it all has a full sprinkler system and alarms.

Breakfast is the main meal; however, Chris serves supper on Friday nights and a four-course dinner on Saturdays. I was lucky enough to be here then, and we had risotto with asparagus, porcini, and basil for the first course. This was followed by a garden salad with champagne vinaigrette and cream biscuits. The next course was peppered fresh tuna on top of garlic spinach with a shallot sauce. Dessert was a bittersweet chocolate soufflé with white chocolate and rum sauce. This is just a sample of Chris's spectacular food.

At breakfast time Chris makes breakfast desserts. Honest. I had one.

How to get there: From Route 30 go north to Historic Route 7A in Manchester. Turn left. Go south about 3 miles to the inn.

Innkeepers: Chris and Ted Sprague
Address/Telephone: Historic Route 7A (mailing address: RR2, Box 3264); (802) 670–2841, fax (802) 362–5176
Rooms: 10; all with private bath and air conditioning, 9 with double whirlpool tub and fireplace.
Rates: $110 to $225, double occupancy, EPB.
Open: All year.
Facilities and activities: Friday-night supper, Saturday dinner by reservation only, BYOB. Hammock, porch. Nearby: golf, bicycling, antiquing, fishing, tennis, hiking, downhill and cross-country skiing.

The Village Country Inn

MANCHESTER VILLAGE, VERMONT 05254

Manchester's favorite front porch beckons you as you arrive at the Village Country Inn, located in the heart of town. The porch is 100 feet long, with wicker furniture and rockers covered with rose chintz. It's full of pink flowers all summer long. It's the icing on this beautiful inn.

This is a French country inn done in shades of mauve, celery, and ecru, and stunning inside and out. Anne was a professional interior decorator, and the inn reflects her expertise. Mauve is a color I adore. The boutique is The French Rabbit, with well-dressed rabbits to greet you. Anne has wonderful taste, and the boutique is full of very nice things.

Tavern in the Green, the bar and lounge, has an upright piano and nice people who play and sing. One night when I was here, a playwright was in this room with a marvelous selection of music and songs. What an unexpected treat. A door from here leads out to the swimming pool and gardens. During the winter the large patio is flooded for ice skating. The inn has a large collection of skates for guests to use, and twinkling lights are hung in the trees all around the patio. In the summertime breakfast and dinner may be served out here.

In the living room is a large fieldstone fireplace dating back to 1889 and comfortable couches and chairs around it. Tables are provided for all sorts of games.

The rooms are magnificent and each one is different. They are done in ice cream colors. Lots of canopied beds, lace, plush carpets, down pillows, and nice things on dressers and tables give the rooms an elegant atmosphere. Good towels are such an important feature to inn guests and, needless to say, they are here.

Dining is a joy in the lovely dining room. The bishop-sleeve lace curtains and trellis alcoves create a cozy and romantic atmosphere for the glorious food. Chilled tomato bisque with dill is excellent. Salads aren't run of the mill, and entrees are creative. Grilled loin of lamb with rosemary and juniper sauce, and medallions of veal with wild mushrooms, shallots, and Madeira in a natural veal sauce are just two of the selections. Vermont lamb chops with black currant cassis and almonds are a house favorite. I chose crème brûlée for dessert. It was grand. Freshly made bread pudding with apples and hazelnuts captivated my dinner companion. Very good indeed. Breakfast is a full one, with many choices.

Affairs of the heart are wonderful up here. Rekindle the romance by having an "Enchanted Evening," an affair for the "too busy" and "too stressed." As the inn literature notes, this "intimate dinner affair is perfect for those of you who: go out to dinner a lot, cook at home a lot, need a break, are looking for a good time and romance." Also offered is the "Blooming Affair," a romantic champagne picnic lunch in the lovely gazebo and formal gardens. These affairs are offered spring, summer, and winter. Christmas, as you can imagine, is very special up here.

How to get there: Coming north on historic Route 7A, you will find the inn on your left in Manchester Village.

Innkeepers: Jay and Anne Degen
Address/Telephone: Route 7A (mailing address: P.O. Box 408, Manchester); (802) 362–1792 or (800) 370–0300
Rooms: 12 standard rooms, plus 21 luxury rooms and suites; all with private bath and phone; some with TV. No smoking inn.
Rates: $150 to $250, per room, double occupancy, MAP. Special packages available.
Open: All year.
Facilities and activities: Bar-lounge, boutique, swimming pool, tennis, ice skating. Nearby: golf, skiing, shopping.
Recommended Country Inns® Travelers' Club Benefit: Stay two nights, get third night free, Sunday–Thursday.

Mid-Atlantic & Chesapeake Region

by Brenda Boelts Chapin

edited by Suzi Forbes Chase

Are you one of those who would sooner travel without your map than without your gold-rimmed wine glasses boxed in velvet? Is your romantic streak searching for a poetic place to fulfill your fantasies?

M. F. K. Fisher once referred to food as love. At country inns we experience multiple layers of love. The savory foods of the Mid-Atlantic—Chesapeake Bay crab, mountain trout, farm-raised lamb, and seasonal vegetables and fruits—are a memorable part of any journey. There are inns to suit every romantic mood and taste. From the Hunt Country of Virginia to the sandy Atlantic shores, from the New York Finger Lakes to Maryland's Eastern Shore, I've selected Victorian inns, mountain lodges, and inns located on historic estates. Some are located in small towns, some in woodland settings, and others in rolling countryside. If you're like us, you enjoy sharing this diversity of style and take pleasure in meandering the byways, learning about local history, and meeting people who you know will be lifelong friends.

I envy you. You are about to explore the places we've enjoyed. To select only twenty-two romantic Mid-Atlantic inns for this inn guide out of the almost 200 inns we've included in *Romantic Country Inns of the Mid-Atlantic and Chesapeake* posed a delicious dilemma—one that required great restraint—which is something you can leave behind. Indulge yourselves. That's how lasting memories are created.

Mid-Atlantic and Chesapeake Region

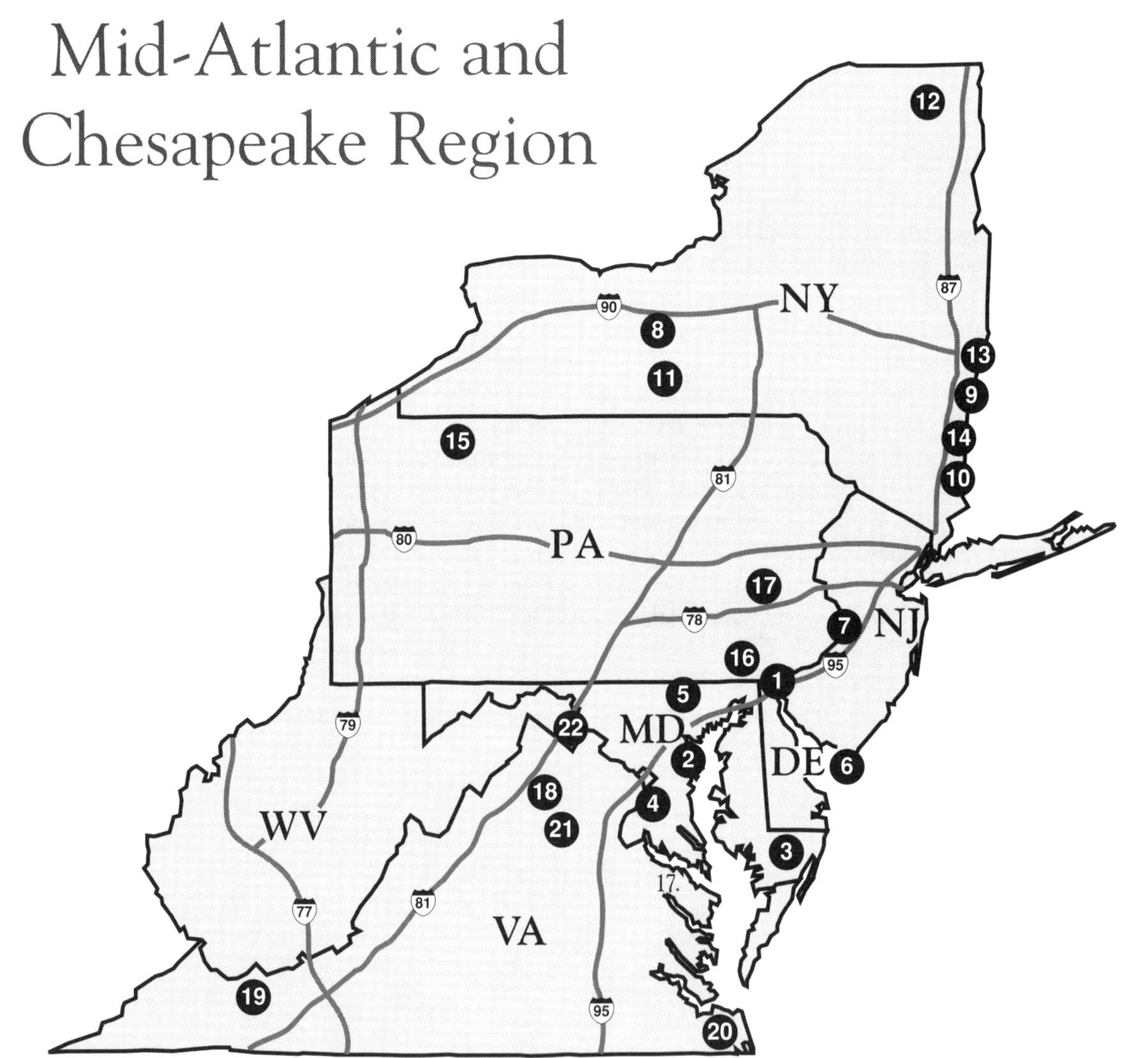

Mid-Atlantic & Chesapeake Region

Numbers on map refer to towns numbered below.

Delaware

1. Montchanin, The Inn at Montchanin Village 52

Maryland

2. Baltimore, Mr. Mole Bed & Breakfast 54
3. Berlin, Merry Sherwood Plantation 56
4. Buckeystown, The Inn at Buckeystown 58
5. Taneytown, Antrim 1844 60

New Jersey

6. Cape May, The Mainstay 62
7. Stockton, The Woolverton Inn 64

New York

8. Canandaigua, Morgan-Samuels B&B Inn 66
9. Dover PLains, Old Drovers Inn 68
10. Garrison, The Bird & Bottle Inn 70
11. Ithaca, Rose Inn 72
12. Lake Placid, Lake Placid Lodge 74
13. Old Chatham, Old Chatham Sheepherding Company Inn 76
14. Standfordville, Lakehouse Inn 78

Pennsylvania

15. Bradford, Glendorn 80
16. Churchtown, The Inn at Twin Linden 82
17. Fogelsville, Glasbern 84

Virginia

18. Charlottesville, Clifton: The Country Inn . . . 86
19. Christiansburg, The Oaks Victorian Inn 88
20. Norfolk, The Page House Inn 90
21. Trevilians, Prospect Hill 92

West Virginia

22. Charles Town, Hillbrook Inn 94

The Inn at Montchanin Village

MONTCHANIN, DELAWARE 19710

Montchanin is a tiny hamlet named for Anne Alexandrine de Montchanin. She was the grandmother of Eleuthère Irénée duPont, founder of the DuPont Gunpowder Company. The inn is located in a cluster of buildings built in the early 1800s to house laborers from the nearby DuPont powder mills. The complex includes several houses, a cluster of cottages, a former blacksmith shop, a schoolhouse, and a massive stone and post-and-beam barn.

The restoration is the ambitious undertaking of local preservationists Missy and Daniel Lickle. When they acquired the property, they sought an adaptive use that would preserve the quaint buildings in their original setting. They achieved this goal admirably.

The restoration is so true to the village's origins that even the original tiny concrete outhouses remain. Connected to the cottages by gardens, these now house mainentance equipment. Privy Lane leads guests from the restaurant (in the former blacksmith shop) to the cottages. The rebuilt barn houses the reception room and a giant reading room with a cathedral ceiling and a massive fieldstone fireplace. The entire six acres are on the National Register of Historic Places.

The romantic guest rooms are luxuriously furnished with antique four-poster and canopy beds, armoires, and painted blanket chests. There are chain-stitched rugs on hardwood floors, graceful moldings, and sponged walls. Eight of the units have fireplaces, and almost all have either a private garden, porch, balcony, or terrace. The beds are swathed in pretty fabrics and dressed in Frette sheets, and the marble baths have every possible luxury, including oversized whirlpool tubs in some. One of my favorites is the Draper Suite, whose bedroom is reached up a tiny stairway and through an angled doorway. It's done in a periwinkle blue faux finish with French toile drapes, pine floors, and a wet bar.

Throughout the inn you'll see eveidence of the owners' collecting passion. Missy collects holstein cows, while Dan collects crows.

The blacksmith shop now houses Krazy Kat's Restaurant. One of the area's top chefs is at its helm; he designed the kitchen as well as the menu. You'll find such dishes as grilled rack of veal chops served with herb-crusted shallots roasted in olive oil, gorgonzola-whipped Yukon potatoes, sautéed jumbo lump Maryland crab cakes, and shrimp mousseline served with whole-grain mustard cream and accompanied by sweet-potato fries.

The inn is in the Brandywine Valley, where the Wyeth family has been painting for years. It's close to Winterthur Museum and Gardens, Longwood Gardens, Brandywine River Museum, and Wilmington. Although there are no sports facilities on the premises, a golf course is located 2 miles away, and this is a terrific area for bicycling.

How to get there: From I–95 take the Concord Pike/Route 202 exit. Travel north on Route 202 to Route 141. Turn left onto Route 141, continuing to the Rockland Road intersection. Turn right onto Rockland Road, passing the DuPont Country Club. Continue on Rockland Road over the Brandywine River and bear left at the fork, just past the river. At the corner of Rockland Road and Route 100, turn right onto Route 100 north. Travel approximately 500 feet and turn into the entrance at Kirk Road and Route 100.

Innkeeper: Brooke Johnson; Daniel and Missy Lickle, proprietors
Address/Telephone: Route 100 and Rockland Road (mailing address: P.O. Box 130); (302) 888–2133 or (800) COWBIRD, fax (302) 888–0389
Rooms: 22 (will increase to 37 in 1997), including 12 suites; all with private bath, air conditioning, telephone, TV, and wet bar, 8 with fireplace, 2 with whirlpool. No smoking inn.
Rates: $125 to $350, double occupancy, EPB. Two-night minimum weekends; 3-night minimum holidays and special events.
Open: All year.
Facilities and activities: Dining room open for dinner daily 5:30–10:00 P.M., entrees $17–$23. Nearby: museums and gardens.
Business travel: Dataport and dual-line telephone in all rooms; 7 with desk; fax available; meeting space for 25 people.

Mr. Mole Bed & Breakfast

BALTIMORE, MARYLAND 21217

Why would someone name a lovely urban inn after a mole? One guest named the inn "Monsieur Molet"—implying that grace and style marked Paul and Collin's bed and breakfast. Of course, many of you have known Mr. Mole since your mother read you the children's book *Wind in the Willows*.

Located in a nineteenth-century brick townhouse in Baltimore, the inn has 14-foot ceilings in three contiguous parlors painted a brilliant yellow that complements the innkeepers' collections: Collin's porcelains and Paul's ecclesiastical antiques and small boxes. An appreciation for the comforts of friends, a delicious hot breakfast, and a knack for storytelling characterize the innkeepers.

Breakfast is served buffet style at the hour you choose the night before. You'll find yourself gathering up rich Amish cake made with walnuts and apples, fresh breads, perhaps a fragrant country cheese, and juices and meats. Then you select a small table for two and compose yourself for the day.

"Guests," admits Paul, "seem to prefer this time for privacy. Most don't really wake up until after they've had their morning coffee and tea. Of course, spontaneous friendships occasionally form, and sometimes we hear total strangers making dinner plans together. Everyone has their own preference."

Each bedroom has a distinctive personality.

The innkeepers obviously had fun developing themes with treasures collected in Amsterdam, Brussels, London, and local markets. Hand-painted wooden fish hang above the fireplace in the Explorers Room, history books and English porcelains are in the London Suite, and stuffed moles of various sizes and descriptions in the Mr. Mole Suite. In the Garden Room a sunporch is filled with flowers and white wicker furniture.

Tucked off to the corner of one parlor is the guest's pantry, with a fridge for storing a bottle of wine and a kettle for preparing yourself a cup of Earl Grey.

Located 5 blocks from Baltimore's light rail, the inn is convenient for touring or business in this easy-to-negotiate city. Should you wish to sequester yourself for the weekend, you might amble up to the coffee shop on the next block and enjoy the urban mix that characterizes the neighborhood.

I love to walk among the bountiful stalls of Baltimore's famed Lexington Market, where some family-owned businesses are a century old, catch a matinee at the Mechanic Theater, and still have time for a sumptuous Italian meal in Little Italy. The next morning I dawdle over breakfast until the nearby antiques shops open.

Where else but at Mr. Mole would you have eighteenth-century antiques and a rubber ducky propped on the rim of the bathtub? Mr. Mole made them do it. Mr. Mole makes them do it all. He's the alter ego of the place. Like him, Paul and Collin had fun collecting all their treasures. The result is an indulgent inn appropriately named for a creature in a book.

How to get there: From I–95 take exit 53 to I–395. Exit onto Martin Luther King, Jr., Boulevard, bearing right, and continue 2 miles. Turn left on Eutaw Street, go 6/10 mile, turn right at fourth stop light, onto McMechen Street. Go 1 block to stop sign at Bolton Street. Inn is diagonally across intersection.

Innkeepers: Paul Bragaw and Collin Clark
Address/Telephone: 1601 Bolton Street; (410) 728–1179, fax (410) 728–3379
Rooms: 5, including 2 suites; all with private bath, air conditioning, and telephone. No smoking inn.
Rates: $97 to $125, double occupancy, EPB. Two-night minimum on weekends March to mid-December.
Open: All year.
Facilities and activities: Enclosed parking. Nearby: Mechanic Theater, Myerhoff Symphony Hall, Lyric Opera House, Antique Row, Walters Art Gallery, Lexington Market, Orioles Park at Camden Yards, Babe Ruth Birthplace, Inner Harbor: Science Museum, National Aquarium.
Business travel: Five blocks from train. Telephone and desk in room; fax available.

Merry Sherwood Plantation

BERLIN, MARYLAND 21811

As we drive under the canopy of sugar maple trees that line the circular driveway, the magnificent seafoam green plantation mansion, trimmed with darker shades of green and sparkling white, looms ahead. A fanciful cupola crowns the confection. We imagine we see Elizabeth Henry Johnson—the young girl for whom the 8,500-square-foot, twenty-seven-room house was built in 1859—surveying her lands while waiting for her husband.

The restoration of the mansion, which is listed on the National Register of Historic Places, was the dedicated work of local businessman Kirk Burbage, whose family has lived in Berlin for some 200 years. He spent two years reviving the former ruin, and his painstaking attention to detail is apparent throughout.

We arrived in time for iced tea, which was being served in the front parlor. In the ballroom creamy, arched marble fireplaces gleam, heavy damask drapes frame doorways, and lace panels cover windows. Priceless antiques include Victorian settees, a square grand piano, and a massive carved chair with lion's-head arms and bearing a brass portrait of Queen Victoria. It's said to have been made for an anticipated visit to the United States by the queen, which never took place. We sat and sipped, talking to the other guests while we all thoroughly enjoyed Stacy's narrative about the house's history and its restoration.

The house contains impressive furnishings and decor throughout. There's a magnificent chandelier in the dining room, the parlor has an organ, and the library has polished paneled walls. There are nine elegant fireplaces. We were especially impressed by several bookcases in the library that open to reveal closets. Some of the books are leather-bound first editions. Beyond the library an inviting side porch contains wicker and rattan furniture and we sat here imagining how gorgeous the gardens must be during the summer. *Southern Living* magazine has been assisting in the development of the gardens and landscaping on the eighteen-acre property. We wished we had been able to come at a time when the flowers and trees were in bloom.

The guest rooms are equally impressive, furnished with museum-quality antiques and lush fabrics. In the Harrison Room, for example, there's a massive Gothic Revival bed and a Victorian fainting couch that can be converted into a double bed. The Chase Room has an unusual bed with 5-foot posts carved into beehive finials. The Johnson Room has a carved canopy bed.

Before going out to dinner, we climbed the mahogany stairs to the cupola, lined with windows, to survey the estate's domain. Later, in the library, we spent a pleasant evening finishing a jigsaw puzzle.

We breakfasted regally the next morning in a formal dining room that boasts a brass chandelier. We were seated at a mahogany Empire-style table with Victorian rosewood chairs. If you're lucky perhaps you, too, will have oatmeal-butterscotch muffins followed by puffed apple-cinnamon pancakes, as we did.

How to get there: From Baltimore and Washington, D.C., follow Route 50 east to Berlin (it's 6 miles before Ocean City). Take the Route 113 exit and travel south for 2½ miles. Merry Sherwood Plantation will be on the right.

Innkeeper: Stacy Kenny; Kirk Burbage, proprietor
Address/Telephone: 8909 Worcester Highway; (410) 641–2112 or (800) 660–0358
Rooms: 8, including 1 suite; all with air conditioning, 6 with private bath, 3 with wood-burning fireplace, 1 with Jacuzzi. No smoking inn.
Rates: $120 to $175, double occupancy, EPB. Two-night minimum weekends.
Open: All year.
Facilities and activities: Nearby: Assateague Island National Seashore, 8 miles away; golf, horseback riding, bird-watching, bicycling; historic Berlin.

The Inn at Buckeystown

BUCKEYSTOWN, MARYLAND 21717

Enter an old-fashioned setting that emits aromatic scents and tender feelings from the moment you step inside. Dan Pelz's general good-naturedness influences the ambience while his cuisine influences the palate; both inspire conversation (either bring a great story or come prepared to hear one).

It's customary to glance at the menu on top of the hall bureau. Dinner begins at 7:30 P.M. with Dan's award-winning soups. Among his eighty-seven soup creations is the famed Jack O'Lantern Soup, a creamy pumpkin soup.

Here's the weekly scenario: Saturday, expect to find a savory veal or beef dish; Wednesday, it's a perfectly baked German duck; Thursday is for beef, as in London broil; and Friday, it's seasonal fish. It's fowl every Sunday, early and by reservation. Each night of the week, a multicourse dinner appears upon antique china around candelit oak tables. Dinner is a single entree served at one shared seating, and it's a bundle of fun.

Buckeystown is a nationally registered historic village on the Monocacy River. In the spring pink and purple azaleas, lilacs, and forsythia accent the lawn. The eighteen-room inn is an Italianate Victorian with two parlors and a wraparound front porch; the woodwork is chestnut and oak, and the floors are heart-of-pine. Sitting on a bureau in your room is Dan and Chase's guide, *'Inn' Joying*. It directs you to the best in Civil War sites, antiquing, golf, walking and cycling tours, orchards, and restaurants.

The inn is filled with collections that reflect Dan and Chase's appreciation for art. The parlors are softly lit with Art Nouveau and Tiffany lamps. There are Phoenix glass and Van Briggle pottery to admire along with Dan's clown collection, which grows as a result of guests' thoughtfulness and generosity. Chase, who has a fine-arts degree, works in oils; when a spare moment appears, he retreats to his studio and paints. It's his green thumb that's nurtured the gardens and makes the orchids flourish throughout the inn.

The attractive rooms are furnished with antiques, and the antique beds have been rebuilt to accept larger mattresses. You find everything from cozy pillows, dolls, Indian paintings, and finely carved jade to handmade quilts and rockers. The honeymoon suite, St. John's Cottage (formerly a chapel), is a gentle walk down the hill. Outside the door is a hot tub graced by wisteria. The loft bedroom, which overlooks the parlor and fireplace, makes you feel sybaritic.

The inn pets include Chagny, the French Briard, and his dear friend Mr. Stubbs, the Scotty dog.

This inn weaves a rich tapestry of friendship, ambience, and cuisine. You bring the wine. The only choice you have to make is the choice to come, and that's the best one of all.

How to get there: From I–270 north of Washington, D.C., exit Route 85 south to Buckeystown. The inn is on the left in town.

Innkeepers: Daniel Pelz, owner/chef; Chase Barnett, partner; Rebecca Smith, manager
Address/Telephone: 3521 Buckeystown Pike (mailing address: General Delivery, Buckeystown); (301) 874–5755 or (800) 272–1190
Rooms: 7, including 2 suites and 2 cottages, all with private bath and desk, 3 with fireplace, 2 with telephone, 3 with TV. No smoking inn.
Rates: $230 to $309, per couple per night (gratuity and tax included), MAP.
Open: All year, but closed Mondays and Tuesdays except holidays and month of December.
Facilities and activities: Dinner Wednesday through Sunday, public invited by reservation ($31 daily except holidays, $35 holidays), BYOB. Two acres of land with pre–Civil War graveyard. Nearby: shops, antiquing, canoeing, bicycling, Antietam Battlefield, Harper's Ferry.

Antrim 1844

TANEYTOWN, MARYLAND 21787

The frosty light of the full moon emerged from the clouds and reflected off the snow as we drove; the farms and fields of rural Carroll County seemed to await passage to warmer days. We, however, found immediate warmth in the elegant Antrim 1844, named by its original builder for Antrim County, Ireland. Richard and Dort added the year it was built to its name.

Today the inn's twenty-three acres surrounding the brick plantation house have given the innkeepers the space to add an outdoor swimming pool, tennis court, croquet lawn, and chipping green. When they purchased the derelict property it lacked even electricity, and the neglected smokehouse, now a restaurant, was in marked disrepair.

The three-story building spans a hillside on the edge of a very small town. It's a large, sumptuous inn filled with antiques that knowledgeable collectors appreciate. After viewing the exquisite bedrooms, elegant mirrored parlor, cozy tavern, and the romantic dining areas, many a bride and groom choose this as their wedding site.

In the evening, Stuart, the maître d', seated us before a blazing fire in the smokehouse for dinner. We began with a mushroom tartlet and then had a fine salad of seasonal greens with Montrachet cheese, roasted peppers, and raspberry vinaigrette. I chose a salmon with an excellent barbecue sauce and a crème brûlée for dessert that came in a heart-shaped terrine with a crusty top, burnished as it should be.

For breakfast Richard might prepare Belgian waffles along with bacon and scrambled eggs. The sun blasts into the high-ceilinged dining rooms through great, lusciously curtained windows. On a winter's day the marble fireplace will be glowing. I think I've never seen such an inn with so many fireplaces.

In the evening, when you go up to your room, chocolates and cordials are served upon a butler's tray. Coffee, a muffin, and the newspaper arrive in the morning on the same tray, so you can emerge from your room slowly. You might have slept in a nineteenth-century rosewood half-tester from New Orleans or the 1790s canopied bed with its lace and ruffles, or the 1820 Honduras mahogany canopy with its 150-pound posts. For pure romance, I love the Boucher Suite with its canopy bed facing the fireplace and two balconies overlooking the gardens. In the marble bath, a two-person cobalt blue whirlpool tub sits on a platform. Even more sybaritic hideaways are found in the Ice House, The Cottage, the Smith House, and The Barn, each tucked away in the gardens and also containing fireplaces and whirlpool tubs.

Climb the ladder in the third-story hallway and take a look at the surrounding hills and town. During the Battle of Gettysburg, General George Meade climbed up here to see how events were progressing.

How to get there: From Baltimore Beltway 695, take exit 19 or 795 north. Exit Route 140 west to Taneytown. In town turn left onto Trevanian Road and go 150 feet to inn on right. From Frederick take 194 north to Taneytown. Turn right at light on Route 140, proceed ½ mile, turn right at fork onto Trevanian Road. Go 150 feet, inn on right. Signs indicate where to park.

Innkeepers: Richard and Dort Mollett

Address/Telephone: 30 Trevanian Road; (410) 756–6812 or (800) 858–1844, fax (410) 756–2744

Rooms: 14, including 5 suites and 4 cottages; all with private bath and air conditioning, 10 with Jacuzzi, 10 with fireplace, 2 with TV. One room wheelchair accessible. No smoking, except in tavern.

Rates: $150 to $300, double occupancy, EPB plus afternoon and evening hors d'oeuvres. Special packages available on holidays. Two-night minimum if stay includes Saturday night.

Open: All year.

Facilities and activities: Tavern, 23 acres, swimming pool, tennis court, croquet lawn, golf-chipping green, volleyball, badminton, horseshoes, formal gardens. Dinner by reservation Wednesday–Sunday (fixed price $50, higher on holidays). Nearby: 12 miles to Gettysburg. Golf courses: Wakefield Valley, Carroll Valley, Bear Creek.

Business travel: Desk in 4 rooms; telephone, fax, and copy machine available; conference rooms; flip charts.

The Mainstay

CAPE MAY, NEW JERSEY 08204

The Mainstay is an inn with a story to tell. It is so famous that Tom and Sue Carroll give visitors an afternoon tour of their landmark lodging, followed by an elegant tea accompanied with sweet pleasures—delicious homemade cakes and cookies—stylishly served either on the summer veranda or in the winter parlor. Advance reservations are a necessity here. If you don't get a room this year, try next year. At the least come for the graciously delicious afternoon tea tour.

The Carrolls purchased The Mainstay in 1976, and it's their dream house. Built in 1872 as a "hotel casino," the former gentlemen's gambling house is a luxurious, high-style Victorian. "We have decorated rather than restored," explains Tom, "and much of the furniture was in place the day we arrived." The scale is grand and impressive, but you can also climb a ladder stairway to the whimsical belvedere room for a view of the town through antique binoculars.

Using scaffolding and patience, the Carrolls created a showcase drawing room papered with wallpaper donated by Bradbury & Bradbury of California (who sought a stunning setting). Unusual furniture—a "tête-à-tête" sofa for facing your companion and a rotating gaming table—furnish the room, along with ornate vases (Sue's taste) and clocks (Tom's taste). You'll probably spot the piece of music on the piano: "Sailing

Down the Chesapeake Bay." In the smaller parlor (furnished in equally commanding style), notice Tom's collection of bisque bathing beauties.

The rooms have handsome Victorian pieces; some have additional Bradbury & Bradbury wallpapers. You can select a room in the neighboring home that the Carrolls have restored. There are rooms with king- and queen-sized beds. In the newly restored Officer's Quarters, located across the street, every contemporary luxury, including fireplaces and whirlpool baths, have been provided.

Cape May has a bounty of excellent restaurants; most ask you to bring your own wines. Menus are available at the inn. You can walk from the inn to the restaurants.

Breakfast is served upon lace placemats with silver coffeepots and lovely china, and everyone begins comparing notes on Victorian manners and morals and basking in the luxurious grandeur. During the summer you might have tea on the veranda, where you can glance up Columbia Avenue and see a perfectly positioned series of front verandas—the Victorians wanted to see who was visiting whom. As you visit with other guests, you bite into Sue's buttermilk orange cupcakes or the memorable lemon bars that come with the iced tea. The ocean breezes blow gently, and you realize this moment will be with you forever.

How to get there: From the Garden State Parkway, merge onto Lafayette Street. Turn left onto Madison, right onto Columbia, to 635 on the right.

Innkeepers: Tom and Sue Carroll; Kathy Moore and Jill Turner, managers
Address/Telephone: 635 Columbia Avenue; (609) 884–8690
Rooms: 16, including 7 suites; all with private bath, 4 suites with fireplace, whirlpool, TV, telephone, and VCR. One room wheelchair accessible. No smoking inn.
Rates: $95 to $245, double occupancy; $10 less for single; EPB, afternoon tea, and beach passes. Additional person, $20. Three-night minimum in season.
Open: All year; reduced number of rooms mid-December to mid-March.
Facilities and activities: Nearby: restaurants, beach, historic Cape May mansions, bicycling, bird-watching, sailing, trolley rides, State Park, lighthouse museum, carriage rides.
Recommended Country Inns® Travelers' Club Benefit: Stay one night, get second night free, Sunday–Thursday, November–April, excluding Thanksgiving and Christmas weeks, subject to availability.

The Woolverton Inn

STOCKTON, NEW JERSEY 08559

In the 1980s The Woolverton Inn was my special secret retreat. I would come on summer afternoons, to sit either on the upstairs porch or on the flagstone veranda, and write. In the evening after dinner, I would play the piano or complete a jigsaw puzzle into the wee hours of the morning. But then the innkeeper moved away and it just wasn't the same.

Therefore, it was with a keen sense of hope that I visited The Woolverton Inn again in late 1994, when I learned that it had been purchased by Elizabeth and Michael Palmer, an enthusiastic couple who had great plans for the majestic, 1792 stone manor house. By early 1996 the renovations were complete, and I found that this magnificent manor house once again met—and exceeded—my expectations. Private baths have been added to every guest room, and two rooms even have two-person Jacuzzis. There are canopy beds, lush fabrics, fireplaces in two rooms, and walls charmingly handpainted with flowers or pastoral scenes. The guest rooms are named for people who have had a connection to the house. My favorite is Amelia's Garden, which has a four-poster cherry bed with a fishnet canopy, a pretty sitting room, and an elegant bath with pink walls and a lovely walnut dresser outfitted with a sink.

Downstairs, in the living room, the piano remains in the corner, and the game table by the window is just waiting for a couple to put a jigsaw puzzle together. The antique furniture is elegantly upholstered, oil paintings embellish the walls, and a fire glows in the hearth in cool weather. On the wicker-filled side porch, guests relax with a book and enjoy the gardens, perhaps while enjoying tea, coffee, or lemonade with cookies, cheese, and fruit, which are offered every afternoon.

A full gourmet breakfast is served in the formal dining room. Elizabeth might prepare a baked apple or poached pear for the fruit course and perhaps an entree of blueberry johnnycakes or creamy scrambled eggs with asparagus and chives.

The inn is located on ten acres. Sheep graze in a meadow. There are a stone spring house, a picturesque barn that may one day be restored, and a carriage house with two guest rooms. Hiking trails meander about, and there's a croquet lawn and a horseshoes pit. For those of us who love country inns with a deep-felt passion, we can add another to our collection of favorites.

How to get there: From New York take the New Jersey Turnpike south to exit 14 and follow I–78 west to exit 29. Follow I–287 south to Route 202 south and take the second Lambertville exit onto Route 29, traveling north to Stockton. Travel through the village to the fork. Veer right onto Route 523 and go for $\frac{2}{10}$ mile. Turn left onto Woolverton Road. The inn is reached along the second driveway on the right.

Innkeepers: Elizabeth and Michael Palmer
Address/Telephone: 6 Woolverton Road; (609) 397–0802, fax (609) 397–4936
Rooms: 10, including 2 suites; all with private bath and air conditioning, 2 with fireplace, 2 with Jacuzzi. No smoking inn.
Rates: $95 to $180, double occupancy, EPB. Two-night minimum weekends; 3-night minimum holiday weekends.
Open: All year.
Facilities and activities: Located on 10 acres with croquet lawn, hiking trails, and horseshoes pit on property. Nearby: Delaware River towpath and park ½ mile, canoeing, rafting, historical sites, boutiques, antiques shops.
Recommended Country Inns® Travelers' Club Benefit: Stay two nights, get third night free, Monday–Thursday.

Morgan-Samuels B & B Inn

CANANDAIGUA, NEW YORK 14424

Were I marking the changing of the seasons, this is where I'd come. In the first bloom of spring, I'd walk between the silver maples that line the lane; as the leaves hinted at harvest colors, I'd visit the fall wineries and select jams and grape pies from the roadside stands; following a snowfall I'd call for a winter's date on the horse-drawn sleigh; and when the first blush of summer heralds its becalming force, I'd canoe across the lake to out-of-the-way places. Whatever the season this refined setting with its placid rural surroundings offers elegant seclusion. A day spent luxuriating in this country house inn is a day complete in itself.

Julie's artistic background has gracefully influenced each room; four have their own fireplaces and one an antique French parlor stove. The suite is a dream. Its two-room bath has a shower, a tub, and a Jacuzzi lit by a window that overlooks the fields. Each piece of furniture opposite the fireplace is inlaid with wood and overlaid with finely carved details.

Julie recommends romantic pleasures. She gives thought to where you might go that would particularly suit your taste. She suggested a canoe ride for the two of us or a summer afternoon lunch in the Sonnenberg Gardens, with its sixty acres of plants, or maybe we just wanted to lounge beside the rose garden while listening to the fountain trickle and savoring our favorite tea.

John is the chef. Early every morning he and

young son Jonathan depart together for the market to purchase the fresh fruits and oranges for juice. If an omelet has crossed his mind on the drive, he selects the six cheeses and green and red peppers that compose this delicious masterpiece. If a meat is called for, his own selection of savory garden herbs is admixed with the sausage that awaits frying.

Some mornings they call upon the nearby monastery for freshly baked whole-grain breads or flours for the fruit or nut pancakes. While all this is occurring, we are sleeping soundly.

The inn is named for Judson Morgan, an actor, and Howard Samuels, who invented the plastic bag. Each owned the mansion at one time. Yes, I should have asked more about the architecture and furnishings. I saw and marveled at the hand-hewn beam in the 1810 section and the stone- and brickwork and wondered who these early craftsmen were. The impressive array of antiques and oil paintings could have prompted innumerable questions as well. But one falls under a spell here and lingers on the patio under the trees or in the breakfast room beside the fire. One sits to breakfast, where the delicious pancakes or fabulous omelets emerge hot from the kitchen.

One steps out the mansion door not expecting to find a black Oriental chicken who busses the ground for seeds while a peacock turns his head sharply and then leisurely fans his massive tail feathers in a paced walk. One hears the rustle of leaves and sees cows peering from behind a stone fence. Or one returns to the library, hears the sound of the fire crackling, and smiles at the beauty of a moment shared with your spouse—whether you've been married for many decades or merely a day.

The location is rural, yet five minutes from Lake Canandaigua and the eponymous town—an ideal setting with articulate hosts.

How to get there: From I–90 East take exit 43 and turn right onto Route 21. Proceed to Route 488 and turn left. Turn right at the first stop sign onto Smith Road and proceed ¾ mile to inn on the right.

Innkeepers: John and Julie Sullivan
Address/Telephone: 2920 Smith Road; (716) 394–9232, fax (716) 394–8044
Rooms: 5; all with private bath and air conditioning, 4 with fireplace, 2 with Jacuzzi, 1 with parlor stove. No smoking inn.
Rates: $119 to $210, double occupancy, May through mid-September; $125 to $255 mid-September through mid-November; lower rates rest of year; EPB. Two-night minimum weekends May through mid-November.
Open: All year.
Facilities and activities: Dinner for 8 or more by reservation (approximately $50 each); BYOB. Forty-six acres, tennis court. Nearby: Horse-drawn sleigh rides during winter, Canandaigua Lake, Sonnenberg Gardens, Rose Hill Mansion, Bristol Playhouse, wineries.

Old Drovers Inn

DOVER PLAINS, NEW YORK 12522

Do you have plans for Valentine's Day? Perhaps, like Alice and Kemper, you'll purchase your favorite inn on the most romantic day of the year. Before this venerable place became theirs, they used to appear on the doorstep when the need for R&R (repose and romance) touched them. Now they make Old Drovers glow with nurturing.

If this building, which dates from 1750, could talk, it would heave a sigh of relief and say thank you for restoring my authentic old beauty, for decorating my windows with colorful chintz, for placing down-filled couches in my cozy parlors, for bringing people back to my hearth.

The Old Drovers is unique in the mid-Atlantic for its authentic character; you intuit a veritable sense of the past. The floors angle slightly and sometimes creak to the step as you descend to the romantic Old Tap Room. The "shell" cabinet in the second-floor library has its mate in the Metropolitan Museum of Art.

In the eighteenth century the drovers herding cattle into New York City would stop here with their herds for watering. "Only," explained Alice, pointing out the tavern sign that reads DROVERS AND ANKLEBEATERS, "the drovers were actually gentry. They came ahead of the ankle-beaters, who performed the cattle-driving work."

This once-rowdy place has settled down. The toughest animals you'll find are Alice's three Yorkies, Gordon Bennett, Goodness Gracious, and Jedediah, who greet everyone as if they were born to hospitality.

Before dinner we visited in the library with a glass of wine (the inn won the *Wine Spectator* Award of Excellence), then descended the stairway to dinner. In the candlelight of the star-patterned hurricane lamps we perused the chalkboard menu. Even before a drink arrived, the deviled eggs came with fresh condiments. Some traditions have remained the same here since 1937, like the double drinks, the condiments and hickory salt, and the turkey hash (healthy, said Alice). I was intrigued, however, by a potato-crusted salmon with vinaigrette and cilantro that was simultaneously moist and crisp; it got superior marks. The chef knows his business. For dessert we ate the naughty but divine Key lime pie.

Our room that night had a double barrel-vaulted ceiling and a fireplace, where we nestled up in the cozy chintz chairs. There were robes in the closet, satin coverlets on the firm beds, and hooked rugs on the floors. And—need I say?—there's nothing historic about the modern bathrooms. Or the inn's membership in *Relais et Châteaux*.

On weekends the chef prepares a full breakfast; midweek there's a fine homemade granola and freshly squeezed juice. The coffee is served in great oversized cups; we filled ours and meandered into the parlor, where the finches were chirping. We admired the rolltop desk and the wall mural painted by Edward Paine.

Soon there will be more of Old Drovers to enjoy—as construction is scheduled to begin on five cottages.

How to get there: From New York City take I–684 to Brewster, then take Route 22 north. On Route 22 a sign for the inn is 3 miles south of Dover Plains. Turn east and drive ½ mile. Inn is on the right; guests park on south side and enter through the porch.

Innkeepers: Alice Pitcher and Kemper Peacock
Address/Telephone: Old Route 22; (914) 832–9311, fax (914) 832–6356
Rooms: 4; all with private bath and air conditioning, 3 with fireplace. Pets by prior approval.
Rates: $320 to $395, weekends per couple, MAP; $150 to $230, double occupancy, midweek, continental breakfast. Two-night minimum if Saturday included.
Open: All year, except two weeks in January.
Facilities and activities: On 12 acres. Dinner Thursday through Tuesday; Saturday, Sunday, and holidays served from noon (entrees: $17 to $35). Nearby: Hyde Park, golf courses, horseback riding, antiquing, country drives, fairs and festivals.

The Bird & Bottle Inn

GARRISON, NEW YORK 10524

New York getting to you? Need out for the weekend?

The Bird & Bottle is where one satiates appetites, where New Yorkers retreat for privacy, where one ventures for Hudson River touring, and where one comes for two- and three-hour-long dinners beside the fire in a historic inn dating from 1761.

Sitting here dining, I imagined the Albany stagecoach driver galloping up to Warren's Tavern (as it was known back then) for fresh horses, the passengers tumbling out and into the inn for good hot food, the staff bustling to serve them in a ruckus while the horses are changed—then the driver shouts the call for New York, everyone reboards, and the creaking of wood and leather and the thudding of hooves against the ground are heard way on up the hill.

The pub, known as the Drinking Room, is framed in wood. A tall man bends down to enter and soon finds a seat near the fire and casts his eyes about the interesting setting.

The rooms are charming and romantic, with fireplaces where you may burn real wood—a rarity in inns today.

The Beverly Robinson Suite is decorated in a peach-and-beige damask that drapes across the canopy bed. Oriental rugs cover the pine floors, and there's a little balcony overlooking the entrance. For the ultimate in privacy, the Nelson

Cottage is tucked away amid the gardens. Its carved canopy bed is festooned in shades of pink and cream, and it has a fireplace.

There are six acres in which to walk, but those of is with a romantic streak will head for the little bridge that crosses the tumbling brook or strike out to explore the remnants of the old stone gristmill.

Every Thanksgiving Day guests arrive all dressed up ready to carve a beautifully roasted turkey at their private table without having lifted so much as a spoon in effort. This has become a traditional feast day at The Bird & Bottle, and an entire turkey is served to parties of six or more. Following dinner the leftovers are individually wrapped for you to carry home. This cozy setting is a delicious way to celebrate a holiday.

The breads here are magnificent; light, white yeast breads and a deeply flavored pumpkin bread (made with fresh pumpkin); you try not to eat too many of these to save your appetite. The pewter serviceware fits with the inn's era. One evening I selected the specials—a spicy dilled tomato soup followed by grilled vegetables served in puff pastry, which created a pleasurable tingling sensation in my mouth. Next a calming, light grapefruit sorbet. Then I sliced into thick scallops filled with slivers of smoked salmon.

The temperature dipped to below freezing that night. But my room was warm, the way I like it, and a fire was laid when I returned from dinner. A note on the bureau asked me to drip the water, and when that was finished, I felt I had done my part to help the inn through the chilly night. Settled into the Emily Warren room, I heard noises—the floor creaking from someone's footsteps, passing voices—then all fell asleep, soundly asleep.

How to get there: From Bear Mountain Bridge take Route 9D north 4½ miles; then take Route 403 to Route 9. Go 4 miles to the inn, which is on the right, well, well off the road.

Innkeeper: Ira Boyer
Address/Telephone: Old Albany Post Road, Route 9; (914) 424–3000 or (914) 424–3283
E-mail: birdbottle@aol.com
Rooms: 4, including 1 suite and 1 cottage; all with private bath, working fireplace, and air conditioning. Limited smoking inn.
Rates: $210 to $240, double occupancy, EPB and dinner credit of $75 per person, plus 12 percent service charge and tax. Two-night minimum weekends.
Open: All year.
Facilities and activities: Dinner Wednesday–Sunday (average $50 fixed price for 4-course dinner exclusive of wine), Sunday brunch, call regarding lunch; pub. Nearby: village of Cold Spring, Boscobel Mansion, historic Hudson River Museum, Kykuit (Rockefeller estate), wineries, nature center, sailing, biking, hiking, antiquing.
Recommended Country Inns® Travelers' Club Benefit: Stay two nights, get third night free, subject to availability.

Rose Inn

ITHACA, NEW YORK 14851

What makes an inn linger in your memory like fine wine? What brings a smile to your lips every time the Rose Inn is mentioned? You could, of course, say it was the sunken whirlpool bath and the beautiful evening with the spring peepers calling away. Or the superb meal of artichoke heart strudel and honey-almond duck enhanced by a Finger Lakes wine. Perhaps it was the myriad adventures you'd enjoyed throughout the day, thanks to Charles and Sherry's recommendations of wineries to visit and the Mackenzie-Childs' pottery shop down the road. But of course, a European-style inn is the culmination of all of the above and that's why you went to Rose Inn.

Sherry, who has earned advanced degrees in microbiology and social planning, has an expert's eye for interior design. Charles trained in Europe and managed seven major hotels before he joined Cornell's School of Hotel Administration. Turning their full-time attention to the Rose Inn, they've created a small, elegant European-style hotel, where your hosts speak eight languages fluently.

The Rose Inn has a mystique in the area. It was known as "the home with the circular stairway" because a museum-quality stairway was crafted from Honduran mahogany by a master craftsman who disappeared without a trace.

The luxury is overt and detailed. Never too much, never too little. Our room, Number 11, was contemporary in design with light and privacy as well as a romantic touch—a sunken whirlpool bath beneath triple Palladian windows and a white brocade love seat near the fireplace.

Dinner at the Rose Inn is served in small dining rooms. You make your selections in advance. Among the choices are smoked oysters in *beurre blanc* on puff pastry, châteaubriand with sauce béarnaise served with a bouquetière of vegetables, and scampi Mediterranean flambéed with brandy and a touch of tomato, curry, and cream. I chose the Chef's Surprise, a tender almond duck (and carried away the recipe). Dessert was a rich multiflavored chocolate-raspberry-hazelnut torte.

Behind the inn is the apple orchard, which is the source of Charles's delicious, long-baked German apple pancakes. His recipe derives from his native Black Forest youth. His breakfasts begin with a tasty freshly squeezed blend of juice from imported oranges.

You enter unpretentiously through the kitchen, but be not deceived—romance lies beyond this unusual entrance. Later you'll say, "Do you remember that evening at the Rose?"

How to get there: From Rochester take I–90, exit 40; follow Route 34S 36$\frac{2}{10}$ miles; the inn is on the left. From Ithaca Airport turn right on Warren Road and go 1$\frac{3}{10}$ miles; turn left on Hillcrest Road for 1$\frac{1}{2}$ miles to the end. Make a right onto Triphammer Road (joins Route 34) and go north 4$\frac{4}{10}$ miles. The inn is 10 miles from Ithaca.

Innkeepers: Charles and Sherry Rosemann; Patricia Cain, manager
Address/Telephone: Route 34N (mailing address: P.O. Box 65766); (607) 533–7905, fax (607) 533–7908
E-mail: roseinn@clarityconnect.com
Rooms: 10, plus 5 suites; all with private bath, air conditioning, and telephone; 4 suites with whirlpool bath, 2 with fireplace. No smoking inn.
Rates: $100 to $150, rooms; $175 to $250, suites, double occupancy; EPB; weekends Easter–Thanksgiving: $125–$175, rooms, $200–$275, suites. Two-night minimum April–November if stay includes Saturday.
Open: All year.
Facilities and activities: Dinner Tuesday–Saturday (prix fixe $50, 4-course). Wine served. Twenty acres with fishing pond, apple orchard, rose garden. Nearby: winery tours, ski Greek Peak, lake mailboat tours, bicycling, cultural events, Cornell University.
Business travel: Desk in all rooms; conference center; secretarial services; fax; e-mail.
Recommended Country Inns® Travelers' Club Benefit: Stay one night, get second night free (tax and service charge excluded), Monday–Thursday, May 1–November 30; Sunday–Friday, December 1–April 30; excluding holidays.

Lake Placid Lodge

LAKE PLACID, NEW YORK 12940

It was a sunny October afternoon when we arrived. We immediately fetched a glass of wine from the cozy bar and retired to Hawkeye, our generous two-level retreat to watch the sunset from our upper deck. As the sun slid behind Whiteface Mountain, it cast its dark reflection in the waters, as we watched the streaking sky change from orange and fuschia to the palest pink. It was then that I realized I could happily stay right here and write for the rest of my life.

This former 1882 Adirondack camp was renovated and opened to guests in 1994. True to its origins, it has a log exterior, and its decks are framed by arching unpeeled birch branches. The guest rooms have beds made of twisted birch trees, and walls made of logs, bark, and beadboard panels. There are twig furniture and sofas and chairs dressed in bright patterns. Most rooms have stone fireplaces with log mantels, and several, including Hawkeye, have two fireplaces. There are six buildings scattered about the grounds, each containing several rooms or suites. Even the smallest rooms on the ground floor of the main lodge seem spacious, and they have their own private patios, with terrific views of the lake.

After watching the evening spectacle, Managing Director Kathryn Kincannon, full of energy and enthusiasm, escorted me through the inn's common rooms, where some guests were playing billiards and others were completing a jigsaw puzzle, and then down to the marina to see the fleet of restored boats. She pointed out a nature trail that leads past trees labeled with identifying tags. We walked to the boat dock, where several couples were just returning from the sunset cocktail cruise on the inn's open-deck sightseeing barge.

It was warm enough at night to eat on the restaurant deck, romantically lighted by flickering candles. Following a dinner of confit of duck leg with sautéed potatoes and foie gras, deliciously ending with a summer pudding with raspberries, we returned to our room to contemplate the difficult decision before us: Should we take a relaxing soak in the two-person Jacuzzi; wrap ourselves against the evening chill and sit on the deck awhile longer, listening to the night sounds; or light the fire in one of the massive stone fireplaces? Reluctant to spoil the mood of this amorous place, we chose the latter and lingered with a port before snuggling into the luxurious feather bed, knowing we would be warm enough to leave the windows open all night as we listened to the loons call across the water.

Bright and early in the morning, as the sun was rising, and with the heavy scent of pine permeating the room, I arose to join Kathryn on the boat deck for tai chi, and my companion did his morning jog around the golf course. We left feeling relaxed, rested, and renewed.

How to get there: From I–87 take exit 30. Travel northwest on Route 73 for 30 miles to Lake Placid. In the village take Route 86 for 1½ miles toward Saranac Lake. At the top of the hill, turn right onto Whiteface Inn Road. Follow it for 1½ miles and turn right at the LAKE PLACID LODGE sign. Travel through the golf course to the lodge.

Innkeepers: Christie and David Garrett; Kathryn Kincannon, managing director
Address/Telephone: Whiteface Inn Road; (518) 523–2700, fax (518) 523–1124
Rooms: 22; all with private bath, Jacuzzi, telephone, TV, and VCR, 18 with fireplace. Children welcome. Pets permitted in 2 rooms at $50 per day. Wheelchair access. No smoking inn.
Rates: $175 to $425, double occupancy, meals extra. Two-night minimum weekends; 3-night minimum holidays.
Open: Year-round.
Facilities and activities: Championship 18-hole golf course, 4 tennis courts, hiking trails, sandy lakeside beach, canoes, fishing boats, paddleboats, Sunfish, open-deck sightseeing barge, mountain bikes, cross-country ski touring center in winter. Nearby: downhill skiing, ice skating, hunting.
Business travel: Desk in room; dataport; fax and secretarial services available, meeting rooms; audiovisual equipment; photocopy services.

Old Chatham Sheepherding Company Inn

OLD CHATHAM, NEW YORK 12136

Is this heaven or am I merely dreaming? We are sitting in a wicker rocker on our private porch looking beyond the sunken garden with its fountain to the lush green pastures brimming with sheep. The quiet is punctuated occasionally by a baby lamb bleating for its mother, but otherwise the air is still. This will always be my first memory of the Old Chatham Sheepherding Company Inn—this and the extraordinary cuisine, that is.

"I'm just a farmer at heart," owner Tom Clark laughed one night in the relaxed but sophisticated living room of the inn, as he tried to describe how he and his wife created their unique inn and its unusual by-products. "From the time I raised and exhibited three sheep at the local Dutchess County Fair," he went on to say, "I've had an interest in sheep."

This interest in sheep has led the couple to create an entirely new American business. Not only does the inn offer overnight lodging and a fine-dining restaurant, but on their 500-acre farm, the Clarks also raise sheep that are producing milk used for cheese, yogurt, ice cream, and other products. Although the dairy is in its infancy, there are great plans for the future. One morning my companion and I rose early to walk down to the Shaker-style sheep barn to watch the 6:30 A.M. milking and to pet the baby lambs. The operation is as modern and as interesting as a large-scale dairy operation.

The inn is gracious and charming—but that's not surprising, since Nancy is an interior designer and also an artist. Her luminous watercolors decorate several guest rooms. Fine antiques are liberally combined with unusual new furnishings, and elegant fabrics cover chairs, love seats, and beds. There are carved four-poster beds padded with fluffy lamb's-wool cushions. A nearby cottage contains two romantic suites that are perfect in every detail. The masculine Cotswold Suite has a high four-poster bed, a brick fireplace, and a private deck, while the Hampshire Suite is charmingly done in shades of pink and yellow. Two more units are being created in the Carriage House.

As elegant as the inn appears, however, innkeeper George Shattuck best described the casual atmosphere when he said, "We want guests to feel comfortable. We know we've achieved our goal when they come to breakfast in their terry robes," and he swears it's actually happened.

The dining room is presided over by Executive Chef Melissa Kelly, a graduate of the Culinary Institute of America and the protégée of such acclaimed chefs as Larry Forgione and Alice Waters. Her rack of lamb was exquisite, as was the grilled ahi tuna. A kitchen garden was being created when we visited, but she is already creating a distinctive new cuisine using sheep's milk instead of cow's or goat's. A separate bakery where the talented pastry chef will have his own ovens and a temperature- and climate-controlled wine cellar will also be completed soon.

The manor house was originally the home of John S. Williams Sr., whose interest in Shaker life was piqued by his home's proximity to several major Shaker communities. He began collecting examples of Shaker artifacts and eventually opened a museum across the street from his home. The museum contains one of the finest collections of Shaker-made articles in the world.

How to get there: From New York City take the Taconic Parkway to Route 295 east to East Chatham. Turn left at the sign for Old Chatham and follow this road for 3 miles. Turn left after the country store onto County Road 13. Follow this road for 1 mile and bear right onto Shaker Museum Road. The inn is ½ mile farther on the left.

Innkeepers: George Shattuck III and Melissa Kelly; Nancy and Tom Clark, proprietors
Address/Telephone: 99 Shaker Museum Road; (518) 794–9774, fax (518) 794–9779
Rooms: 8, including 2 suites; all with private bath and air conditioning, 2 with fireplace, 1 with whirlpool. Wheelchair accessible. No smoking inn.
Rates: $150 to $325, double occupancy, EPB. Two-night minimum June–October; 3-night minimum selected holiday weekends.
Open: All year except January.
Facilities and activities: Walking and hiking on 500 acres; seminars and events throughout the year, ranging from sheep-shearing demonstrations to cooking classes and wine dinners; tennis court is being installed. Nearby: Shaker Museum is across the street.

Lakehouse Inn
STANFORDVILLE, NEW YORK 12581

Judy and Richard Kohler owned a Victorian gingerbread house that they called the Village Victorian Inn in Rhinebeck for many years, but when they built this contemporary home overlooking tiny Golden Pond in 1991, they created a thoroughly sophisticated, elegant and utterly romantic retreat, as different from the fussy Victorian as Dr. Jeckyll is from Mr. Hyde.

At first sight the cedar-sided house appears modest and unremarkable; even when we walked along the flying-bridge entrance to the house, we were unprepared for the gracious and urbane interior. The house envelops its guests in country charm but also offers luxurious and spacious private retreats. For a total getaway from the fast-paced city, I can't imagine a more relaxing sanctuary.

The living room is decorated with flair in gentle earth tones. The vaulted, rough-sawn pine ceiling and the wall of view windows toward the lake give the room a warm, inviting glow. It's furnished with antiques, Oriental rugs on oak floors, twig furniture, comfortable sofas, piles of magazines and books, and an ornately carved oak English bar on which Victorian flow blue china is displayed. It's surrounded by a wraparound deck overlooking the lake.

Lakehouse Inn is the ultimate romantic retreat. The Casablanca Suite, for example, has its own fireplace, laid with logs and ready to be lighted, and a private deck. There's a pink damask sofa on which to watch the flames with a loved one while sipping a glass of wine chilled in the refrigerator. The canopy bed is swathed in lace. A television, VCR, and CD player hide in a pine armoire. In the bath, a Jacuzzi for two has a serene view and is surrounded by a lip holding an array of fat candles.

The equally spacious Master Suite, located downstairs, has a private deck offering a view of the lake. Oriental rugs cover oak floors, another lace canopy decorates the bed, fat shutters shield the windows, and the pink-tile bath has another Jacuzzi. Each of the rooms is so large and so well equipped that it's possible to spend an entire weekend in the room and never feel claustrophobic.

Every possible amenity is provided. As Judy explained, "We just want our guests to be comfortable. We're too far from a town for them to run out for a soft drink, so we provide all of that in the room. We have soft drinks, wine, cookies, appetizers such as smoked salmon, truffles, and even Baby Watson cheesecakes in the refrigerator in case someone has a late-night sweet-tooth craving."

In the morning our breakfast was delivered to our room in a covered basket. One day it included an individual quiche with fresh fruit and breads. Another day we had cheese blintzes and chicken Chardonnay.

If guests do venture forth, they will find rowboats and paddleboats for use on the lake, hammocks, trails through the twenty-two-acre property, and a VCR library that includes almost 150 selections. Historic mansions, local wineries, and superb restaurants are located nearby.

How to get there: From New York City take the Hudson River Parkway north to the Saw Mill River Parkway, and then travel north on the Taconic Parkway to the Rhinebeck/Route 199 exit. Turn right onto Route 199 and go ½ mile. Take the first right onto Route 53 (South Road). Go 3 ½ miles. Turn right onto Shelly Hill Road and go exactly 9/10 mile. Turn into paved driveway. The Lakehouse Inn is the second house.

Innkeepers: Judy and Richard Kohler
Address/Telephone: Shelly Hill Road; (914) 266–8093
Rooms: 5; all with private bath, air conditioning, telephone, TV, stereo, CD player, minirefrigerator, wet bar, coffeemaker, balcony or deck, fireplace, and Jacuzzi. No smoking inn.
Rates: $295 to $495, double occupancy, EPB. Two-night minimum weekends.
Open: All year.
Facilities and activities: Rowboats, paddleboats, hiking. Nearby: historic Hyde Park home of Franklin Roosevelt, Wilderstein, Montgomery Place.
Business travel: Fax, computer, and copy machine available.

Glendorn

BRADFORD, PENNSYLVANIA 16701

Imagine yourself on the private porch of a secluded stone cabin tucked away among stands of hemlock and maple. In the hush of this misty morning, you've already watched several deer graze on the lawn, and you scarcely breathed when you saw a red fox dart from the woods to race across the clearing. A family of rabbits is still nibbling on the flowers in the beds. Just beyond, a stone bridge crosses a gentle stream, and you believe you saw several trout hugging the shady waters under the overhanging bank. It's this seamless communication with nature that we experienced on our visit to Glendorn.

Once the family retreat of the Dorn family, founders of Forest Oil Corporation, the family converted their 1,280-acre estate into a country inn in 1995. Clayton Glenville Dorn began building the complex in 1930 with the construction of the Big House, a remarkable all-redwood structure that contains a 27-by-45-foot great room with a 20-foot-high cathedral ceiling and a massive two-story sandstone fireplace. The dining area is now located at the end opposite the fireplace. Additional cabins with fireplaces (one even has three fireplaces) were added for family members over the years. These, and the Big House, now contain guest rooms.

The guest rooms at Glendorn are far from ordinary. Reminiscent of the style that the Dorns enjoyed in the 1930s and 1940s, they are spacious and elegant. They feature butternut- or chestnut-paneled walls, oil paintings, and beds, chairs, and sofas covered in floral prints and checks. The rich, warm woods give the rooms a soft glow, and even in the Big House, most have stone fireplaces. We loved the Dorn Suite in the Big House, which has a fireplace in both the living room and the bedroom as well as a private sunroom.

The ultimate romantic hideaway, however, is The Hideout, a one-bedroom cabin sequestered among evergreen trees high on a mountaintop and reached by a steeply climbing, ½-mile-long private road. A stone fireplace warms the chestnut-paneled livingroom, and guests sunggle into ¾-sized beds tucked into cozy alcoves.

All meals are included in the room price, as is the use of all the recreational facilities, which are extensive. Indeed, it would take weeks to sample them all. There are fishing streams, three stocked lakes for fishing, 20 miles of marked trails for hiking and cross-country skiing with promontories offering romantic picnic sites with views (the inn will pack a lunch), three tennis courts, an archery range, canoes, and bicycles; a gymnasium and a half-basketball court; a 60-foot outdoor swimming pool, snowshoeing, and a game room.

Few places in America offer an escape from the workaday pressures in such a serene setting. The Dorns have long known that their retreat offered a unique, environmentally sensitive sanctuary that had an ability to restore the spirit and renew the psyche. Now we are able to share it.

How to get there: From I–80 exit onto Route 219 at DuBois. Go north on Route 219 to Bradford. In Bradford take the Elm Street exit. Follow Elm Street to Corydon Street. Travel for 5 miles to the Glendorn gate, which is just after a bright red barn. The complex is 1½ miles farther on a private paved road.

Proprietors: The Dorn Family; Linda and Gene Spinner, managers
Address/Telephone: 1032 West Corydon Street; (814) 362–6511 or (800) 843–8568, fax (814) 368–9923
Rooms: 11, including 4 suites and 5 cabins; all with private bath and telephone, 9 with TV, minirefrigerator, and fireplace (several with multiple fireplaces). Wheelchair accessible.
Rates: $295 to $895, double occupancy, AP, including all recreational facilities. Two-night minimum for some cabins and weekends July–October as well as holiday weekends. No credit cards.
Open: All year except March.
Facilities and activities: Tennis, skeet and trap shooting, archery, canoes, fishing, bicycling, swimming, hiking, cross-country skiing, snowshoeing, billiards and pool. Nearby: golf, downhill skiing, horseback riding, licensed guides for deer and bird hunting, the Allegheny National Forest.
Business travel: Desk in room; fax, copier, audiovisual equipment available; conference center.

The Inn at Twin Linden

CHURCHTOWN, PENNSYLVANIA 17555

Our physical state of arrival—hot and exhausted—improved so swiftly that we wondered: Did the outside world exist any longer? If it did, we'd forgotten, having stepped into the small world of the stone mansion inn. Bob had smiled in his direct, relaxed manner and led us up the stairs to our quarters. Along the way we admired his photographs of Italy, Ireland, Maine, and the farmlands surrounding Twin Linden. Sweet indulgence—the tenor of our visit—focused on the palate and the garden and tea on the patio. We could have been on a ship in the sea, contentedly marooned with a chef and photographer at the helm.

The inn is in Philadelphia's breadbasket, Lancaster County, where the rich farmland produces strawberries the size of a fist; vegetables are consumed within hours of picking; and choice meat, fowl, and fish can be had from a number of local purveyors. It's also convenient to Temple University, where Bob teaches photography.

Our suite was a study in light and grace with a comfortable sitting area; the Palladian window overlooked fields, a distant farm, and a low mountain range beyond. I concluded that winter here must be as cheering as the warm months. I envisioned myself perusing a book of photography, Chardonnay in hand and woolen lap afghan in place, while toasting in front of our room's wood-burning stove and occasionally gazing outside at Mother Nature's frosty finery.

Many of the rooms have handmade four-poster beds, which were delivered upon a horse-drawn sleigh. The walls are ivory with Colonial-green woodwork. Donna has added Laura Ashley quilts and handmade afghans, warm touches that beckon.

After a soak in the Jacuzzi in our room, we went to tea, which was served in the large foyer, where a three-tiered tray held luscious cookies and sweets. Some couples settled in the parlor, others at nearby tables or on the patio, which overlooks the linden trees and garden—a small, spectacular affair of benches and bushes, flowers, and ornamentals. Nearby are more benches for observing the fields beyond. We would come here after dinner with our cordials to watch the soft summer breeze sway the corn and wish for a falling star.

Dinner was served in the Hunt Country Restaurant, where travelers in search of innovative, vibrant tastes savor Donna's creations. (The menu changes weekly.) It was elaborate. We began with summer-asparagus tips with lemon and herbs in pastry, followed by Belgian endive with tortellini, pesto, and red peppers. For an entree I was presented with the scrumptious grilled jumbo shrimp, served with fresh-roasted red-pepper coulis. My companion chose the jumbo sea scallops with a heavenly champagne and tarragon sauce, baked under a flaky, light pastry lid. For dessert the freshest of strawberries arrived with rich whipped cream.

Breakfast began with fruits, fresh-squeezed juice, and pastries; then came an elaborate cheese omelet. We learned that Donna was invited to cook at the prestigious James Beard House in New York City, an engagement offered only to outstanding American chefs.

Two souls have put together their talents, and the outcome is a place done right.

How to get there: From the Pennsylvania Turnpike take exit 22 (Morgantown) to Route 23 (less than 1/10 mile) and proceed west 4 miles into Churchtown. Inn is on the left, in the center of village.

Innkeepers: Bob and Donna Leahy

Address/Telephone: 2092 Main Street; (717) 445–7619, fax (717) 445–4656

Rooms: 7, including 1 suite; all with private bath, air conditioning, and TV, 3 with fireplace, 2 with Jacuzzi. No smoking inn.

Rates: $100 to $210, double occupancy, EPB and afternoon tea. Two-night minimum if Saturday included and holidays.

Open: All year except January.

Facilities and activities: Dinner served Friday and Saturday ($16 to $24 Friday, $37 fixed price Saturday) by reservation. BYOB; garden and gift shop. Nearby: The People's Place and Old Country Store in Intercourse, Railroad Museum in Strasbourg, country quilt shops, factory outlets, Artworks Complex, farmer's markets.

Glasbern

FOGELSVILLE, PENNSYLVANIA 18051-9743

Had I passed by chance, I'd have stopped and driven down the cobblestone lane, intent on discovering what purpose this visually compelling structure held.

Beth Granger gave the inn its name, Glasbern, meaning "glass barn." It's a Pennsylvania German barn architecturally transformed in 1985 by the Grangers to create a unique contemporary inn amidst the serenity of a stream, a pond, and the green hills of the countryside.

You enter the Great Room, the heart of the inn. Intact are the original haymow ladders. The beams in the vaulted ceiling are exposed, and the stone walls were cut open with a diamond-edged saw to let in the sunlight. The lighting reminded me of a cathedral designed by Le Corbusier I once visited in France. The Great Room is an elegant setting within a former hand-hewn "bank" barn.

The inn is a good place to commune with nature. On a clear fall day, you can board a hot-air balloon that departs from the inn. Walk along the inn's country paths. Travel to the nearby antiques markets or the sights of Historic Bethlehem. Then return, this time perhaps on a winter's eve after a day of skiing, and ease into the whirlpool with the warmth of the nearby fireplace for total bliss. You may never leave the place.

The carriage-house suites have fireplaces framed either in stone or barn-wood siding. In the corner suites two-person whirlpools are surrounded by windows opening out to the countryside. The rooms are a blend of today's comforts, good lighting, and quality-built furnishings tastefully selected by Beth.

By evening guests gather in the Great Room, where you must reserve in advance, since the chef has a following. First you have a drink around the great stone fireplace. Once you're seated hot fresh breads are served with crisp salads. You might have ordered a New York strip steak brushed with olive oil and rosemary, then broiled; perhaps you selected a range chicken or Dover sole sautéed with country-style vegetables, tomatoes, herbs, in a reduced sweet cream sauce and served with lemon angel-hair pasta. Later comes a light cheesecake soufflé coated with raspberry sauce. Some guests enjoy a liqueur upon returning to the stone fireplace or go for a walk around the pond.

Breakfast is served, in leisurely style, in the sunroom. That morning we ate whole-wheat pecan pancakes coated with maple syrup and thick slices of bacon. We felt recharged. And we noticed others looked that way too. Was it the fresh air, the country walks, the fine meal, the whirlpool and the fireplace? Or had someone anointed us with newfound energy during the night?

How to get there: From I–78 take Route 100 north short distance to Tilghman Street and turn left. Go ⅓ mile and turn right on North Church Street; go 7⁄10 mile and turn right on Pack House Road. The inn is 8⁄10 mile on the right.

Innkeepers: Al and Beth Granger; Erik Sheetz, manager
Address/Telephone: 2141 Pack House Road (mailing address: R.D. 1); (610) 285–4723, fax (610) 285–2862
E-mail: innkeeper@glasbern.com
Rooms: 24, including 13 suites; all with private bath, air conditioning, TV, VCR, and telephone, 11 with fireplace, 17 with whirlpool bath. Two wheelchair accessible rooms. Designated nonsmoking rooms.
Rates: \$105 to \$315, double occupancy; \$95 to \$160, single; EPB. Additional person, \$20. Two-night minimum on certain weekends.
Open: All year.
Facilities and activities: Dinner nightly (entrees \$19 to \$38), service bar. Outdoor swimming pool, pond, hot-air balloon rides, 16 acres farmland. Nearby: Hawk Mountain Sanctuary, antiquing in Kutztown and Adamstown, ski Blue and Doe mountains, wineries, Historic Bethlehem.
Business travel: Telephone and desk in all rooms; fax, photocopies, dataport available; conference rooms.

Clifton: The Country Inn

CHARLOTTESVILLE, VIRGINIA 22911

We walked down to the lake and then along the wide pathway through the woods. We passed the tennis court and the lap pool. Near the gazebo were eight touring bikes. We saw the map that directs you on a day ride to Monticello, Michie Tavern, and Highland House, once the home of James Monroe. But first we must settle in.

Clifton is a white-columned mansion on the National Register of Historic Places. Secluded among forty acres of woodland, it overlooks the distant Rivana River and a lake. Monticello can be spied in the distance through the trees. This proximity was convenient for Thomas Jefferson, whose daughter, Martha, was the lady of the manor. She had married Thomas Mann Randolph, who, at various times, was governor of Virginia, member of the Virginia House of Delegates, and a U.S. congressman.

You enter a large hallway, and to the left is the small library, where you imagine the household affairs were conducted. Positioned near the fireplace are a pair of green leather wingback chairs; a hunting horn sits on the mantel above the fireplace. Opposite is the large parlor with a grand piano at one end. You like the feel of the place, indoors and out.

Next you're led to your room. On the beds are exquisite cotton fabrics and (in winter) down comforters. Each room has a fireplace and views of trees or the lake.

Among my favorite spots are the picturesque guest rooms in the livery stable. They have their original bead-board walls and are decorated with a splashy cabbage-rose fabric. The rooms are on two levels, have a fireplace in the sitting room, and overlook the lake. Other favorites, however, are the rustic but tender honeymoon cottage, with an exposed-beam ceiling, skylights, and a loft bedroom; and the carriage house, a suite so large it even has a grand piano in the sitting room.

Before dinner guests will have a seat in the large parlor, and Craig may tell the history of the house and describe dinner. On weekends a Celtic harpist or another instrumentalist often plays.

Craig is an outstanding chef who also teaches cooking classes in the large kitchen. A graduate of the Culinary Institute of America, he doesn't just prepare food, he celebrates it. A typical seven-course dinner may start with poached medallions of North Atlantic salmon served over fresh arugula with a sun-dried tomato-pear vinaigrette, then go on to a soup that's an essence of asparagus with watercress oil and fleurons. There will always be two choices of entree. maybe a roasted rack of Summerfield Farms (local) lamb crusted with garlic and served with a sauce Robert or a pan-seared swordfish with a red-bell-pepper coulis and sorrel pesto. For dessert a dark chocolate pôt de crème may be served with fresh berries.

You'll be seated in the formal dining room, in a small sunroom, or in the French café–style room that overlooks the trees. After dinner you might walk down to the lake, return to the parlor for a liqueur, or play a game of croquet in the balmy moonlight. You'll feel like it's your private estate for the weekend.

How to get there: From I–64 east of Charlottesville, exit Route 250 south, go 2 miles, turn right on Route 729, go ¼ mile, and turn left at the discreet sign.

Innkeepers: Craig Hartman; Mitch and Emily Willey, proprietors
Address/Telephone: 1296 Clifton Inn Drive; (804) 971–1800 or (888) 971–1800, fax (804) 971–7098
Rooms: 14, including 7 suites; all with private bath, air conditioning, and fireplace. Wheelchair access. No smoking inn.
Rates: $185 to $245, double occupancy, EPB, and afternoon tea. Two-night minimum weekends.
Open: All year.
Facilities and activities: Prix-fixe dinner Friday and Saturday, $58; Sunday–Thursday, $48. Forty acres, lake, tennis court, bikes. Nearby: Monticello, Ash Lawn, University of Virginia, wineries.
Business travel: Desk in 6 rooms; telephone, dataport, fax, PC, copy machine, laser printer available; meeting rooms.

The Oaks Victorian Inn

CHRISTIANSBURG, VIRGINIA 24073

The Oaks is named for seven ancient oak trees. Margaret and Tom have received a grant to preserve the trees with the help of experts from the America the Beautiful program. The oldest, a white oak, is estimated to be around 400 years old and has the girth to back up that estimate.

Exteriorwise, the inn's description is simple: It's the queen of Christiansburg. A classic, in fact—a Queen Anne Victorian, now painted buttercup yellow, which was designed by a New York architect in 1889 for Major W. L. Pierce and his wife and seven children. The original beauty of gleaming hardwood floors, stained glass, and trim is intact.

The bedrooms are oases of comfort and style. You might go up to the third floor and select Lulu's Lair, painted in red and cream, or Lady Melodie's Turret, a skylit room with a king-sized canopy bed, gas fireplace, and sunset view. The inn has inviting common areas (which perhaps explains why the inn ended up in a PBS television special). They include the wraparound porch with rocking chairs; the backyard patio with garden and fish pond; a second-story sun deck; and a sunroom with a fireplace, well stocked with books, games, and movies.

When at last you do depart from your oasis for lunch or dinner, Margaret and Tom help you make a wise choice. They might suggest a mountain vineyard, where the vintner is also a French chef and the wine and dining have consistently won awards, or a Brazilian place with exotic international flavors.

One guest once asked, "Margaret, what's your philosophy of art?" It's more a response to beauty than a particular philosophy. Together the Rays select what inherently pleases them. As a result, there's a Joe King above the fireplace that's an evocative depiction of the painter's wife; there are photographs by Darvish and sculptures and prints. "The human spirit needs the sensitivities of the arts," Margaret once said.

Breakfast is served in a style conducive to conversation. The place mats are handmade lace, the china (inherited from Tom's grandmother) is Dresden, and the coffeepot is an unusual heirloom, a silver-over-porcelain piece. You might receive a dish of curried eggs laced with shiitake mushrooms and wine sauce or a broccoli-lemon quiche and apricot-and-pumpkin tea bread or Southern buttermilk biscuits. Meats, if you wish, range from ginger-braised chicken to herbed sausages. One tends to linger over breakfast, even though the patio beckons and the hummingbird feeder is busy.

How to get there: From I–81 take exit 114. Turn left if approaching from the south and right if coming from the north, and you will be on Main Street. Continue for approximately 2 miles to fork at Park and Main streets. Bear right onto Park, then left into The Oaks driveway.

Innkeepers: Margaret and Tom Ray
Address/Telephone: 311 East Main Street; (540) 381–1500 or (800) 336–OAKS, fax (540) 382–1728
Rooms: 7; all with private bath, air conditioning, telephone, and TV, 5 with fireplace, 2 with Jacuzzi. No smoking inn.
Rate: $115 to $140, double occupancy, EPB. Additional person $15. Two-night minimum in October and special-event weekends.
Open: All year, except first week in January.
Facilities and activities: Parlor, patio, hot tub. Nearby: 24 miles to Blue Ridge Parkway; Transportation Museum in Roanoke, antiquing, outlet shopping, Long Way Home Outdoor Drama. Bicycling, hiking, Mill Mountain Theatre, Virginia Tech University, Radford University.
Business travel: Telephone with dataport, desk, and minirefrigerator all rooms, valet service, parking on premises; corporate rates.

The Page House Inn

NORFOLK, VIRGINIA 23507

"Champagne tastes and jogging shoes," my companion said as Stephanie, wearing an attractive warm-up suit, swung open a highly polished oak door to an elegant foyer. We beheld other guests in the formal dining room; they were laughing, sipping cappuccino, and savoring the cookies. We couldn't believe our good fortune at finding The Page House in Ghent—Norfolk's prestigious historic neighborhood. It is within walking distance of the Chrysler Museum, the opera, and the Hague, a tranquil canal where boats lie at anchor year-round.

Stephanie introduced us to a pair of small black-and-white Boston terriers named Charlie and Tootsie, who went off to their private lodging while we followed her up the wide oak staircase. She presented to us a "definitive" honeymoon suite. We admired the boldly printed wallpaper and window furnishings and the canopied bed with its antique handmade spread and coverlets. We had hardly caught our collective breath when Stephanie opened the door to the commodious sitting room with love seat and bay windows. Here, as in the other rooms of the inn, were lovely antiques.

Returning down the stairs, Stephanie pointed to a basket full of goodies for guests, should hunger strike at any time of the day. A collection of games, books, and magazines were organized beside a rocking chair.

Meanwhile I tried to determine what made the inn's design style so vigorous yet different. "I have an aunt who's a decorator," explained Stephanie. "She helped me arrange our family collection of antiques and art." The result is an inn that's a balanced creation of personal vision. Stephanie's husband, Ezio, a retired contractor and woodworker, renovated the three-story Georgian Revival building. He artfully reworked the interior: new plumbing, wiring, and safety features were part of his masterful transformation, which also included quality oak woodwork installed according to historic preservation guidelines.

Stephanie named the inn for Herman L. Page, the man who first laid out and developed the Ghent area in the late 1800s. But Stephanie is a mover and shaker in her own right. She had to break through the town's codes, which prohibited a historical bed and breakfast, to create her first-class, award-winning restoration.

We rose early for a breakfast of perfectly textured scones and fruit jams, homemade granolas, and bagels served in the formal dining room. (We wore jeans.)

Stephanie's dog, Charlie, wearing a mildly spiked collar befitting his breed, licked my hand when I stooped to pet him as we left.

"Lucky dog," remarked my companion as we said goodbyes.

How to get there: From I–63 East or West take exit for I–264 (toward downtown Norfolk) and follow signs (staying in left lane) to exit 9, Waterside Drive. Continue on Waterside Drive, which curves and becomes Boush Street. Turn left onto Olney Street (after Grace Street). Continue for 2 blocks and turn left onto Mowbray Arch, go 1 block to Fairfax Avenue, and turn right. Inn is on the left; park behind.

Innkeepers: Stephanie and Ezio DeBelardino
Address/Telephone: 323 Fairfax Avenue; (804) 625–5033, fax (804) 623–9451
Rooms: 6, including 2 suites; all with private bath, telephone, TV, and air conditioning, 3 with fireplace, 2 with whirlpool bath. No smoking in rooms.
Rates: $85 to $150, double occupancy, continental breakfast and afternoon refreshments. Two-night minimum weekends April–October.
Open: All year.
Facilities and activities: Rooftop garden. Nearby: Chrysler Museum; Virginia Opera, Symphony, and Stage Company; Naval Base Tour; Hampton Roads Naval Museum; Mariner's Museum; Harbor and Sailing Tours; Virginia Beach.
Business travel: Telephone and desk in all rooms; fax and copier available; meeting rooms; corporate rates.

Prospect Hill

TREVILIANS, VIRGINIA 23093

Michael Sheehan greets you with a firm handshake and ushers you into this former plantation house, which dates back to 1732. This is reputedly the oldest continuously operating plantation in America; it traces its roots to the 1600s. As families grew and plantation activities increased, dependency buildings were added to the grounds: a smokehouse, carriage house, and summer kitchen, to name a few. These structures have been turned into charming guest rooms, all connected to the main house by a stone pathway.

One of my favorites is the Boy's Cabin, a log cabin that dates back to 1699. It has log walls, a brick fireplace, and a simple bed that is covered with a quilt; nevertheless, the bath is large and absolutely modern. Anther favorite is the Overseer's Cottage, which has a four-poster bed, a fireplace, and a step-down sitting room with a private deck. Each of the cottages is impeccably furnished in a style that is appropriate to its original use, but with all the comforts we love today. There are five rooms in the plantation house as well; these are the most elegant.

Bill and Mireille Sheehan created the inn in 1977. Eventually, they eased out of hands-on innkeeping, and their son Michael stepped into the innkeepers' shoes. When I asked if he and his wife, Laura, are training their daughter and son to eventually assume the responsibility, he replied they wear T-shirts that read: "Innkeeper in training."

Behind the inn stretches a lawn shaded with massive old leafy trees. A hammock is suspended between the trees. A pool and cabana entice sun-lovers on warm days. Large white wicker chairs cuddle the afternoon reader on the small porch in back, while the Board Room downstairs, with its soft leather chairs and fireplace, serves the purpose in cool weather. There's also a formal living room with a stereo to listen to classical music.

Dinner at Prospect Hill is an experience that should not be missed. For many years Mireille was the chef, preparing meals inspired by the foods of Provence, where she grew up. Today Michael prepares classically inspired French cuisine spiced up with a bit of Provence, as his mother used to, but with his own twist. He uses herbs from his kitchen garden and garnishes each dish with flowers, making them as pretty as they are delicious.

The dining rooms (there are three separate rooms) are charmingly decorated, as if they were plucked directly from the French countryside. There are wide-plank polished floors, fireplaces in two the rooms, and French antiques and fabrics used throughout.

Dinner begins with a wine reception. The five-course menu changes every night, but typically it will include a creative appetizer, then a soup, followed by a salad. The entree may be a pan-seared tenderloin of veal forestière. For dessert perhaps Michael will have prepared a blackberry-and-Drambuie cheese torte served with a blackberry coulis. All this is accompanied by wines from the extensive slection. It's a wonderfully romantic way to spend an evening.

Prospect Hill is one of my favorite inns—an enchanting getaway in the country, where exceptional food, gracious innkeepers, charming rooms, and a relaxed style blend to create a perfect stay.

How to get there: Take exit 136 from I–64 to Route 15 south to Zion Crossroads. Turn left on Route 250 east. Go 1 mile to Route 613, turn left, and go 3 miles to Prospect Hill on the left. Fly-in: Gordonsville Airport.

Innkeepers: Michael and Laura Sheehan
Address/Telephone: 2887 Poindexter Road; (540) 967–2574 or (800) 277–0844, fax (540) 967–0102
Rooms: 13, including 3 suites and 5 cottages; all with private bath, air conditioning, and fireplace, 8 with whirlpool bath. Wheelchair accessible.
Rates: $245 to $325, double occupancy, MAP; 10 percent discount Monday–Thursday. Two-night stay may be required on weekends.
Open: All year.
Facilities and activities: Dinner daily ($35 to $40 for the public), wine served. Swimming pool. On 45 acres. Nearby: carriage rides, fishing, golfing, horseback riding, tennis, winery tours, hot-air ballooning, Monticello, Ash Lawn, antiques shops.
Business travel: Desk, coffeemaker, and minirefrigerator in most rooms; fax and copier available; meeting room.

Hillbrook Inn

CHARLES TOWN, WEST VIRGINIA 25414

Hillbrook is a romantic European hideaway in the lush gentle countryside of West Virginia, where you're smitten by the peace and solitude. After traveling and working around the world and staying in inns, Gretchen Carroll arrived by happenstance one rainy afternoon; the rest is champagne and candlelight.

Hillbrook was built during the Roaring Twenties of stone, timber, and stucco and was terraced with these materials to form a grand country house. Entry is into the living room, with fireplace burning, Oriental rugs, and artworks to be appreciated; an atmosphere of casual elegance reigns. You notice the theme of people's faces in Gretchen's artwork and find interesting books on foreign travels adjacent to carvings, pottery, and prints.

Two bedrooms are off the living room; one is reached by climbing a stairway, where a private balcony gives you a superior view. The downstairs room has a small private porch and fireplace. A third room is near the library. The rooms are uniquely furnished with antique or brass beds, down comforters, and Gretchen's worldly treasures, such as an antique Vuitton trunk.

Dinner is an absolute affair with flavors. It's served by reservation at a fixed price and set menu; it is a seven-course palatable event. We began with a tasty tapenade artfully arranged, then came a creamy, tangy carrot-and-orange soup, after that an absolutely delicious hot pasta. The entree was veal served with tastefully seasoned broccoli and squash; then a salad arrived, followed by a superb cheese plate with English crackers; last came a perfect chocolate cake. Each table in the room was set differently; ours had black candles that burned exuberantly until after midnight, when we finished our brandies and congratulated the chef for a fine meal.

For daytime excursions Gretchen suggests a route that takes you past several wonderful antiques shops and an excellent winery, where you can have a picnic lunch (conveniently prepared by the first antiques shop). You might prefer to remain at the inn, walk through the garden with Gretchen, to admire the Chippendale bridge with its iron lion's heads, take a nap in the hammock down by the stream, sip a glass of wine on the patio, delve into a basketful of books beside the fireplace, or simply lie back and catch up on your daydreams.

How to get there: From I–270 take I–70 west to Route 340 west. Past Harper's Ferry take Route 51 west to Charles Town. Continue on Route 51 West to Route 13 (Summit Point Road), which bears off to left at west end of town. Go 4⁸⁄₁₀ miles on Route 13 to the inn on your left (past elementary school on right). Watch for stone pillars.

Innkeeper: Gretchen Carroll
Address/Telephone: Route 13 (mailing address: Route 2, Box 152); (304) 725–4223 or (800) 304–4223, fax (304) 725–4455
Rooms: 6; all with private bath, telephone, and air conditioning, 2 with fireplace, 1 with whirlpool.
Rates: $198 to $450, double occupancy, MAP, including wine.
Open: All year.
Facilities and activities: On 17 acres with pond and stream. Dinner (by reservation) for guests not spending the night ($60 to $68). Nearby: antiquing, tour Shepherdstown or Harper's Ferry, Summit Point Raceway, bicycling, and hiking on C&O Canal towpath.
Business travel: Desk in two rooms; fax and copier available; meeting room.
Recommended Country Inns® Travelers' Club Benefit: Stay two nights, get third night free, Monday–Thursday.

The South

by Sara Pitzer

What's more romantic—a starry evening watching boats on the Mississippi River or a night in an elegant suite in Georgia with real gold fixtures in the bath? You can't really answer for anyone but yourselves because places aren't romantic—people are. It's what you bring to an inn that makes it romantic: your personal taste, your ideas of pleasure. A romantic getaway is to share the pleasures you enjoy most with someone special in a way that lets you be together at your best.

My parents took a two-week camping-canoe trip down the Delaware River on their honeymoon. It was, they've always assured me, truly romantic. (And that's before insect repellent was invented!) My own memorable romantic time was a vacation my husband and I took years ago, staying in an inexpensive room with shared bath, getting dressed to the nines, and eating outrageously expensive dinners in a gourmet restaurant every night. At the end of each meal, we'd sip our liqueurs and sigh with pleasure.

If romance means being in special places, you almost can't go wrong in good Southern inns. Each one offers pleasures you just don't find everywhere. To choose well, all you need do is reflect on what appeals to you. Seclusion? How about Little St. Simons Island? Opulence? Maybe the Gastonian. Casual accommodations on top of a mountain from where you see no other man-made structures? Hickory Nut Gap Inn. Gourmet food, lots of privacy, museum-quality art and antiques, city pleasures, unspoiled nature—you can find it all in Southern inns.

Moreover, the fact that the inns are in the South adds an extra dimension of romance—Southerners pride themselves on the romance of the past, the charm of their present, and the graciousness of their hospitality. Here are twenty-two inns, each different from the others, each special in its own way, and all romantic in the Southern style. I've provided lots of details about each place. Those that sound like they'd make *you* feel good will make you feel romantic, too.

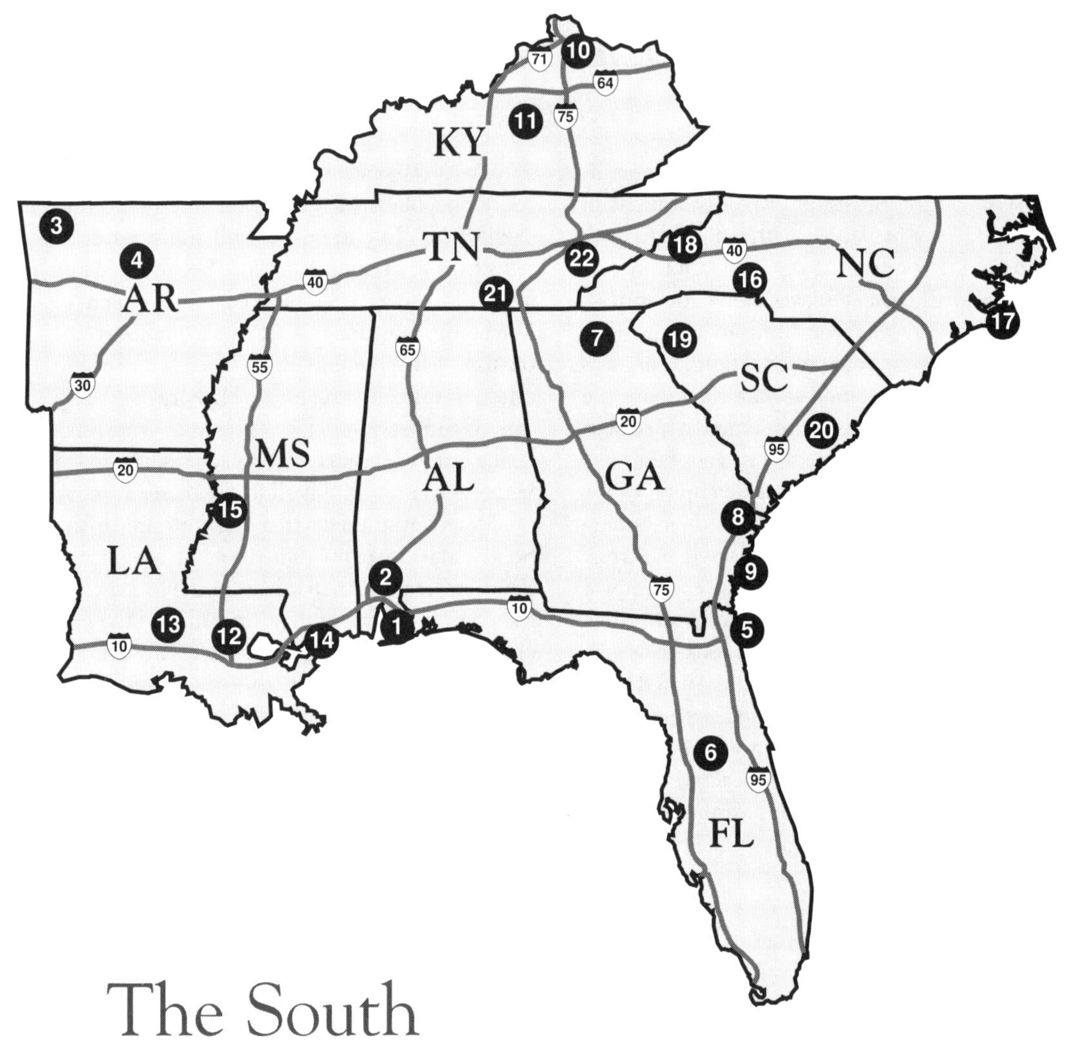
KY
TN
NC
AR
SC
MS
AL
GA
LA
FL
71
64
75
40
55
65
30
20
95
10
1
2
3
4
5
6
7
8
9
10
11
12
13
14
15
16
17
18
19
20
21
22

The South

The South

Numbers on map refer to towns numbered below.

Alabama

1. Fairhope, Bay Breeze Guest House 100
2. Mobile, Malaga Inn 102

Arkansas

3. Eureka Springs, Heartstone Inn and Cottages 104
4. Heber Springs, Oak Tree Inn 106

Florida

5. Amelia Island, The 1735 House 108
6. Lake Wales, Chalet Suzanne 110

Georgia

7. Clarksville, Glen-Ella Springs 112
8. Savannah, The Gastonian 114
9. St. Simons Island, Little St. Simons Island 116

Kentucky

10. Covington, The Amos Shinkle Town House 118
11. Versailles, Shepherd Place 120

Louisianna

12. Burnside, Tezcuco Plantation 122
13. St. Francisville, Barrow House 124

Mississippi

14. Biloxi, The Father Ryan House Bed & Breakfast Inn 126
15. Natchez, Weymouth Hall 128

North Carolina

16. Bat Cave, Hickory Nut Gap Inn 130
17. Beaufort, Langdon House 132
18. Clyde, Windsong 134

South Carolina

19. Anderson, The Evergreen Inn and 1109 South Main Restaurant 136
20. Charleston, Ansonborough Inn 138

Tennessee

21. Monteagle, Adams Edgeworth Inn 140
22. Sevierville, Von-Bryan Inn 142

Bay Breeze Guest House

FAIRHOPE, ALABAMA 36533

Here is a place romantically secluded yet close to everything you could want for fun.

The inn sits on a three-acre site right on the shores of Mobile Bay. The grounds are filled with mature shrubs and trees that give you a feeling of being in the woods. The stucco building was built in the 1930s and has been variously remodeled and enlarged over the years to accommodate the family's changing needs. It works beautifully as an inn.

The entire downstairs—a sitting room with fireplace, glassed-porch bay room, living room, and kitchen—is devoted to guests. (The Joneses have private quarters upstairs.) Most of the furnishings in the main house are family heirlooms going back as far as five generations. The mix of wicker, stained glass, and hooked and oriental rugs produces a romantic feel no designer could duplicate. "And everything has a story," Becky says. Flowers bloom romantically everywhere.

For perfect privacy, try the cottage suite. It has pickled white-pine walls, old brick floors, vaulted ceilings, and lots of generously sized windows. The cottage is decorated with just the right combination of antiques, oriental rugs, new sofas, and good beds. You feel comfortable but not overwhelmed with stuff. Becky has been careful to keep the suite light and spacious. Staying in the cottage is a lot like playing house—but without the responsibility, because Becky takes care of everything.

As a hostess, she knows how to find out what you like and provides it without apparent effort: a special jelly, a particular bread or coffee or drink. And if you come back again, she'll remember what you liked and have it ready for you. This is what a good Southern hostess prides herself on. Romance Southern style.

How to get there: From I–10 take U.S. Highway 98 toward Fairhope and exit right onto Scenic/Alternate Highway 98 at the WELCOME TO FAIRHOPE sign. At the third traffic light, turn right onto Magnolia Avenue. Go 4 blocks and turn left on South Mobile Street at the municipal pier. Bay Breeze Guest House is about a mile farther, on the right.

Innkeepers: Bill and Becky Jones
Address/Telephone: 742 South Mobile Street (mailing address: P.O. Box 526); (334) 928–8976
Rooms: 3 in main house, plus 1 cottage suite; all with private bath and TV, cottage suites with phone, small kitchen, and wheelchair access. Third room available in main house for large parties. No smoking inn.
Rates: $95 to $105; full breakfast.
Open: All year.
Facilities and activities: Private pier, decks, and beach on Mobile Bay. Nearby: walking distance to downtown historic Fairhope, restaurants, and shops.

Malaga Inn

MOBILE, ALABAMA 36602

If you find romance in grand old love oaks dripping with Spanish moss and in old city townhouses in the deep South, try Malaga Inn, in Mobile.

Although Malaga looks pretty much like a hotel now, it started out as two three-story townhouses built in 1862 by two brothers-in-law. Had the outcome of the Civil War been different, they might still stand as two townhouses. Instead, the two homes have been restored, beginning in 1968 with a patio and garden and space for new accommodations between them.

Twenty of the guest rooms are in the restored homes. Some of these still have the original wallpaper and hardwood floors. One has the remains of a fine marble fireplace. The rooms are furnished comfortably with both traditional furniture and some good antiques. The other twenty rooms, in the newer addition, are more elaborate but perhaps less interesting because they have less history. Many of the rooms overlook the courtyard, a pretty, spacious, tiled area with a fountain and lots of plants. A courtyard is romantic in the best old Southern sense.

The Malaga is one of the relatively few inns in the South that have full-service restaurants on the premises. The Malaga's restaurant, Mayme's, offers contemporary cuisine, emphasizing coastal ingredients with a French flair. For instance a popular appetizer is crawfish cakes with aioli and tarragon mayonnaise, while entree choices range from risotto-stuffed quail with apricot sauce to potato-crusted red snapper with curry beurre blanc.

How to get there: Traveling east on I–10, take the Canal Street exit. Cross Canal to Jackson Street and follow it to Church. Turn left on Church. Traveling west on I–10, take the Government Street exit from Bayway through the Bankhead Tunnel. Follow Government Street to Claiborne, turn left, go to Church Street, and turn left again. From I–65 take I–10 East and follow the directions for traveling east on I–10. You will come to the inn almost immediately.

Innkeeper: Julie Beem
Address/Telephone: 359 Church Street; (205) 438–4701 or (800) 235–1586
Rooms: 40; all with private bath, TV, and telephone, some with refrigerator. Some with wheelchair access. No-smoking rooms available.
Rates: $52 to $59, single; $62 to $69, double; coffee and daily newspaper; breakfast is extra.
Open: Year-round.
Facilities and activities: Restaurant, cocktail lounge, swimming pool. Nearby: located in historic district of downtown Mobile; within walking distance of the Museum of the City of Mobile, Mobile Civic Auditorium, Conde-Charlotte House Museum; Oakleigh Period House Museum, The Cox-Deasy House, The Minnie Mitchell Archives, The Fine Arts Museum of the South, Fort Conde Military Museum; short drive to Bellingrath Gardens and Home and USS *Alabama* Battleship Memorial Park.

Heartstone Inn and Cottages

EUREKA SPRINGS, ARKANSAS 72632

The Heartstone Inn gets its name from a large, flat, vaguely heart-shaped stone that the Simantels found on the property. They play with the heart theme, using the phrase "Lose your heart in the Ozarks" and a heart-shaped logo in their brochure. The doors have heart-shaped welcome signs. The stone that justifies it all rests in the front garden, surrounded by flowers.

As far as I'm concerned, the Simantels have such heart they could use the theme even without the stone.

They came to the Ozarks from Chicago to become innkeepers. They love Eureka Springs. They love their inn. They love their guests.

The Simantels offer all kinds of romantic extras. For instance, you might stay in the Jacuzzi suite and ask to have flowers in the room, along with a heart-shaped cake and champagne. Iris will make it happen. Couples celebrating anniversaries oftem will make appointments for massages in the massage therapy room, thus adding perfect relaxation to the romantic mix. Breakfast is always a pampering affair, with such delights as strawberry blintzes and delicate coffeecake, plus several kind of fruit.

And if you like getting out and around, the Simantels will pack a picnic for you to enjoy in a sunset lake cruise or arrange a carriage ride for you in one of Eureka Spring's white "wedding" carriages.

Of course, the Heartstone is in a romantic town, too. Eureka Springs has become known as a "wedding destination" where hundred of couples come to be married in one of its wedding chapels. You could say that here romance in always in the air.

The inn is pretty. It's an Edwardian house, painted pink, with a white picket fence and lots of bright pink geraniums and roses all around.

Most of the rooms are furnished with elegant antiques, though a couple are done in country style. One favorite is an especially elegant Jacuzzi suite. Such outdoor niceties as decks and a gazebo means there are always glorious places for special gatherings such as weddings.

Many couples enjoy the privacy afforded by the two cottages. The smaller one has its own garden with a deck and a garden swing that become your own romantic hideaway. The larger Victoria house has a fireplace in the bedroom.

The Simantels have been enjoying a good bit of "discovery," applause from magazines and newspapers and other innkeepers for doing such a good job. The praise, Iris says, has not gone to their heads. They are still keeping their prices moderate because they don't want to attract snobs who go to places only because they are expensive. Not that Bill and Iris could be snobs if they wanted to. That Simantel humor bubbles too close to the surface. In fact, Iris says there are lots of new jokes between them but some, she thinks, may not be suitable for print.

They love jokes and they love to laugh. An inn filled with love and laughter can't help but be romantic.

How to get there: From the west, take the first 62B exit off Route 62: From the east, take the second 62B exit. Follow 62B through town until it becomes Kingshighway.

Innkeepers: Iris and Bill Simantel
Address/Telephone: 35 Kingshighway; (501) 253–8916, fax (501) 253–6821
E-mail: eureka@intellinet.com
Rooms: 7, plus 3 suites and 2 cottages; all with private bath.
Rates: Rooms $65 to $82; suites and cottages $87 to $120, single or double, full breakfast. Inquire about winter discounts.
Open: Year-round.
Facilities and activities: Gift shop, massage/reflexology therapist available by appointment. Located in the historic district, within walking distance of downtown Eureka Springs tourist activities; golf privileges at private course. Nearby: restaurants.
Recommended Country Inns® Travelers' Club Benefit: 10 percent discount, Monday–Thursday, for rooms, gift shop, and massage-therapy services.

Oak Tree Inn

HEBER SPRINGS, ARKANSAS 72543

This inn is romantic in an unusual way. Remember the saying, "All the world lvoes lovers?" Here they're the innkeepers. Freddie Lou has been at the Oak Tree Inn since 1983. She's recently remarried, and she and her husband Jerry together enjoy serving guests. The Quists want the inn to be a place for couples who wish to escape daily routines and converse without distractions. There are no televisions in the guest rooms, but there are fireplaces and private whirlpool baths inviting you to relaxation and intimate conversation.

If you need accommodations with wheelchair access or you just can't get along without a television, even for the sake of romance, you might prefer one of the river cottages. Each cottage has a fireplace and is self-sufficient with a dishwasher, microwave, washer, and dryer. Each cottage is spaced far from the others for seclusion and privacy. A hammock, grill, and canoes give you a chance to savor the woods and river.

For the time when you want some activity away from the inn, Freddie Lou and Jerry have placed in your room a list of restaurants they recommend along with a list of interesting things to see and do in the area. There's plenty. Heber Springs is an easy place to be in. It has a population of approximately 5,000 neighborly people at the foothills of the Ozark Mountains. These are the kind of people who wave when they see you whether they know you or not and slow their cars if they see you're taking a photograph across the road. The inn is close to Greers Ferry Lake—45,000 acreas of recreational potential. Also close, Little Red River is stocked with trout. Good hiking trails are nearby. After enjoying the Quist's generous breakfast of waffles or eggs Benedict or some other treat, you can spend a romantic day playing in the great outdoors, then at the end of the day, return to the inn patio and relax in the shade of huge oak trees with the dessert served by Freddie Lou and Jerry each evening. Their most popular specialty is homemade hot fudge sauce over ice cream or cake.

How to get there: State Highway 25 Business goes into Heber Springs. From 25, take Highway 110 West, which is also Main Street, to the inn.

Innkeepers: Freddie Lou and Jerry Quist
Address/Telephone: 1802 West Main Street; (501) 362–7731 or (800) 959–3857
Rooms: 4 in inn, all with private whirlpool bath and fireplace; 3 cottages with fireplace and television, 2 with wheelchair access.
Rates: $75 to $85 per room, full breakfast and dessert; $10 less Sunday through Thursday; $110 to $160 per cottage.
Open: Year-round.
Facilities and activities: Swimming pool and tennis courts. Nearby: restaurants, area noted for fall foliage and spring dogwood, 45,000-acre Greers Ferry Lake, trout fishing on Little Red River.
Recommended Country Inns® Travelers' Club Benefit: Stay two nights, get third night free, subject to availability.

The 1735 House

AMELIA ISLAND, FLORIDA 32034

So you'd like to sail away to a desert isle but you can't quite pull it off. Here's something almost as good. The 1735 House is a Cape Cod–style inn directly facing the ocean, furnished with antiques, wicker, and neat old trunks. All the suites face the ocean.

Maybe there will be no room at the inn, and you'll stay instead in the lighthouse. Its walls are covered with navigation maps. As you enter, you can either step down into a shower-and-bath area or take the spiral stairs up to the kitchen. A galley table and director's chairs make a good spot for playing cards, chatting, or ocean gazing, as well as eating. The stairs keep spiraling up to a bedroom with another bath, and finally up to an enclosed observation deck, which is the ultimate spot for romantic ocean gazing for two.

Wherever you stay, in the evening all you have to do is tell the staff what time you want breakfast and they'll deliver it right to your room in a wicker basket, along with a morning paper.

The physical setup is uncommon, but the staff have the true inn spirit. They'll give you ice, towels for the beach, bags for your shell collection or wet bathing suit, and just about anything else you need. All you have to do is ask.

The staff are full of helpful recommendations about good eating places, of which there are many on Amelia Island, too. The Down Under Seafood Restaurant, under the Shave bridge on A1A, is in keeping with the nautical mood of the inn and the lighthouse. The seafood is all fresh from the Intracoastal Waterway. There's a boat ramp with a dock, and the atmosphere is correspondingly quaint. You can enjoy cocktails and dinner.

If staying at The 1735 House gets you in the mood for more inns, you're welcome to browse through a large, well-used collection of books about inns in the office.

How to get there: Amelia Island is near the Florida/Georgia border. Take the Yulee exit from I–95 onto Route A1A and follow the signs toward Fernandina Beach. The inn is on A1A.

Innkeepers: The Auld family
Address/Telephone: 584 South Fletcher; (904) 261–5878 or (800) 872–8531, fax (904) 261–9200
Rooms: 5, plus 1 suite in lighthouse; all with private bath and TV.
Rates: $100 to $150, single or double. Breakfast extra.
Open: Year-round.
Facilities and activities: Cooking and laundry facilities, beachfront. Nearby: restaurants, downtown historic Fernandina Beach shopping and sightseeing, boating from the marina, golf, tennis, shopping, horseback riding.
Recommended Country Inns® Travelers' Club Benefit: 10 percent discount, Monday–Thursday.

Chalet Suzanne

LAKE WALES, FLORIDA 33859

Chalet Suzanne releases a photograph for publicity along with this caption: "Through wrought-iron gates one can view the unlikely hodgepodge of towers, turrets, and gables that ramble in all directions." Well, yeah, that too.

Everyone who writes about the place falters under the burden of trying to describe what they've seen—a collection of whimsical, odd buildings assembled over a number of years by Carl Hinshaw's mother, who got into innkeeping and the restaurant business trying to keep body and soul together after being widowed during the Great Depression. I've seen the words "Camelot," "phantasmagoria," "fairy tale," "magical," in the reviews of writers trying to capture the mood of the place. Any and all will do. Staying here is a great giggle for anyone who doesn't like too many straight lines, who enjoys walks and walls that tilt, and who appreciates the kind of humor represented by a potted geranium atop the ice machine.

I stayed in the Orchid Room, a roughly octagonal space where sherry and fruit were set out on a small table between two comfortable chairs. Live plants and fresh flowers were scattered throughout the room and its bath, and the furniture was painted various shades of aqua, cream, and deep orchid. The bath had black-and-gray tile and an improbable little bathtub of brick-colored ceramic tile. The tub was really too straight up and down to sit in; I used the shower and afterward appreciated finding a blow dryer to try to tame my hair.

Chalet Suzanne is famous for its award-winning restaurant, in which the tables are all set with different kinds of china, silver, and glasses collected by the Hinshaws over years of travel. Carl's Romaine soup, Vita's broiled grapefruit garnished with chicken livers, and the shrimp curry are all much-extolled selections, so I tried them all with a nice house wine dispensed in generous servings. I enjoyed everything, including being served by waitresses in costumes that looked Swiss in the Swiss dining room, where European stained-glass windows provide a focal point.

A waitress told me that Carl Hinshaw's soups—which have become so popular that he started a cannery on the premises for people who want to take soup home—have made it to the better gourmet shops and even to the moon with the *Apollo* astronauts—not necessarily in that order.

So there you are, in a wacky, unreal environment, eating multistar-winning food that must be famous by now on the moon, served by waitresses dressed like Snow White, and you're sleeping in a room that looks as though it came out of a Seven-Dwarfs coloring book . . . how are *you* going to describe it? I give up.

How to get there: Chalet Suzanne is 4 miles north of Lake Wales on Chalet Suzanne Road, which turns off Highway 27. Signs clearly mark the turns.

Innkeepers: Carl and Vita Hinshaw
Address/Telephone: U.S. Highway 27 (mailing address: 3800 Chalet Suzanne Drive); (914) 676–6011; for reservations, (800) 433–6011
Rooms: 30; all with private bath, TV, and telephone, 5 with Jacuzzi.
Rates: $135 to $195, single or double, full breakfast. Pets $20 extra.
Open: Year-round.
Facilities and activities: Lunch, dinner, wheelchair access to dining room; restaurant closed Monday. Cocktail lounge, wine cellar open for sampling, gift shop, antiques shop, ceramics studio, swimming pool, lake, soup cannery, airstrip. Nearby: golf, tennis, fishing, Cypress Gardens, Bok Tower Gardens.
Business travel: Conference facilities, access to fax, telephone in room.

Glen-Ella Springs

CLARKSVILLE, GEORGIA 30523

I think I'm in love!

Usually country inns are elegant or they are rustic. This one-hundred-year-old place is both. The suites are beautifully finished and furnished, with fireplaces; refinished pine floors, walls and ceilings; local mountain-made rugs on the floors; whirlpool baths; and such niceties as fresh-cut pansies floating in crystal bowls. Some of the less-expensive rooms are simpler, though perfectly comfortable, with painted walls and showers in the bathrooms.

The fireplace in the lobby is made of local stone, flanked with chintz-covered chairs.

An especially nice swimming pool, surrounded by an extra-wide sundeck that seems posh enough for any Hyatt hotel, overlooks a huge expanse of lawn that ends in woods. Both the pool and the lawn are great for kids.

The dining room is what I would call "subdued country," but there is nothing subdued about the food. It is simply spectacular—some of the best I've had anywhere in the South.

Because I sat with a large group for dinner, I had an opportunity to taste many more entrees and appetizers than usual. I remember scallops wrapped in bacon served in a honey-mustard sauce; a low-country shrimp and grits entree; fresh trout sautéed and then dressed with lime juice, fresh herbs, and toasted pecans; and rack of lamb. I sampled desserts the same way and gave my vote to the delicious homemade cheesecake.

The story here is that Barrie, a wonderful cook, had wanted a restaurant for a long time. But the Aycocks also wanted to work and live away from the city. They bought Glen-Ella even though the old hotel needed a tremendous amount of renovating.

They figured that here Barrie could have her restaurant, and since the inn was so far out in the country, lots of guests would spend the night. They do. And lots of other guests, who come for longer stays just to be in the country, enjoy the added pleasure of five-star quality food.

The Glen-Ella gift shop has the *Glen-Ella Cookbook*, with some of the inn's best recipes, for sale. I use mine whenever I want something unusual and good. You can order it by calling or writing the inn.

If you've been here before, you'll find the place has a new look in many of the rooms. Barrie calls the redecorating "a face-lift."

And now one more bragging point for Barrie and Bobby. The hotel has been added to the National Register of Historic Places.

How to get there: From Atlanta, take I–85 north to I–985, traveling through Gainesville. Stay on this four-lane road past Cornelia and Clarkesville heading toward Clayton. It will become U.S. 441. In the town of Turnersville, turn left on G. Hardman Road, then turn right back onto Historic Old 441. After ¼ mile turn left on Orchard Road and follow the signs for 3½ miles to the inn. From Clarkesville, go north on Historic Old 441 for 8½ miles to Orchard Road. Follow the signs for 3½ miles.

Innkeepers: Barrie and Bobby Aycock

Address/Telephone: Bear Gap Road, Route 3 (mailing address: Box 3304); (706) 754–7295 or (800) 552–3479 outside Georgia

Rooms: 16 rooms and suites; all with private bath, some with fireplace, some with wheelchair access.

Rates: $95 to $160, single or double, continental breakfast and full breakfast Saturday. Inquire about discounts for weeknights and stays of more than 3 nights.

Open: Year-round.

Facilities and activities: Dining room, with wheelchair access, open to guests and public most days; reservations requested; available for private parties; brown bagging permitted. Gift shop, conference room. Swimming pool, 17 acres with nature trails along Panther Creek, herb and flower gardens, mineral springs. Located in northeast Georgia mountains near historic sites. Nearby: restaurants, golf, horseback riding, boating, rafting, tennis, hiking.

The Gastonian
SAVANNAH, GEORGIA 31401

I first heard about The Gastonian from Jeff Simpson, a student in a class I was teaching at the University of North Carolina in Charlotte. Jeff said that he'd read about the inn and decided to check it out when he visited Savannah. He couldn't afford to stay there but stopped in anyhow, and he was treated to a full tour with commentary by Hugh Lineberger. That's what's special about The Gastonian. It's also astonishingly elegant—I'll tell you more about that—but, more important, the Linebergers are here, personally, involved in the daily activities of the inn and its guests. Often an inn of this opulence turns out to belong to absentee owners, or to a group of owners who hire a staff to run the place. A staff may be perfectly competent, but it's not the same as being in an inn with innkeepers who've poured their passion into the property. And that sure describes Hugh and Roberta.

It's not just passion they've poured in, but also money—a million and a half of their own and $900,000 of the bank's, Hugh says, calling it a poor investment but a "hell of a love affair."

How could you not love it? The inn comprises two 1868 historic buildings sitting side by side and a two-story carriage house, joined by a garden courtyard and an elevated walkway.

The guest rooms are filled with English antiques, exotic baths, Persian rugs, and fresh flowers. The most outrageous bath is in the

Caracalla Suite (named for a Roman emperor); it has an 8-foot Jacuzzi, sitting on a parquet platform draped with filmy curtains, next to a working fireplace. The fixtures here are of solid brass. In another room, they are of sculptured 24-karat gold. Each bath is unique and styled to complement the theme of its room—French, Oriental, Victorian, Italianate, Colonial American, or Country. All the inn's water runs through a purification system, which means, Hugh says, that you have to go easy on the bubble bath.

The public rooms are equally lavish, furnished with English antiques, satin damask drapes, and Sheffield silver. This kind of thing can easily be intimidating, but not when you're under the same roof with the Linebergers, who figure that having raised five daughters, a history-laden inn is a retirement pushover and jolly good fun at that. "It beats standing around with a golf club in my hand," Hugh says.

How to get there: From I–95, take I–16 to Savannah. Take the Martin Luther King exit and go straight onto West Gaston Street. The inn is at the corner of East Gaston and Lincoln streets.

Innkeepers: Hugh and Roberta Lineberger

Address/Telephone: 220 East Gaston Street; (912) 232–2869 or (800) 322–6603, fax (912) 232–0710

Rooms: 14, plus 2 two-room suites; all with private bath, fireplace, TV, and telephone, 1 with wheelchair access.

Rates: $125 to $285, single or double, full sit-down Southern breakfast or silver-service continental breakfast in your room, afternoon tea, wine and fresh fruit on arrival, and nightly turn-down service.

Open: Year-round.

Facilities and activities: Sundeck, hot tub, off-street lighted parking, garden courtyard. Nearby: restaurants, carriage tours of historic district, Savannah Riverfront shops, museums, beach, wildlife refuge.

Little St. Simons Island

ST. SIMONS ISLAND, GEORGIA 31522

This is truly a special place. It is a 10,000-acre barrier island still in its natural state except for the few buildings needed to house and feed guests. You can get there only by boat. Such creature comforts as nice bathrooms and ice machines have been added, but they rest unobtrusively in the natural scene.

When my late husband and I visited, we felt welcomed as though we'd been visiting there for years.

I still marvel at how much we did in a short time. The permanent staff includes three naturalists. One of the naturalists loaded us into a pickup truck and drove us around the island to help us get oriented. We walked through woods and open areas and along untouched ocean beaches. I saw my first armadillo. I gathered more sand dollars than I've ever seen in one place before. We saw deer, raccoons, opossums, and more birds than I could identify. Serious birdwatchers plan special trips to Little St. Simons to observe the spring and fall migrations.

We rode horseback with one of the naturalists. I was scared to death because I'd never been on a horse before, but they got me up on a mild-mannered old mare, and she plugged along slowly. By the end of the ride, I almost felt as though I knew what I was doing.

We canoed out through the creeks. When a big wind came up, I had a notion to be scared again, but the naturalist directed us into a sheltered spot where we could hold onto the rushes until the weather settled; then we paddled on.

When we weren't out exploring the island, we sat in front of the fire in the lodge, chatting with the other two guests and inspecting the photographs on the walls. They're standard hunting-camp pictures: rows of men grinning like idiots and holding up strings of fish, hunters with rifles grinning like idiots, and people climbing in and out of boats grinning like idiots.

One of the best meals we had while we were there was roast quail, served with rice pilaf and little yellow biscuits. As I polished off an unladylike-sized meal and finished my wine, I realized that *I* was grinning like an idiot. After dinner, with no thought of television, I retired to the comfortable bed in a simple, pleasant room and fell asleep instantly, still grinning.

How to get there: When you make your reservations, you will receive instructions on where to meet the boat that takes you to the island.

Innkeeper: Debbie McIntyre
Address/Telephone: St. Simons Island (mailing address: P.O. Box 21078); (912) 638–7472, fax (912) 634–1811
E-mail: 102063.467@compuserve.com
Rooms: 2 in main lodge with private bath; 4 in River Lodge, all with private bath; 4 in Cedar House, all with private bath; 2 in Michael Cottage share bath.
Rates: $200, single; $425, double; all meals, wine with dinner, island activities, and ferry service. Minimum two-night stay. Inquire about longer-stay and off-season discounts.
Open: Year-round.
Facilities and activities: Bar in lodge; collection of books about native birds, plants, animals, and marine life; swimming pool, stables, horseshoes, ocean swimming, birding, naturalist-led explorations, beachcombing, shelling, fishing, canoeing, hiking biking, fly-fishing schools.
Recommended Country Inns® Travelers' Club Benefit: 10 percent discount, weekdays, May–September.

The Amos Shinkle Townhouse

COVINGTON, KENTUCKY 41011

If you share the preservationists' enthusiasm for the romance of fine old architecture in excellent condition, you'll enjoy a stay at the Amos Shinkle Townhouse.

This is the house the entrepreneur Amos Shinkle and his family lived in during the Civil War while his castle was being finished. A tour brochure for the historic district calls the structure a "modest Italianate home." Compared to a castle, maybe. But unless *you* are accustomed to castle life, you'll find The Amos Shinkle Townhouse posh.

The ceilings are 16 feet high, with Rococo Revival chandeliers, plaster moldings, and cornices. Beyond the front entry a mahogany staircase, still with the original murals on the walls, and crown moldings that continue on the second-floor landing, ascends to guests rooms furnished with antiques. The master bedroom has a fireplace, a four-poster bed, and a maroon-tiled bath with a crystal chandelier and a whirlpool tub.

Downstairs, comfortable couches and chairs clustered near the fireplaces make elegant places to read or chat. You're welcome to play the baby grand piano, too.

Behind the main house in the carriage house are simpler rooms decorated in Early American style. This building served as stable quarters in the 1800s. The horse stalls have been turned into sleeping accommodations for children.

A brick-and-grass courtyard between the two buildings includes places to sit under umbrellas when the weather is nice. During the growing season, pots of geraniums, petunias, and black-eyed Susans brighten the area. Tall hollyhocks and mature shrubs soften the austere lines of the carriage house.

Quite apart from the visual and architectural interest of the townhouse, staying here evokes a sense of romantic old Southern hospitality. I talked at length with the resident innkeeper, Bernie Moorman. He used to be the mayor and maintains active involvement with the community. He likes to tell guests how special the area is historically and culturally, and he'll do almost anything to make sure you like it here. Bernie says everyone at the inn will help you arrange everything from restaurants to tickets for the horse races.

Even breakfast reflects their willingness to cater to your schedule. You order, from a full menu, anytime from 7:00 to 9:30 A.M. Your eggs, pancakes, French toast or whatever come to you cooked to order. Be sure to try the goetta, a regional sausage-like dish of cooked ground pork, pinhead oatmeal, and spices. Bernie says their goetta, made by Dick Fink, is the best in the area. I say if you wanta spenda day in romantic luxury you gotta getta night here.

How to get there: From I–75/71 take exit 192 onto 5th Street, which is one-way going east. Drive 9 blocks to where 5th street ends at Garrard Street. Turn left and go 2½ blocks north. The inn is on the left.

Innkeepers: Don Nash and Bernie Moorman
Address/Telephone: 215 Garrard Street; (606) 431–2118 or (800) 972–7012
Rooms: 7, 3 in main house, 4 in carriage house; all with private bath and TV. Smoking and no-smoking rooms available.
Rates: $73 to $130, double; $10 less, single; full breakfast. Children under 12 free in room with adults.
Open: Year-round.
Facilities and activities: Located in historic district across the bridge from downtown Cincinnati. Meeting space for groups up to 15. Nearby: walking distance to restaurants; Ohio River recreation, boating, cruises.

Shepherd Place

VERSAILLES, KENTUCKY 40383

On five rural acres in the middle of Bluegrass Country, the Yawns keep fifteen sheep. Don't go thinking lamb chops, though; you'd have it all wrong. These sheep are for guests to enjoy watching and petting, for shearing, and for loving. Their wool, as far as Sylvia is concerned, is for spinning and knitting. She shears the sheep only once a year, even though twice a year is possible, so that the wool will be longer and more suited to her handcrafts.

If you spend time here, you're bound to learn about the sheep, to want to see Sylvia spin, and probably to buy some yarn or order a hand-knit sweater for yourself. In this situation the choices are so personal that you can even request a sweater from Pearl's or Abigail's or Sabrina's wool, and Sylvia will see that the appropriate yarn is set aside to knit your sweater. Obviously you won't get it in a week or two, but a garment so uniquely your own seems worth waiting for.

In busy times you might have to wait to book a night at the inn, too, but the experience, like a sweater of Sabrina's wool, is worth the wait.

To give you an idea, an old-fashioned swing sways on the porch. The downstairs parlor once had French doors. These have been converted to floor-to-ceiling windows that let in a glorious amount of light. The light is picked up by 12-inch-high baseboards painted white. Spice-brown walls keep the overall effect from being glaring. Queen Anne–style chairs are set off by formal English sofa lamps, and a red-and-blue Oriental rug unifies all the room's elements.

The guest rooms are uncommonly large, 20 feet by 20 feet, with bathroom facilities fitted into alcove rooms in their corners.

As pleasing as all this is, the real kick comes from Sylvia's pleasure with it all. In every way she's thrilled with being an innkeeper in her old Kentucky home. She's proud of the smooth gleam of interior paint Marlin (who used to be a professional painter) has accomplished. She enjoys cooking huge breakfasts, which often include Kentucky ham and such delicacies as whole wheat pancakes with walnuts. She loves the sheep and working with their wool. And, most significant of all, she enjoys the guests. "We get such *good* guests. We have a bulletin board full of cards and letters they send after they've been here," she said.

How to get there: Coming from Knoxville on I–75, take exit 104 onto the Lexington Circle; from Cincinnati, take exit 115. From the Lexington Circle take exit 5B onto U.S. 60. Drive 6 miles to Heritage Road and turn left. The inn is at the corner of U.S. 60 and Heritage Road.

Innkeepers: Marlin and Sylvia Yawn
Address/Telephone: 31 Heritage Road; (800) 278–0864
Rooms: 3; all with private bath; TV available on request. No smoking inside.
Rates: $65, single; $75, double; $85, triple; full breakfast.
Open: Year-round.
Facilities and activities: Pond with ducks and geese. Nearby: restaurants, Lexington, Shakertown.

Tezcuco Plantation

BURNSIDE, LOUISIANA 70725

How about a couple of nights of Southern-style romance on an old Louisiana plantation? You can enjoy all the old-time ambience without the bother of hoop skirts or the stickiness of the state before air conditioning.

Tezcuco Plantation tries to give guests a feeling of what it would have been like to live on a working sugar plantation in the 1800s. The original plantation house is an antebellum raised cottage (cottages were a lot bigger in those days) built about 1855 from cypress grown and cut on the property and from bricks made in the plantation's kiln.

All but three of the original outbuildings remain. The others, long since gone from the grounds, have been replaced by moving in appropriate ones found on other plantations.

The overnight cottages are restored slave quarters, doubtless improved since slaves lived in them, with ruffled curtains, air conditioning, antique furnishings and artifacts, pecky cypress paneling, and the work of Louisiana artists on the walls.

Altogether there are thirty buildings on the plantation now, including a children's playhouse, a greenhouse and potting shed, an old shop with antique tools, a Civil War museum, and an African-American museum.

Guests sit in rockers on the porches of the little cottages, chatting back and forth from cottage to cottage in the old-time way.

For dinner, the people at Tezcuco will certainly suggest that you drive a couple of miles to Lafitte's Landing Restaurant next to the Sunshine Bridge on the Mississippi River, where John D. Folse, a chef much admired in the area, serves up wonderful, rich, and well-seasoned gourmet meals in his historic building.

On the grounds, the Tezcuco Plantation Restaurant is open from 8:00 A.M. to 3:30 P.M. to serve breakfast and lunch. The offerings range from such comfortably familiar dishes as shrimp salad to more exotic choices, including fried alligator.

How to get there: Tezcuco is between Baton Rouge and New Orleans, near I–10. Coming from the north or the south on I–10, take exit 179 onto L.A. 44 south to Burnside. The plantation is 1 mile north of Sunshine Bridge on L.A. 44. Write for brochure with map.

Innkeeper: Debra Purifoy
Address/Telephone: Burnside (mailing address: 3138 Highway 44, Darrow, LA 70725); (504) 562–3929
Rooms: 17 cottages; all with private bath and TV, some with kitchen and fireplace.
Rates: $60 to $160, single or double, tour of plantation house and grounds, bottle of wine, and full Creole breakfast. $20 for each extra adult, $12.50 for each extra child.
Open: Year-round.
Facilities and activities: Victorian-style restaurant, antiques-and-gift shop. Nearby: restaurants, plantation tour homes and historic sites, Mississippi River.

Barrow House

ST. FRANCISVILLE, LOUISIANA 70775

Loosen your girdle and listen to this: crawfish salad, chicken Bayou La Fourche (stuffed with crabmeat), jambalaya rice, pecan praline parfait. Served on good china with sterling silver flatware by candlelight on a flower-decorated table in the formal dining room, under the old punkah "shoo fly" fan. Oh, be still my heart!

I can tell you lots more about Barrow House, and I'll get to it, but how can Louisiana food like that, served with such style, come anywhere but first? You have to arrange for such dinners ahead of time, and you select from a number of different possibilities for each course.

After a meal—next day maybe—you can do penance by jogging down Royal Street with the locals, an enjoyable thing to do even if all you ate the night before was half a Big Mac.

"We want people to have a good time here," Shirley said. And they do. Beyond the food there's the house, an 1809 saltbox with a Greek Revival wing added in the 1860s that's listed on the National Register of Historic Places and furnished with 1860s antiques. Next to it, the Printer's House was built for the monks who founded the town. It dates from about 1780.

In the saltbox, the gorgeous antiques include a rosewood armoire by Prudent Mallard and a *queen-sized* Mallard bed with a *Spanish moss* mattress. You don't have to sleep in that bed unless you want to, but one man, a doctor with a bad back, said it was the most comfortable bed he'd ever had.

Spanish moss was the traditional mattress filler used in Louisiana for two hundred years. Shirley's informal tour of the house gives you a chance to learn how the mattress was made and to see all the fine antiques.

Similarly, the professionally recorded Historic District walking tour (with Mozart between stops) Shirley wrote guides you from Barrow House to twenty-three historic stops.

Food and antiques and tours matter, but unless good people are involved, it's probably more fun to go to Disney World. This will give you an idea about Shirley. Her inn came to my attention partly through an article on inns in the magazine *Louisiana Life*. Barrow House was included in the article because when the editor was married in St. Francisville, she dressed for the wedding at Barrow House. By the time she drove off, everybody who should have been crying was crying properly, and Shirley was carrying the bride's train. Shirley was crying, too.

Some people don't want too much personal fuss. Shirley says that she has to know when guests would rather be left alone. You'll get whatever amount of attention you want—no more. Probably the ultimate in privacy is in the rooms and suites at the Printer's House. Here, the Empire and Victorian suites are the very best accommodations. Wherever you stay, expect to leave happy.

Shirley said, "It's great to have guests, and when they leave they hug you."

How to get there: Barrow House is behind the courthouse in the St. Francisville Historic District. You will receive a map after you make reservations.

Innkeepers: Shirley Dittloff and Christopher Dennis
Address/Telephone: 524 Royal Street (mailing address: P.O. Box 700); (504) 635–4791, fax (504) 635–4769
E-mail: staff@topteninn.com
Rooms: 5, plus 3 suites in 2 buildings; all with private bath and TV, telephone on request.
Rates: $85 to 95, double; $115 to $135, suites; inquire about single rates. Continental breakfast, wine, and cassette walking tour of Historic District. Full breakfast available at $5 extra per person. Cash and personal checks only.
Open: Year-round except December 22–25.
Facilities and activities: Dinner for guests by advance reservation. Located in St. Francisville Historic District. Nearby: tour plantations and historic sites.
Recommended Country Inns® Travelers' Club Benefit: Stay two nights, get 50 percent off third night, subject to availability.

The Father Ryan House Bed & Breakfast Inn

BILOXI, MISSISSIPPI 39530

Poetry is the lanuguage of romance. Here is an inn devoted to the momory of its resident poet and embellished by a bright decor and lots of creature comforts that will make you feel romantic even if you don't care about poetry.

> Just a hundred feet away
> Seaward, flows and ebbs the tide;
> And the wavelets, blue and grey
> moan, and white sails windward glide
> o'er the ever restless sea.
>
> — Father Abram Ryan, *Sea Rest*

So Father Ryan described this place. He was the poet laureat of the Confederacy and a close friend of Jefferson Davis, president of the Confederacy. Father Ryan wrote some of his best-known poetry while he lived in this house, which was built about 1841. Standing just 20 feet from the beach, this is one of the oldest remaining structures on the Gulf Coast, and it has been faithfully restored according to information in Father Ryan's letters and other contemporary sources.

To further heighten the mood, his poetry, written in calligraphy, is displayed throughout the house, as are books about him, some of his letters, and more poetry, and Margaret Mitchell's *Gone with the Wind*, open to her mention of Father Ryan's visit.

But don't suppose that the historicity of the house means it's dark and gloomy. In fact one guest who saw it for the first time said, "How did you make it so light?"

Windows, mainly. Roseanne says that the English architect who designed the second floor "went crazy with windows," an uncommon approach at the time, because homes were taxed according to the number and size of their windows. "Apparently it didn't matter," Roseanne says.

The guest rooms in the house, including the ones that once would have been Father Ryan's bedroom, study, and a room for an orphan boy he took in, are quietly elegant, almost understated, furnished with handcrafted beds and antiques dating back to the early 1800s. All the comforters and pillows are of down.

The inn has several appealing common areas. Upstairs a large room that runs all the way from the north to the south side of the house overlooks the Gulf on one side and the courtyard and swimming pool on the other. Downstairs, the library has floor-to-ceiling shelves filled with books, including many about the South and Mississippi. Rolling ladders help you reach the high shelves. Empire furniture from the 1860s, upholstered in a light cream-colored fabric, lends dignity without being overbearing. In addition to a formal dining room, there is the Lemon Room–a bright closed-in porch with Mexican tile floors, high ceilings, and paddle fans–where breakfast is served unless you request (free) room service.

No matter where you take your breakfast, it will be special. Anita, the chef, was trained in San Francisco and brings a California flair and expertise with herbs to the kitchen. Each breakfast includes a savory or fruit bread, fruit prepared in various ways–poached pears or yogurt-fruit soup, for instance–and a main dish that may be anything from cheese blintzes to puffy oven pancakes with fruit. That's a breakfast that gives you zing for a romantic day.

How to get there: The inn is on Highway 60, 6 blocks west of the I–110 off ramp, 4 blocks west of the Biloxi Lighthouse, and 2 blocks east of the main Keesler entrance. You will receive a brochure with a map when you make a reservation.

Innkeeper: Rosanne McKenney
Address/Telephone: 1196 Beach Boulevard; (601) 435–1189 or (800) 295–1189, fax (601) 435–1189
Rooms: 9 in main house, 2 in beach cabin; all with private bath, cable TV, and telephone. Smoking outside only.
Rates: $85 to $130, double; single $15 less; full breakfast.
Open: Year-round.
Facilities and activities: Swimming pool, Gulf of Mexico ocean beach, bicycle rentals. Nearby: restaurants, Biloxi Lighthouse, Keesler Air Force Base, Jefferson Davis home at Beauvoir, Gulf Shores National Seashore, golf courses, floating gambling casinos.
Business travel: Excellent work space and light in rooms; direct telephone lines, data ports, fax available.

Weymouth Hall

NATCHEZ, MISSISSIPPI 39120

Gene calls Weymouth Hall a "gem of Natchez" because of its unique architecture and fine millwork and bridge work, and, most of all, because of its spectacular view of the Mississippi River. Even before we had looked around inside, Gene showed me the backyard of the inn, where guests can sit in the evening to watch the sun set and the lights come on along the river. "When you've got a view like this, who cares about the house?" he said.

That's a deceptive line. I've never met an innkeeper more involved with the restoration and furnishing of a building than Gene. His collection of antiques by John Belter, Charles Baudoine, and Prudent Mallard is so impressive that even other innkeepers talk about it. The rococo furniture in the double parlor looks as though it had been bought new as a set and kept intact ever since, but Gene spent a lot of time assembling it from wherever he could find it, a piece at a time.

It's worth mentioning that at Weymouth Hall all the guest rooms (which have showers in the private baths) are in the house, not in adjacent buildings or added wings as is the case with some of the larger tour homes. And breakfast is served at a Mississippi plantation table in the main dining room. Gene says that in conversations many guests have said that "living" in the house is important to them.

On a more frivolous note, Gene keeps a player piano from the 1920s, partly to reflect his sense that the inn should be fun, not a museum.

Nor does Gene's involvement stop with the inn and its furnishings. He knows how to entertain guests. He knows the area well. Gene used to take guests on personal tours (and probably still would if you asked), so he is a great source of information about where to go and what to see.

You may decide not to leave the property for any kind of tour, however, once you take in the view of the Mississippi River from Weymouth Hall's backyard. It's unquestionably one of the best vistas in Natchez. And the grounds keep getting more pleasing as the shrubbery and gardens mature. Sitting high on the hill catching the breezes and enjoying the view here can be entertainment aplenty, especially if you're with good company.

How to get there: From Highway 65 and 84 (John R. Junkin Drive) on the south side of Natchez, go north on Canal Street as far as you can. Make a left and a quick right onto Linton Avenue and follow Linton Avenue to Cemetery Road. The inn is directly across from the cemetery, on a small hill.

Innkeeper: Gene Weber
Address/Telephone: 1 Cemetery Road (mailing address: P.O. Box 1091); (601) 445–2304
Rooms: 5; all with private bath, some with wheelchair access. No smoking inn.
Rates: $85, double; rate adjusted for singles; full plantation breakfast, house tour, and beverage on arrival.
Open: February 1 through December 31.
Facilities and activities: Nearby: restaurants, Mississippi riverboat tours, tours of many historic Natchez homes.

Hickory Nut Gap Inn

BAT CAVE, NORTH CAROLINA 28710

From this mountaintop inn, elevation 2,200 feet, at the top of Hickory Nut Gorge, you can look out over mountains in all directions and not see another man-made structure. You can sit on the 80-foot screened porch and watch hummingbirds. Bettina (known to all as B.) and her husband Easy and I were doing that one afternoon as the sun came out toward the end of a rain shower. "I think it will make a rainbow," Easy said.

He was right.

When the moment had passed, I asked questions about the inn. B. said it was built in 1950 as a mountain retreat by a well-to-do businessman and that she inherited it from a later owner. She and Easy have put years of work into refurbishing the place. They've concentrated on keeping such features as the cathedral ceiling and stone fireplace of the great room, and cleaning up the wood paneling throughout. If you know your wood, you'll recognize maple, cherry, poplar, black walnut, and red and white oak, as well as cedar in the closets.

B.'s decorating has grown from her own interests and history and from her respect for what was already in the building. For instance, the eighty-six characters of the Cherokee alphabet, mounted high on the walls, circle the recreation room. They were hand carved in wood by the Cherokee artist Goingback Chiltoskey.

The owner from whom B. inherited the

place was part Native American. You find Native American arts and crafts throughout the inn, mixed in with such surprising items as a camel saddle used as a footstool, a trunk used as a coffee table, and an honest-to-goodness hand-woven hippie dress used as a wall decoration. The dress was B.'s. "Remember when everything we wore had to make a statement?" she said.

This eclectic decor works partly because of B.'s skill in putting things together without over-doing it and partly because of the spaciousness of the building to begin with. The effect is too sophisticated to call rustic and too comfortable to call exotic.

In this inn space, B. and Easy, two social and articulate people, try to see that you have whatever you need and, at the same time, try to keep out of your hair if what you need most is privacy.

The atmosphere here is just enought out of the ordinary to encourage romance, even if you don't have a word for description. I was searching for a word to describe them and their inn, not having much success. "How would *you* describe it all?" I asked.

They answered almost in union.

"Laid back."

How to get there: In Bat Cave, where Highway 64 splits off from Highway 74A and goes west toward Hendersonville, follow Highway 64 ½ mile. On the right two pillars made of river rock mark the entrance to the inn. A narrow drive winds 7/10 mile up to the inn. You'll know you've made the right turn when you see the inn's small sign about 15 feet up the drive.

Innkeepers: Bettina Spaulding and Easy Batterson
Address/Telephone: P.O. Box 246; (704) 625–9108
Rooms: 4, plus 1 suite; all with private bath. No smoking inn.
Rates: $75, double; $70, single; $110, suite; continental breakfast. No credit cards.
Open: April through December 10, weather permitting.
Facilities and activities: Musical instruments; VCR; recreation room with bowling lane, sauna, pool table; hiking trails. Nearby: restaurants; crafts and antiques shops; short drive to Chimney Rock and Lake Lure, boating, golf, shopping.

Langdon House

BEAUFORT, NORTH CAROLINA 28516

I find this place intensely romantic because of its almost Zen-like simplicity and because of the warmth of the innkeeper. This is an inn that bears no stamp of the "sameness" that inevitably creeps into any business, from restaurants to retail to inns after a new idea becomes popular. There is no other inn even remotely like this one.

The first thing you notice as you walk in is the beautifully restored red-amber heart-pine flooring. Jimm Prest did some of the refinishing himself, "working way too close to the ground." He has created a comfortable hostelry in this 1732 home, which has verandas on the first and second floors that almost demand some stargazing. The furnishings are comfortably Colonial, with bentwood wing-back chairs and an Edwardian oak dining table that stretches to 8 feet with all its leaves and can seat fourteen. Many of the antiques, paintings, and musical instruments scattered throughout the inn were donated by earlier residents to support his authentic restoration and furnishing of the place.

It happens as it does because this is Jimm Prest's place. The well-restored and -maintained building, the comfortable furnishings and good beds with simple white spreads, are the stage he's created upon which he plays the role of innkeeper with unique style and verve. Take Jimm out of it, and it would still be a comfortable place, but it wouldn't be Langdon House.

Consider his list of amenities, for instance.

Alphabetically arranged and running to at least a couple dozen entries, it includes bikes, beach baskets, car music, cortisone cream, fishing gear, ice chests, jumper cables, portable gas grills, and tennis rackets. Nor does he promise anything he can't deliver. He says that the advantage to running so small an inn is that he's able to cater to your whims and provide any service you might need, pretty much one-on-one.

Or consider his breakfasts. Cooking is a skill he developed in college when he volunteered to cook weekend breakfasts for his housemates and the people who stayed over, because he figured if he cooked, he wouldn't have to clean. He will accommodate any dietary restriction if you warn him ahead of time, but his signature offering is Belgian waffles in such combinations as orange-pecan or cranberry-nut.

Jimm serves breakfast on plain white dishes that won't compete with the appearance of the food, because food "is to be looked at as well as consumed." And that, he figures, is a pretty good use of his college degree in fine arts.

If he went back now, they'd probably give him one in history, or maybe storytelling, too, because he knows the local lore in detail and tells it with wit. He knows about the old burying ground where the oldest, early 1700s graves face east, so the dead will face the sun when they rise on Judgment Morning; he knows about the British Revolutionary War soldier buried standing up, because he swore he would never lie down on foreign soil; he knows the best restaurants and assures you you'll recognize the Net House, because it has a big crab on the front. And he likes to sit on the porch and "trade words."

What it adds up to is that the luster of the heart-pine floors may be the first thing you notice when you arrive, but when you leave, what you'll remember is Jimm Prest.

How to get there: From Highway 70 take the Morehead drawbridge into Beaufort. Turn right at the first light onto Turner Street, where you'll see a sign for the Historic District. Go 1 block. The house is on the corner of the intersection facing Craven Street. Park in front of the house or in the side yard parking area.

Innkeeper: Jimm Prest
Address/Telephone: 135 Craven Street; (919) 728–5499
Rooms: 4; all with private bath.
Rates: Weekdays: $115, double with full breakfast; $103, single with full breakfast; $106, double with continental breakfast; $94, single with continental breakfast; $83, double or single with morning coffee only. Weekends in season: two-night minimum stay, $120 to $128, single or double, continental breakfast. All rates include tax.
Open: Year-round.
Facilities and activities: Bicycles. Nearby: restaurants, North Carolina Maritime Museum, Beaufort Historic Site Tours, Mattie King Davis Art Gallery, access to Outer Banks.

Windsong
CLYDE, NORTH CAROLINA 28721

I like this place so much that if I use every word of praise that comes to mind you'll think it's too good to be true. Donna and Gale built the rustic log building specifically to be a small inn and their own home. It has light pine-log walls and floors of Mexican saltillo tile. The rooms are large, with high, beamed ceilings. Skylights and huge windows let in light on all sides. The building perches on the side of a mountain at 3,000 feet so that looking out the front windows in the direction the guest rooms face, you get a panoramic view of woods and rolling fields below; looking out the back from the kitchen and entry, you see more wilderness higher up and, closer to the house, the perennial gardens, terraces, and recreational facilities.

In addition to sliding glass doors to let you look down the mountain, each guest room has either a deck or a ground-level patio where you can sit to admire the lower mountain peaks that seem to roll on forever.

Donna decorated the guest rooms in witty, sophisticated styles, using mostly items her family has gathered living in distant places: hence the Alaska Room with Eskimo carvings and art and a dogsled in the corner; hence the Santa Fe Room with Mexican furniture and a steerhide rug. I like the Safari Room. Mosquito netting is draped over the head of the bed, and the room is decorated with primitive artifacts, vines, and bamboo. Dieffenbachia and other junglelike plants flank the big soaking tub in the corner. A little sculptured giraffe with extra-long legs peers out at you from the greenery.

This place has some interesting live animals, too. The Livengoods' daughter Sara manages the beautiful herd of llamas, which not only adorn the surrounding hills but also are the focus of dinner treks on the inn property on Tuesdays and Fridays.

Above the area where the llamas live, higher on the hill, the two-bedroom cottage with kitchen, loft bedroom, and woodstove that would be nice for a family or two couples.

How to get there: From I–40, take exit 24. Go north on U.S. 209 for 2½ miles. Turn left on Riverside Drive and go 2 miles. Turn right on Ferguson Cove Loop and go 1 mile, keeping to the left. You'll be driving straight up some narrow, unpaved roads. The distance will seem longer than it is.

Innkeepers: Donna and Gale Livengood
Address/Telephone: 120 Ferguson Ridge; (704) 627–6111, fax (704) 627–8080
Rooms: 5; all with private bath, separate vanity and soaking tub, deck or patio, and fireplace. No air conditioning (elevation 3,000 feet). No smoking inn. One cottage.
Rates: $99 to $140, double; single and weekly rates 10 percent less; full breakfast. Extra person in room, $20. Cottage: $140 to 160.
Open: Year-round.
Facilities and activities: VCRs and extensive videocassette library, guest lounge with refrigerator and wet bar (brown bagging), piano, pool table; washer and dryer on request; swimming pool, tennis court, hiking trails, llama treks. Nearby: restaurants, Great Smoky Mountain National Park, Asheville and historic sites, Biltmore House, crafts and antiques shops, horseback riding.
Recommended Country Inns® Travelers' Club Benefit: Free bottle of red wine with three-day booking.

The Evergreen Inn and 1109 South Main Restaurant

ANDERSON, SOUTH CAROLINA 29621

"This is delicious. How's yours?"

"Wonderful."

"Couldn't be better."

It was early dinnertime, and I was eavesdropping shamelessly as I ate my way through an appetizer of smoked goose breast with raspberry sauce, a perfect Belgian-endive salad sprinkled with Roquefort cheese, and a really well-prepared piece of fish in a green-peppercorn sauce.

People at neighboring tables had ordered beef and veal, and I wondered if those dishes were as good as what I had. Apparently they were.

This is the place to stay if your notion of romance is good dining, nice wines, and an elegant guest room to retreat to after dinner without having to get back int your car. The South doesn't have a lot of these places, especially with so good a resident chef.

Peter Ryter is the chef. He learned his trade in Switzerland and then worked many years in good restaurants across America. No matter what I tell you about the menu now, he'll probably be serving something else when you visit The 1109 because he prides himself on changing his offerings regularly in response to what's in season and what's looking especially good at the farmer's market in Atlanta, where he goes to buy produce. But you can always count on the freshness of his vegetables and fish and the delicacy of his sauces.

Peter has been selected for membership in La Chaîne des Rôtisseurs, a worldwide French gourmet society founded in 1234. This is an honor from his peers.

Each dining room is done in different colors and patterns, giving you more the sense of a home that feeds many people graciously than of a public restaurant.

The guest rooms are in Evergreen Inn (a building next door dating from 1834), a companion to The 1109.

My favorite room in this second house is a huge, nearly octagonal room with wallpape of peacocks and greenery and lots of built-in w nut and mahogany shelves. There are specialty rooms, including one for honeymooners in pink and rose velvet with an exotic navy satin canopy and huge antiques.

How to get there: Going south on I–85, take exit 27 (Highway 81) toward Anderson. Turn left on Main Street and go 8 blocks. If you are traveling north on I–85, take exit 11 (Highway 24) toward Anderson. Turn left on Main Street and continue 4 blocks. The inn is on the left. Turn the corner on Hampton Street to park in the rear.

Innkeepers: Myrna and Peter Ryter
Address/Telephone: 1109 South Main; (803) 225–1109
Rooms: 7; 6 with private bath, 4 with television.
Rates: \$52, single; \$65 to \$70, double; continental breakfast and cocktail or wine.
Open: Year-round.
Facilities and activities: Dinner and bar open to guests and the public by reservation, restaurant closed Sunday and Monday. Nearby: public tennis courts, Lake Hartwell, fishing, swimming, boating.

Ansonborough Inn

CHARLESTON, SOUTH CAROLINA 29401

Like so many Charleston inns, this one had a different function in its earlier time. It was a three-story stationer's warehouse built about 1900. The building's renovation not only kept the heart-of-pine beams and locally fired red brick, which are typical of the period, but actually emphasized them. The lobby soars three stories high, with skylights; the original huge, rough beams are fully visible, an important part of the decor.

The original plan to use the renovated building as a condo complex didn't work out, which probably was bad news for some investors; but it's great for inn guests now, because the rooms, which are really suites, are huge. At least one wall in each features the exposed old brick. The ceilings are about 20 feet high. Because all the rooms were fit into an existing shell, no two rooms are exactly the same shape or size. Nothing is exactly predictable. The resulting little quirks, nooks, lofts, and alcoves add a lot of interest.

The living rooms are furnished in period reproductions with comfortable chairs and sleeper sofas to accommodate extra people. What's more, you really can cook in the kitchens. If you ask for place settings and basic kitchen utensils when you make your reservations, the kitchen will be ready when you arrive. The inn is just across the road from an excellent Harris Teeter supermarket housed in an old railroad station. I don't think it would be appropriate to whip up corned beef and cabbage or deep-fried chittlins in this environment, but the arrangement is great for preparing light meals—a good way to save our calories and your dollars for some sumptuous dinners in Charleston's excellent restaurants.

Clearly this isn't the kind of place where everyone sits around the breakfast table comparing notes about dinner the night before, but the continental breakfast (with sweet breads baked at a plantation in Walterboro) and the evening wine and cheese are set up in the lobby so that guests can sit in conversational clusters. If someone on the staff thinks that you may have something in common with another guest, he or she will take the trouble to introduce you. Indeed, the staff here is personable and helpful—attitudes you don't always encounter in Charleston hostelries. A visitor from a Scandinavian country said that if this is Southern hospitality, he likes it.

How to get there: From I–26 East, take the Meeting Street/Visitor Center exit. Go 1²⁄₁₀ miles to Hasell Street. Turn left and go through the next traffic signal. From Route 17 South, take the East Bay Street exit, go 1³⁄₁₀ miles to Hasell and turn left. From Route 17 North, after crossing the Ashley River, exit to the right and go through the first traffic signal onto Calhoun Street. Drive 1⁴⁄₁₀ miles to Easy Bay Street, turn right, and go to the second traffic signal (Hassel Street) and turn left. The inn is on your right.

Innkeeper: Eric A. Crapse
Address/Telephone: 21 Hasell Street; (803) 723–1655 or (800) 522–2073
Rooms: 37 suites; all with private bath, telephone, TV, and kitchen. No-smoking rooms available.
Rates: Spring and fall, $89 to $130, double; summer and winter, $89 to $119, double; continental breakfast and afternoon wine and cheese. $10 for each extra adult in suite. Children 12 and under free. Inquire about discounts for singles, long-term stays, and corporate rates.
Open: Year-round.
Facilities and activities: Free off-street parking. In heart of waterfront historic district. Nearby: historic sites, restaurants, shuttle transportation to visitor center. Walking distance to antiques shops and downtown Charleston.
Business travel: Located minutes from business district. Telephone, computer and modem setup, excellent work area in room; fax, copy service available; meeting room.

Adams Edgeworth Inn
MONTEAGLE, TENNESSEE 37356

Occasionally someone opens an inn that seems destined from the beginning to become a classic. I believe Edgeworth is such an inn. David and Wendy put uncountable hours of study, thought, and travel into defining the kind of inn they wanted. Then they put at least that much into finding the right building in the right location. They wanted a good-sized inn, in a rural setting, elegant but not formal. They wanted a full-service inn, serving dinner as well as breakfast.

The three-story Victorian house, nearly one hundred years old, on the grounds of the Monteagle Assembly (sometimes called "the Chautauqua of the South"), is perfect because it was built as an inn. Outside, David and Wendy expanded established perennial gardens to enhance the sense of rural seclusion. It looks like everything has been growing here forever.

Inside, they refurbished and brightened the interior without hiding the wood floors or changing the inn's warm character. They brought a large, eclectic collection of museum-quality art, as well as antiques and interesting mementos they and their grown children have picked up in world travel. Also, they have some wonderful items from the years Wendy's father spent as a United States ambassador, including the gold-edged ambassadorial china upon which Wendy serves dinner. She has even found some of the antiques that were originally in the inn and returned them to their proper places.

Some of the guest rooms have been designed around quilts made by her mother and grandmother that Wendy uses as bedcovers. The library and guest rooms overflow with books. Classical music deepens the feeling of serenity in the sitting areas and floats out onto the shady porches.

If you prefer an active retreat to a sedentary one, the state park and wilderness areas offer more possibilities than you could explore in a lifetime. Because David has family with homes on the Assembly grounds, he knows the area intimately and takes pleasure in sharing. You can, he asserts, even find places to go skinny-dipping. The facilities of the Assembly offer more sedate versions of swimming and walking.

After your daytime exertions, you definitely should plan on a dinner at the inn. Wendy dims the lights in the formal dining room and you dine by candlelight, often to live piano or guitar music. Some of the offerings are chicken Florentine, fresh salmon, and angel-hair pasta with Wendy's secret sauce. Wendy's cuisine includes lots of fresh herbs, lightly cooked and sauced fresh vegetables, fine cheeses, and delicate desserts. Each dish looks as good as it tastes.

How to get there: From I–24 take exit 134 into Monteagle. In the center of the village you will see a steel archway with a MONTEAGLE ASSEMBLY sign. Turn through the arch. Once on the grounds, follow the green-and-white CENTENNIAL CELEBRATION signs to the inn, 2/10 mile from gate.

Innkeepers: Wendy and David Adams
Address/Telephone: Monteagle Assembly; (615) 924–4000
Rooms: 13, plus 1 suite with kitchenette; all with private bath, some rooms with fireplace or wheelchair access. Smoking on verandas only.
Rates: $85 to $195, single and double, full breakfast. Two-night minimum on weekends.
Open: Year-round.
Facilities and activities: Five-course candlelight dinner by reservation. Gift shop. On grounds of Monteagle Assembly. Nearby: golf, tennis, Tennessee State Park, wilderness and developed hiking trails, Sewanee University of the South, Monteagle Wine Cellars.

Von-Bryan Inn

SEVIERVILLE, TENNESSEE 37862

Von-Bryan Inn is on top of a mountain near the Great Smoky Mountains. Not near the top, *on* it. The view includes the Smokies and Wears Valley and treetops in the clouds. The inn is set up to make the most of the view, especially the garden room, a room on three levels with a reading loft and many windows from which you can look out over the hills and watch the sunset. The outdoor pool seems to float above clouds and mountains, and from there the view is panoramic. And the large hot tub by the pool is a great place to relax while you watch the stars at night. While I was here, I saw men stand in the yard looking across the valleys and deciding, without even going inside, that this was a place to which they must bring their wives.

I could've told them that it's nice inside, too. The living room has a stacked-stone fireplace and attractive, unobtrusive furniture grouped for conversation.

The suite is interesting. It has lots of glass, a pine floor, a queen-sized canopy bed, and a reading loft. Each of the other guest rooms has a special delight, a special view or an unusual bed, for example, but the Red Bud Room is unlike anything I've ever seen. It has a king-sized bed against a natural paneled wall, windows along another wall, a sitting area with a love seat, and a big cherry-red hot tub in the corner. Red simply dominates the room. Jo Ann says that it's one of the most requested rooms and theorizes that folks who would find a red hot tub just too racy at home get a kick out of it on vacation.

Speaking of Jo Ann, if personable innkeepers are important to you, you'll enjoy this inn. Jo Ann is thoroughly competent and produces a gourmet breakfast without a flick of the eyelid, but she's easy, chatty, and comfortable, all at the same time. D. J. has a green thumb and also is a good conversationalist. When I visited, I lingered much too long over breakfast because we got to talking about everything from food and plants to our earlier careers, and I couldn't make myself leave.

Among the nice little treats you can arrange for yourself if you stay here are helicopter pickup and delivery to the inn. I didn't experience the helicopter trip, but given the view and the height of the mountain, I think it would be a sensational experience.

One treat you don't have to arrange. Jo Ann unobtrusively sets out lemonade, tea, and desserts each evening for all who want them.

How to get there: From Highway 321, turn onto Hatcher Mountain Road (the inn's sign marks the turn) and follow inn signs all the way to the top of the mountain. Ask for a map and more detailed instructions when you make reservations.

Innkeepers: D. J. and Jo Ann Vaughn
Address/Telephone: 2402 Hatcher Mountain Road; (423) 453–9832 or (800) 633–1459, fax (423) 428–8634
Rooms: 5 in main house, plus 1 three-level suite; all with private bath, some with whirlpool. Separate chalet with whirlpool, 3 bedrooms, kitchen, living room, fire place, decks, hot tub.
Rates: In main house, \$90 to \$135, double; \$20 each additional person; full breakfast and afternoon refreshments. In chalet, \$180 for up to 4 people; \$20 each additional person. Two-night minimum stay in chalet.
Open: Year-round.
Facilities and activities: Upstairs television lounge in main house, swimming pool, hot tub. Nearby: restaurants; short drive to Pigeon Forge, Gatlinburg, and Great Smoky Mountains National Park; Glades Craft Community.
Recommended Country Inns® Travelers' Club Benefit: Stay two nights, get third night free, December–February.

The Midwest

by Bob Puhala

One only needs to think back to the heartrending love story embodied by the best-selling book and box-office hit film, *The Bridges of Madison County* (set in Iowa), to realize that the Midwest holds tremendous romantic potential.

From restored farmhouses given new life as a couples' getaway to renowned Victorian hotels elegantly restored to resemble their 1800s grandeur, Midwest wanderers can discover hideaway retreats boasting roaring fireplaces, huge whirlpool baths, and candlelight dining—all designed to offer opportunities for otherwise life-hurried humans to relax and hone their lovey-dovey skills.

Two of the most romantic retreats my wife, Debbie, and I have ever visited are located in the Midwest. Canoe bay, a twelve-room masterpiece in Chetek, Wisconsin, combines its 280 acres of private, natural wonderlands with some of the most luxurious and elegant inn rooms of the Midwest. At the other end of the size-scale is The American Club in Kohler, Wisconsin, boasting 236 rooms and a five-star rating—the only such rated resort hotel in the region. It more resembles a baronial estate than a hotel—with all the finery and lavishness you'd expect at a titled English retreat.

But it's not just the surroundings that make an inn score high on the romance scale. There's ambience and pampering, too. Some inns offer breakfast baskets delivered right to your door. Others boast candlelight breakfast meals in a formal and highly romantic atmosphere—and that includes a crackling fireplace nearby.

You can't even imagine the variety of the rooms! There are see-through fireplaces looking onto king-sized beds. Huge Jacuzzis located in the middle of rooms beneath skylights. Even an "environmental enclosure" where inside you can relax and push buttons to choose what kind of "weather" it's going to be—from soft rain showers amid warm breezes to hot sunlight.

Yes, there are many opportunities for couple to enjoy a romantic rendezvous in the Midwest. And here are some of the best places I know.

The rest is up to you!

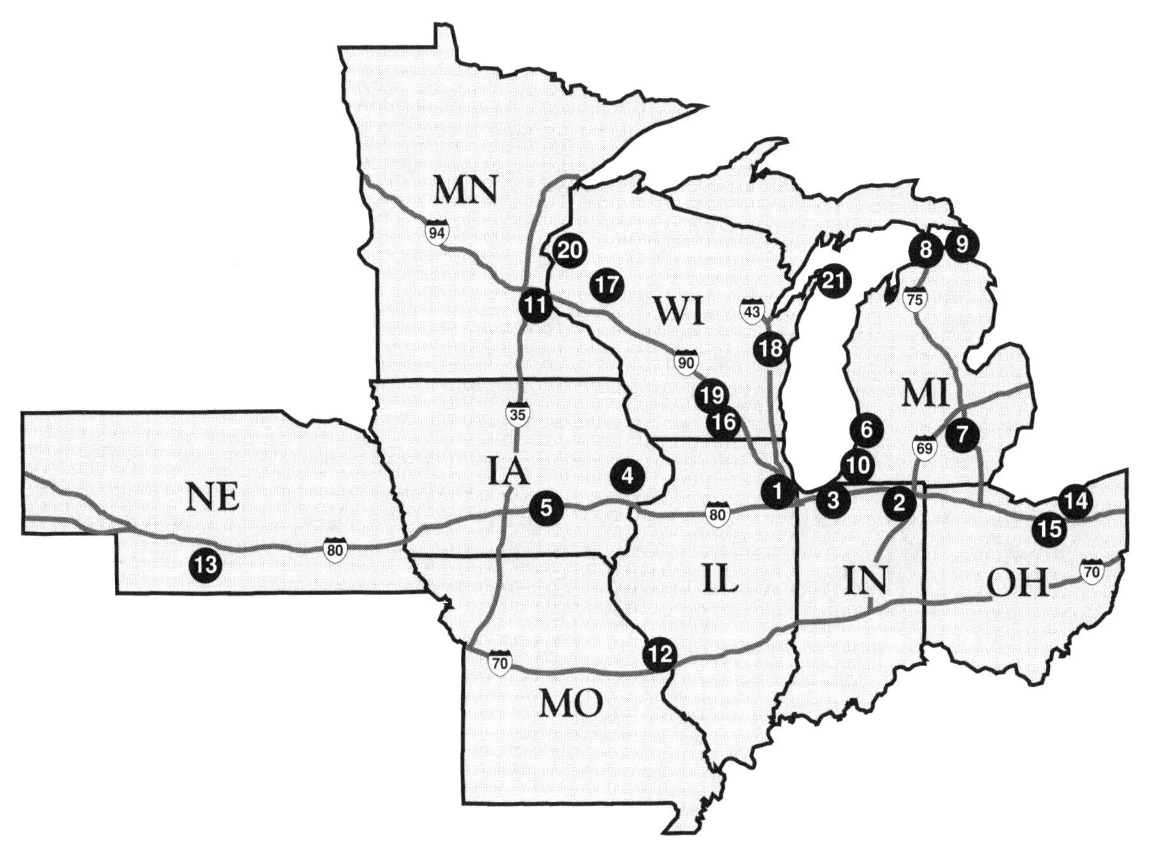
MN
94
20
17
11
WI
43
21
8
9
75
18
90
MI
19
35
16
6
7
69
IA
4
10
NE
1
3
2
14
5
80
15
13
80
IL
IN
OH
70
12
70
MO

The Midwest

The Midwest

Numbers on map refer to towns numbered below.

Illinois

1. Wheaton, The Wheaton Inn 148

Indiana

2. Goshen, The Checkerberry Inn 150
3. Michigan City, The Creekwood Inn 152

Iowa

4. Maquoketa, Squiers Manor 154
5. Newton, La Corsette Maison Inn 156

Michigan

6. Douglas, The Rosemont Inn 158
7. Fenton, Pine Ridge Inn 160
8. Harbor Springs, Kimberly Country Estate . . . 162
9. Mackinac Island, Grand Hotel 164
10. Union Pier, Pine Garth Inn 166

Minnesota

11. Hastings,
    Rosewood Inn 168
    Thorwood Inn 170

Missouri

12. St. Charles, St. Charles House 172

Nebraska

13. Cambridge, The Cambridge Inn 174

Ohio

14. Chagrin Falls, The Inn at Chagrin Falls 176
15. Sagamore Hills, The Inn at
    Brandywine Falls 178

Wisconsin

16. Belleville, Rose Bed and Breakfast 180
17. Chetek, Canoe Bay 182
18. Kohler, The American Club 184
19. Lodi, Victorian Treasure
    Bed and Breakfast 186
20. Osceola, St. Croix River Inn 188
21. Sturgeon Bay, White Lace Inn 190

The Wheaton Inn

WHEATON, ILLINOIS 60187

With a little imagination, romantic nights can be yours at the Wheaton Inn, which weaves so well today's sophistication with yesterday's elegance. Completed in 1987, it relies on opulence in the Colonial Williamsburg tradition for its distinctive flair.

Attractive rooms are named after famous Wheaton citizens. Cuddlers note that eleven have gas fireplaces, many boast Jacuzzi tubs, and each has an elegantly distinctive personality. All have European towel warmers in their bathrooms—another thoughtful touch, especially for coosome twosomes who venture out in Chicago winters.

Rooms have oversized styles often found in European concierge hotels. The Woodward Room is one of my favorites, with its Jacuzzi situated in front of a large bay window that overlooks the inn's gardens. (Go ahead and use your imagination.) The fireplace marble came from the face of Marshall Field's department store in downtown Chicago. (By the way, the room's namesake, Judge Alfred Woodward, is the father of newspaperman Bob Woodward, who broke the Watergate scandal for the *Washington Post* along with Carl Bernstein.)

Vaulted ceilings in the third-floor McCormick Room, along with its huge four-poster bed and windows overlooking the garden, make this a "romance" favorite. Another charmer is the Morton Room, with its alcoved ceiling, cozy fireplace, and 4½-foot-deep Jacuzzi, perfect for couples who yearn for a relaxing soak.

Especially romantic nights can be yours in the Rice Room, where a Jacuzzi sits almost in the middle of the room, in front of a fireplace, and two skylights let you gaze at the stars above.

Only the Ottoson Room, named after the inn architect, departs from the Williamsburg theme. A brass-topped, black iron-rail bed is dwarfed by cathedral ceilings that harbor a skylight.

In a cheery, window-lit breakfast room, couples enjoy the innkeeper's European-style buffet of imported coffee and teas, hot egg dishes, seasonal fruits, and delicious pastries and muffins. Personal service is a trademark here, so expect amenities like afternoon cheese and crackers, freshly baked cookies and milk, twenty-four-hour coffee, and bedtime turndown service with chocolate treats left on your pillow.

Other "personal" service is up to you!

How to get there: From Chicago, take I–294 to Roosevelt Road, then go west to the inn.

Innkeeper: Dennis Stevens
Address/Telephone: 301 West Roosevelt Road; (708) 690–2600
Rooms: 16; all with private bath and air conditioning, some with Jacuzzi. Wheelchair access.
Rates: $99 to $195, single or double, EPB. Weekend packages.
Open: All year.
Facilities and activities: Patio, lawn area with croquet course and gardens, sitting room, dining area. Nearby: McCormick's Cantigny war museum, Prairie Path hike and bike trail; Herrick Lake paddle boating and fishing; Wheaton Water Park; Fox River and Geneva famous shopping districts; horseback riding; Morton Arboretum; Wheaton College's Billy Graham Center; golf courses; tennis courts; polo grounds. Also a short drive to Drury Lane Theatres.
Business travel: Located about 30 miles west of Chicago. Corporate rates, conference rooms, fax.

The Checkerberry Inn

GOSHEN, INDIANA 46526

"We wanted to create a European feel to the inn," Susan said. "After all, being surrounded on all sides by Amish farmlands is more than enough country ambience."

The fine appointments of this northern Indiana inn do remind me of intimate, romantic European hotels I've stayed at. In fact, the handsome photographs adorning inn walls were taken by John during his travels in the French Bordeaux region.

Amish straw hats hang over beds, lending a cozy regional touch to luxurious guest rooms that boast fine-arts prints, furniture with definite European flair, wide windows that allow views of the rolling countryside, and amenities like Swiss goat's milk soap in the baths. Rooms are named for flowers; my favorite is Foxglove, with its sitting-room fireplace, whirlpool bath, and six windows—an almost perfect lovers' retreat.

Queen Anne's Lace is another handsome room; its most interesting feature is a primitive secretary, made in the 1850s. It consists of 1,200 individual pieces, and it took three years to complete. Its geometric designs put that craftsman far ahead of his time.

The inn's restaurant leans toward country-French cuisine. Four-course meals begin with a fresh garden salad, followed by a fresh fruit sorbet, entree, and dessert. An inn specialty is double duck breast sautéed and served over sweet onions, topped with an orange and port wine sauce, accompanied by *pommes Anna* and a bouquet of fresh vegetables. The vegetables, herbs, and spices are grown specially for the inn. Other favorites include chicken basil, veal medallions, and rack of lamb served off the bone with herb cream-and-garlic cheese.

Checkerberry sits on one hundred acres, so there's plenty of quiet and relaxation. It's just a walk through French doors to the swimming pool, and the woods contain numerous hiking trails. And the inn provides Indiana's only professional croquet course. So now is the time to perfect your game.

Unless you're too busy enjoying each other.

How to get there: From Chicago, take the Indiana Toll Road (I–80/90) to the Middlebury exit (#107). Go south on Indiana 13, turn west on Indiana 4, then go south on County Road 37 to the inn. It's 14 miles from the toll-road exit to the inn.

Innkeepers: John and Susan Graff, owners; Sheila Reed, manager
Address/Telephone: 62644 County Road 37; (219) 642–4445
Rooms: 13, including 3 suites; all with private bath and air conditioning. Wheelchair access.
Rates: Sunday through Thursday, \$80 to \$275; Friday and Saturday, \$100 to \$325; single or double, continental breakfast.
Open: May through December; limited time February through April; closed January.
Facilities and activities: Full-service dining room, swimming pool, arbor, croquet course, tennis court, hiking trails, cross-country ski area. In the midst of Amish farmlands; offers horse-drawn buggy tours of Amish surroundings, sleigh rides in winter. Near Shipshewana auctions, Middlebury festivals.
Recommended Country Inns® Travelers' Club Benefit: 10 percent discount, subject to availability.

Creekwood Inn

MICHIGAN CITY, INDIANA 46360

The Creekwood Inn is nestled amid thirty-three acres of walnut, oak, and pine trees near a fork in tiny Walnut Creek. The winding wooded roadway leading to the inn is breathtaking, especially in the fall, when nature paints the trees in glorious colors.

Done in English Cottage design, the inn is romantic, cozy, and classically gracious. Massive hand-hewn wooden ceiling beams on the main floor were taken from an old area toll bridge by the original owner, who built the home in the 1930s. The parlor has a large fireplace, surrounded by comfortable sofas and chairs—a perfect setting for afternoon tea or intimate midnight conversation. Wood planking makes up the floors. And you can gaze out a bay window that overlooks the estate's lovely grounds.

Mary Lou said she wanted to combine the ambience of a country inn with the romantic pampering that people have come to expect. She has done better than that; she has established a first-class retreat. Twelve large guest rooms and a suite are tastefully decorated in a mixture of styles; incurable romantics should note that some have fireplaces and terraces. All have huge beds, overstuffed chairs, and mini-refrigerators.

Couples should visit the Conservatory, overlooking the inn's pond and gardens, which offers both a comfy spot to enjoy nature and a chance to luxuriate in the whirlpool or hit the exercise room.

Mary Lou visited Oxford, England, and was inspired to plant an English perennial garden on the east side of the inn. Things just keep getting better.

One winter my wife and I stayed here during an especially snowy stretch. We simply walked out the front door, slipped on our touring skis, and beat a path to the inn's private cross-country trails, which wind through deep woods and past Lake Spencer, the inn's private lake. Average skiers, we completed the loops in about twenty minutes, returning with a hearty breakfast appetite. Mary Lou served us a tasty continental breakfast of freshly baked breads, pastries, fruit, and coffee. It was one of the most romantic winter mornings we ever spent together.

Late-afternoon tea in the parlor offers cookies and some delicious pastries. You may even have a cup of hot chocolate at bedtime on a blustery winter night, stretching before the fire with your partner and toasting your toes.

Mary Lou now serves dinner every night at the inn's American Grille. Be prepared for savory delights from chef Kathy deFuniak, who came from Ambria's in Chicago's Lincoln Park. These might include New Zealand lamb loin with basil whipped potatoes and summer tomato salad; crispy soft-shell crab with citrus vinaigrette; Portobello mushroom lasagna; herb-roasted chicken with sweet corn and garlic polenta; and much more.

Desserts might include anything from simple fresh-fruit tarts to "gooey chocolate" treats—her husband's favorite.

How to get there: Heading northeast to Michigan City on I–94, take exit 40B. Then take an immediate left turn onto 600W, and turn into the first drive on the left. The inn is at Route 20/35, just off the interstate.

Innkeeper: Mary Lou Linnen
Address/Telephone: Route 20/35 at Interstate 94; (219) 872–8357
Rooms: 13, including 1 suite; all with private bath and air conditioning. Wheelchair access.
Rates: $112 to $156, double; $104 to $149, single; $166, suite; continental breakfast.
Open: All year except 2 weeks in mid-March and Christmas Day.
Facilities and activities: A short drive to southeastern shore of Lake Michigan, Indiana Dunes State Park, Warren Dunes State Park in Michigan. Charter fishing, swimming, boating. Antiquing in nearby lakeside communities. Area winery tours. Old Lighthouse Museum. "Fruit Belt" for fruit and vegetable farms.

Squiers Manor

MAQUOKETA, IOWA 52060

Nothing prepares you for the romantic splendor of this 1882 house, listed on the National Register of Historic Places.

The handsome Queen Anne home boasts fine wood everywhere. There's a walnut parlor, a cherry dining room, and butternut throughout the rest of the house.

Fine antiques are everywhere, too; some, such as the 1820s Federal four-poster mahogany bed in the Harriet Squiers Room, are of museum quality.

That's not surprising, since Cathy and Virg also own a nationally renowned antiques store just a few miles out of town.

Romantics should try the Jeannie Mitchel Bridal Suite. Its canopied brass bed stands more than 7 feet tall. (Note the mother-of-pearl on the footboard.) And the Victorian Renaissance dresser with marble top is another treasure.

Did I mention that the suite has a double whirlpool bath?

So does the J. E. Squiers Room; there a green marble floor creates a path leading to a cozy corner whirlpool for two. What better way to spend an evening on a romantic getaway.

And Opal's Parlor (named after a longtime resident of the manor when it rented its rooms as apartments) features not only 1860s antiques and hand-crocheted bedspreads but also a Swiss shower that acts "like a human car wash," said

Cathy. (Create your own romantic fantasies here.)

Every common room bespeaks luxury and splendor. The parlor's fireplace, with tiles depicting characters in Roman mythology, is unusual. Look at the fabulous hand-carved cherry buffet in the dining room. The dining room's 10-foot-tall, hand-carved jewelers' clock is another conversation starter.

And the library, an enclave done entirely in butternut paneling and graced with its original fireplace, is flat-out gorgeous.

Not only do you get great atmosphere; Cathy's breakfasts are terrific, too. Consider pumpkin pecan muffins, black-walnut bread, eggs Katrina, pecan-stuffed French toast, seafood quiches, apple pudding, and more.

But the newest wrinkle is "candlelight evening desserts." Imagine nibbling on Cathy's chocolate bourbon pecan pie, delicious tortes, or Grandma Annie's bread pudding, a guest favorite. Other kinds of nibbling is optional.

And there are two fantastic new suites reclaimed from the house's grand ballroom. The Loft boasts a gas-log fireplace for instant romance, a 6-by-4-foot whirlpool tub, wicker sitting room—with breakfast delivered to your bedchamber.

The Ballroom (that's the other suite's name) is an incredible 1,100 square feet of luxury, with a whirlpool tub nestled in a "garden" setting, king-sized bed, cathedral ceiling, massive sitting room, reading nook, and lots more surprises.

Maybe this is your own "Garden of Eden."

How to get there: From Dubuque, take U.S. 61 south to U.S. 64, then turn east into town. One block past the second stoplight, turn right, then go 1 block to the inn.

Innkeepers: Cathy and Virl Banowetz
Address/Telephone: 418 West Pleasant Street; (319) 652–6961
Rooms: 8, including 3 suites; all with private bath and air conditioning.
Rates: $75 to $100, single or double; $150 to $185, suites; EPB.
Open: All year.
Facilities and activities: Library, parlor, porch. A short drive to Mississippi River towns; Dubuque, site of low-stakes riverboat casino gambling; and Galena, Illinois, a Civil War–era architectural wonderland.
Recommended Country Inns® Travelers' Club Benefit: Stay two nights, get third night free, Sunday–Thursday, excluding holiday weeks.

La Corsette Maison Inn

NEWTON, IOWA 50208

My wife, Debbie, and I sat in front of a roaring fire in an elegant parlor, enjoying a romantic gourmet-style breakfast.

First Kay brought us a delightful fresh fruit compote of pink grapefruit, mandarin orange slices, grapes, and kiwi. Her home-baked apple muffins with strudel were next. (We could have eaten four apiece, they were so delicious.)

We sipped on raspberry and orange juice, which washed down authentic English scones, another of Kay's specialties. Then came a wonderful frittata with two cheeses—and some special La Corsette French bread.

It was one of the ultimate bed-and-breakfast experiences for lovers.

It's also no wonder that Kay's inn has received a 4½-star rating from the *Des Moines Register* and has been hailed as a "gleaming jewel in the crown of fine restaurants."

The mansion itself is a 1909 Mission-style masterpiece built by an early Iowa state senator. Not much has changed in the intervening years. Gleaming mission oak woodwork, Art Nouveau stained-glass windows, and other turn-of-the-century architectural flourishes make La Corsette a special place.

We overnighted in the Windsor Hunt Suite; the massive bedchamber has a huge four-poster bed (you use a stepstool to reach the high mattress), and the sitting room boasts its own fireplace—which we used for a romantic end to the day—as well as a two-person whirlpool bath.

Other rooms are imbued with their own particular charms. The Penthouse bedchambers, for instance, are located in the tower and surrounded by beveled-glass windows. Use your imagination here.

Kay's romantic five-course gourmet-style dinners, prepared by both herself and a new chef (a graduate of the Culinary Institute of America, by the way), are renowned. The first person to make reservations for the evening sets the night's menu. Choices include the likes of French veal in cream, broccoli-stuffed game hen with Mornay sauce, and roast loin of pork with prune chutney.

Maybe you'd rather have a romantic basket dinner delivered to your door during weekday visits. This three-course treat might included stuffed pork chops, fancy veggies, home-baked breads, and more.

Or choose to stay at the 100-year-old Sister Inn next door. Here Kay features double whirlpools and antique soaking tubs. Imagine the fun . . .

How to get there: From the Quad Cities, take I–80 to Newton (exit 164), and go north until the second light (Highway 6); then turn right and continue 7 blocks to the inn.

Innkeeper: Kay Owen
Address/Telephone: 629 1st Avenue; (515) 792–6833
Rooms: 5, including 2 suites; all with private bath and air conditioning. No smoking inn.
Rates: $65 to $80, single or double; $75 to $170, suites; Sister Inn, 2 bedchambers, $145 and $170; EPB. Multinight minimum during Pella, Iowa, Tulip Festival and some other special events. Pets allowed by prearrangement.
Open: All year.
Facilities and activities: Gourmet 5-course dinners. Two sitting rooms with fireplace; porch. Nearby: Maytag Company tours, tennis courts, golf courses, horseback riding, cross-country skiing. A short drive to Trainland, U.S.A.; Prairie Meadows Horse Track; Krumm Nature Preserve.

The Rosemont Inn

DOUGLAS, MICHIGAN 49406

The last time I spoke to Joe and Marilyn, they'd just completed their newest addition to the inn—a Victorian gazebo on the front lawn facing Lake Michigan. "We've already had our first gazebo wedding, too," noted Marilyn.

It's certainly the perfect spot for any kind of romantic celebration or weekend getaway. Winds rustle tall trees, which shade the inn's landscaped grounds from a bright sun. Waves crash on the lakeshore, just across the tiny road and down a steep bluff. And an expansive wraparound porch invites peace and relaxation.

In fact, the Rosemont Inn stands like an inviting friend, a turn-of-the-century Queen Anne Victorian that got its start as an 1886 tourist hotel. Enter through French doors opening onto a formal sitting room; the handsome antique hardwood fireplace signals the elegance you will find throughout the inn.

Joe and Marilyn continue to add even more pampering touches to this already wonderful place. Relax on the enclosed front porch, overlooking the lake. I love the Garden Room, perhaps my favorite inn spot out back; it's bright and sunny, with cathedral ceilings and a ceiling-to-floor glass wall that looks out over the gardens and swimming pool. There are also a sauna and whirlpool in the back, overlooking the pool.

Check out the fireplace here, great for warming up guests on cool spring and autumn nights, to say nothing of Michigan winters. Of course, the inn is perfect headquarters for cross-country ski adventurers.

And the deck, with its colorful umbrella tables, is another addition that's become a favorite guest gathering place.

The Garden Room serves as the location of the innkeepers' buffet-style continental breakfasts. Count on juices, croissants, muffins, delicious quiches, bagels, cereals, and more. Marilyn and Joseph can also suggest some fine dinner spots in nearby Saugatuck.

Country Victorian antiques and reproductions fill the delightful guest rooms, each unique in design; nine have gas fireplaces, which add a cozy touch. I especially liked our room, with its brass bed adorned with a charming crazy quilt, a pinch of colorful pizzazz. Some rooms have a view of the lake through the tall maples that ring the grounds.

Two of three common areas also feature wet bars.

One summer Debbie, Kate, and I, along with some relatives, spent a glorious long weekend at the inn. Especially inviting was the swimming pool, where the kids splashed and played endlessly. It made for good memories. Especially when we were blessed with Dayne about nine months after our stay here!

How to get there: From Chicago, take I–94 north to I–196 north. At exit 36, near Douglas, take Ferry Street north to Center Street. Turn west on Center Street and go to Lakeshore Drive; then turn north to the inn.

Innkeepers: Joseph and Marilyn Sajdak

Address/Telephone: 83 Lakeshore Drive (mailing address: P. O. Box 214, Saugatuck, 49453); (616) 857–2637 or (800) 721–2637

Rooms: 14; all with private bath and air conditioning, 10 with gas fireplace. Wheelchair access. No smoking inn.

*Rates:*May through mid-June and mid-September through October, $70 to $115, single; $80 to $145, double; mid-June through mid-September, $125 to $175, single or double; November through April, $60 to $95, single; $70 to $125, double. Continental breakfast. Off-season rates available.

Open: All year.

Facilities and activities: Garden room, swimming pool, screened porch, Victorian gazebo. Across the road from Lake Michigan. Nearby: charter fishing, boating, scenic supper cruises; golf, hiking the Lake Michigan dunes, dune rides; summer theater; cross-country skiing in winter. Fine restaurants, art galleries, antiques shops, boutiques.

Pine Ridge Inn

FENTON, MICHIGAN 48430

If ever there was a setting for privacy and romance, this is it.

Secluded in a very remote forty acres amid swaying pine trees and rolling hills, the Pine Ridge Inn is an exclusive hideaway. No phones. No pets. Just you and your honey for a luxurious and romantic interlude.

Guest rooms are elegant and huge, with lovey-dovey relaxation kept in mind. Those king-sized beds are actually firm waterbeds. Whirlpools are massive, measuring 7 by 7 feet. And a romantic fire in the hearth is only a fingertip away, thanks to gas-log fireplaces that light up the room with a very romantic glow.

They say you "never have to leave your room" at the Pine Ridge. Sure enough. A gourment snack tray is delivered to your bedchamber each evening. And a delicious continental breakfast tray will be found at your door come morning.

For those who do venture outside, walk along a cozy forest path marked with red hearts. Or gaze longingly at the inn's pond. Winter visitors might cross-country ski on a blanket of newly fallen snow.

But when your guest room has all of the above, plus stereo and remote-control television, why bother ever leaving until it's time to leave?

How to get there: From east or west, take I–96 to U.S. 23. Turn north and continue to White Lake Road exit; turn left, then turn left immediately onto Old U.S. 23, and continue to inn.

Innkeeper: Jim and Val Soldan
Address/Telephone: N-10345 Old U.S. 23; (810) 629–8911 or (800) 353–8911
Rooms: 4; all with private bath, whirlpool tub, and fireplace.
Rates: $145, single or double, Monday through Thursday; $195, single or double, Friday through Sunday and holidays; continental breakfast.
Open: All year.
Facilities and activities: Walking paths through forest and by pond. Less than an hour's drive to Pontiac Silverdome, Henry Ford Museum and Greenfield Village, and metro Detroit.

Kimberly Country Estate

HARBOR SPRINGS, MICHIGAN 49740

Ronn and Billie's inn could be a romantic showcase for *House Beautiful*.

That's not surprising, I guess; Ronn, an interior designer, has transformed this Southern plantation–style home into an elegant retreat that offers some of the most extraordinarily luxurious inn surroundings possible.

We got the red-carpet treatment (literally) as we mounted steps to the house, set atop a gentle hill and surrounded by fields and farms.

Inside, Chippendale and Queen Anne–style furniture, Battenburg linens, Laura Ashley fabrics, and exquisite antiques collected by the innkeepers over forty years add to the elegance.

The Lexington Suite is the epitome of romanticism, with its four-poster bed and Battenburg linens lending touches of sophistication; this room also has its own sitting area, wood-burning fireplace, and Jacuzzi.

Le Soleil is another of our favorites, with its walls of windows, sunny yellow color, and hand stenciling. And four of the rooms open onto a shaded veranda overlooking the inn's 22-by-40-foot swimming pool.

The library is a most stunning common room. It's entirely paneled with North Carolina black walnut—milled on the spot as the house was built, Billie told me.

Pampering is legion here. Guests find a decanter of sherry in their rooms upon arrival, with an invitation to join Ronn and Billie for afternoon tea and hors d'oeuvres—sometimes at poolside in good weather. At night they return to their rooms to discover beds turned down and chocolate truffles on the pillows.

Weekend breakfasts are another Southern-tinged plantation treat. Billie might serve fresh fruit compote, scrambled eggs, smoked turkey sausage, home-baked muffins, and more.

If you want to experience the "estate of the art" in romantic country inn living, make your reservations now.

How to get there: From Petoskey, take U.S. 31 north to Michigan 119, continue north toward Harbor Springs; turn right at Emmet Heights Road, then left on Bester Road, and continue to the inn.

Innkeepers: Ronn and Billie Serba
Address/Telephone: 2287 Bester Road; (616) 526–7646 or 526–9502
Rooms: 6, including 3 suites; all with private bath. Wheelchair access.
Rates: $135 to $250, single or double, EPB and afternoon tea. Two-night minimum on weekends. Special packages. No smoking inn.
Open: All year.
Facilities and activities: Living room, library, lower-level entertainment room, terrace, swimming pool. Nearby: golf, biking, hiking; sailing and other water activities on Little Traverse Bay. A short drive to chic shops in Harbor Springs, downhill skiing at Boyne Highlands and Nubs Nob.

Grand Hotel

MACKINAC ISLAND, MICHIGAN 49757

The Grand Hotel, built in 1887, has been called one of the great hotels of the railroad and Great Lakes steamer era. Its location high on an island bluff provides magnificent vistas over the Straits of Mackinac waters. And it also was the location for one of the most romantic period movies ever made—*Somewhere in Time*—which still draws fans to the historic hostelry.

Its incredible, many-columned veranda is 660 feet long (it claims to be the longest in the world) and is decorated with huge American flags snapping in the wind, bright yellow awnings that catch the color of the sun, and colorful red geraniums hanging everywhere. Many guests simply sit in generous rockers, sip on a drink, relax, and enjoy cooling lake breezes. We also like to admire the hotel's acres of woodland and lawns, finely manicured with exquisite flower gardens and greenery arrangements.

At the Grand Hotel, guests feel immersed in a long-ago era of luxury and romance. Even the attire of hotel attendants harkens back to a long-ago era; they're dressed in long red coats and black bow ties. Once Debbie and I rode the hotel's elegant horse-drawn carriage (the driver wore a black top hat and formal "pink" hunting jacket) from the ferry docks, up the long hill, to the grand portico. That was one of the most romantic journeys we've ever taken.

Inside, the hotel boasts Victorian-era colors

and decor—greens, yellows, and whites, with balloon draperies on the windows, high-back chairs and sofas everywhere in numerous public rooms, and a healthy dash of yesteryear memorabilia hanging on hallway walls. (One 1889 breakfast menu especially caught my eye, listing an extraordinary selection of foods, including lamb chops, lake fish, stewed potatoes in cream, and sweetbreads.)

Special services are legion and include complimentary morning coffee, concerts during afternoon tea, romantic horse-drawn-carriage island tours, hold-me-close dinner dances, and much more. It seems as if the pampering never stops.

Many of the guest rooms have spectacular lake views that induce lots of lovey-dovey musings. Rates include breakfast and candlelight dinners, with Lake Superior whitefish an evening specialty. A dessert treat—the Grand pecan ball with hot fudge sauce—is a sweet confection best shared with your special honey. The rest of the evening's romantic bliss is up to you.

How to get there: From either Mackinaw City from the Lower Peninsula or from St. Ignace on the Upper Peninsula, a thirty-minute ferry ride brings you to Mackinac Island. Dock porters will greet your boat. There's an island airstrip for chartered flights and private planes.

Innkeeper: R. D. Musser III, corporation president
Address/Telephone: Mackinac Island; (906) 847–3331 or (800) 334–7263 (reservations)
Rooms: 324; all with private bath.
Rates: $145 to $275, per person, May through mid-June; $170 to $275 mid-June through late October. Children in same room with 2 persons, $35 to $99 per child; MAP. Special packages available.
Open: Mid-May to late October.
Facilities and activities: Main dining room, Geranium Bar, Grand Stand (food and drink), Audubon Bar, Carleton's Tea Store, pool grill. Magnificent swimming pool, private golf course, bike rentals, saddle horses, tennis courts, exercise trail. Carriage tours, dancing, movies. Expansive grounds, spectacular veranda with wonderful lake vistas. Nearby: museums, historic Fort Mackinac, Mackinac Island State Park, and other sites, guided tours; specialty shops. There are no motor vehicles allowed on historic Mackinac Island; visitors walk or rent horses, horse-drawn carriages and taxis, and bicycles.

Pine Garth Inn

UNION PIER, MICHIGAN 49129

When we first came to this stretch of shifting sands in southwestern Michigan almost 20 years ago, all we found was an empty Lake Michigan shoreline, sleepy towns, and small cottages.

How times have changed.

Now there's a huge marina crammed with massive cabin cruisers, luxury townhouses stacked one atop the other, and a small-town "Main Street" that's increasingly filled with tony shops to lure big-city spendthrifts.

And those small cottages—they're more likely to have four-bedroom summer mansions as next door neighbors than somebody's clapboard cabin.

Yet, Harbor Country, a 50-mile swath of white-sand beaches stretching from Michigan City, Indiana, to Harbert, Michigan (and beyond), somehow manages to retain its small-town charm and be a big attraction (especially for stressed-out Chicago folks) at the same time.

In fact, Harbor Country is now the cool weekend place to be, with a wave of lodgings, stores, and restaurants hitting the beaches and environs.

One of the best ways to enjoy the region is by staying at the romantic Pine Garth Inn—the only bed and breakfast in Harbor Country nestled on the lakeshore. Located on a high bluff, six of the seven rooms in the 1905 inn offer breathtaking vistas of Lake Michigan and the hostelry's private white-sand beach below.

Rachel's Room boasts flamingos perching on the headboard and an entire wall of windows overlooking Lake Michigan—and opening out to a private terrace.

Or go upstairs to Melissa's Room, done in Laura Ashley blues and yellows. Another favorite of guests because "it's so romantic," it features a canopied bed and deck overlooking the lake. Even the bathroom boasts a lake view.

Of course, all lovers understand the lure of the private beach, reached by walking down a terrace of stairs clinging to the bluff. We looked for shells and ran around in the sand. Spending time together—life can't get much better than that.

How to get there: Take the I–94 to Michigan exit 6, which is the Union Pier exit. Turn right (on Towline Road) and proceed west toward the lake and go to the flashing red light, which is Red Arrow Highway. *Do not turn.* Continue on Townline Road to the next stop sign, which is Lakeshore Road. Turn right and proceed about 1/4 mile to the inn (it'll be on your left).

Innkeepers: Russ and Paula Bulin
Address/Telephone: 15790 Lakeshore Road (mailing address: P.O. Box 347); (616) 469–1642
Rooms: 7; all with private bath. No smoking inn.
Rates: $110 to $145, single or double, EPB.
Open: All year.
Facilities and activities: Gathering room, screened porch, five decks overlooking Lake Michigan, 200 feet of private sugar-sand beach with beach chairs. Short drive to New Buffalo arts and antiques stores, skiing, water sports, restaurants.
Recommended Country Inns® Travelers' Club Benefit: Stay two nights, get third night free, Sunday–Thursday, November–April, excluding holidays, subject to availability.

Rosewood Inn

HASTINGS, MINNESOTA 55033

This handsome Queen Anne, built in 1878, now houses one of the most romantic getaways imaginable. That's not really surprising, since Pam and Dick's other Hastings hideaway (the Thorwood Inn) reflects similar pampering-inspired luxuries.

As soon as you see Rebecca's Room, you'll get the idea. This is a stirring romantic retreat, with a marvelous all-marble bathroom highlighted by a double whirlpool bath resting in front of its own fireplace. There's a second fireplace opposite an inviting four-poster antique bed. And a four-season porch offers views of the inn's rose garden.

Or consider the Vermillion Room, with a see-through fireplace that warms both an ornate brass bed and a sunken double whirlpool bath.

If you want shameful opulence, try the Mississippi Room. As large as an apartment, it offers skylights over a sleigh bed, its own fireplace, baby grand piano, bathroom with both a copper tub and double whirlpool—and a meditation room where "people can either relax or be creative," said the innkeeper. "We've even had several guests do paintings here." A collection of some of those works are hanging about the room.

The breakfasts are added treats. And the mealtime flexibility is unusual: They'll serve whenever guests are hungry, between 6:00 and 11:00 A.M. Eat in one of the dining areas, on the porch, in your room, or in bed—the choice is yours.

The feast might include homemade breads and blueberry muffins, cheese strata, wild-rice gratiné, cherry strudel, raspberry coffee cake. . . . Aren't you hungry just thinking about all this food?

Another chance to feast: The inn offers gourmet dinners in the formal parlor—or in your own room. The meal might feature delights such as beef Wellington and a raspberry strudel with chocolate and vanilla sauce. The cost is $44.70 to $56.70 per couple.

The innkeepers are also happy to arrange an in-room "hat box" supper, or to package a delightful evening with dinner at one of the town's fine restaurants, including limousine service. And they occasionally arrange dinner at the inn featuring Minnesota-accented recipes accompanied by live chamber music.

How to get there: From the Twin Cities, take U.S. 61 south into Hastings and exit at Seventh Street; then turn left and proceed 1½ blocks to the inn.

Innkeepers: Pam and Dick Thorsen
Address/Telephone: Seventh and Ramsey; (612) 437–3297
Rooms: 8, with 4 suites; all with private bath and air conditioning; TV and phone upon request. No smoking inn.
Rates: $87 to $217, single or double, EPB. Two-night minimum on weekends. Special packages available.
Open: All year.
Facilities and activities: Dinner by reservation. Sitting room, parlor, library, porch. Nearby: historic river-town architecture, arts and crafts, stores, antiques shops, specialty boutiques, Mississippi River water activities, bluff touring on bikes and hikes, St. Croix Valley Nature Center, Alexis Bailly vineyard winery, downhill and cross-country skiing, snowshoeing, golf.

Thorwood Inn

HASTINGS, MINNESOTA 55033

Perhaps Thorwood's ultimate romantic retreat is the Steeple Room, with its see-through fireplace and double whirlpool—set in the house's steeple. The steeple rises 23 feet above the tub and boasts a ball chandelier hanging from the pinnacle. Ooh, la la!

Others swear by Sarah's Room, with its bedroom-sized loft, window views of the Mississippi River Valley, and skylight over a queen-sized brass bed. Or Maureen's Room, with its unusual rag-rug headboard, fireplace, country-quilted bed, and double whirlpool bath.

However, my favorite lovers' lair is Captain Anthony's, named for the original owner's son-in-law, who operated a line of steamboats on the Mississippi. It has a canopied four-poster brass bed and Victorian rose-teal-and-blue Laura Ashley fabrics. Though the Lullaby Room (the house's historic nursery) with its double whirlpool bath is a close runner-up.

The house itself, fashioned in ornate Second Empire style and completed in 1880, is a testament to the innkeepers' restoration prowess and romantic notions. When I saw the marble fireplaces, ornate rosettes and plaster moldings on the ceilings, and elegant antiques and surroundings, it was difficult to imagine that the house had once been cut up into several apartments. For more fine detail, just look to the music room. Pam said that maple instead of oak was used for flooring because it provided better resonance for live piano concerts, popular with society crowds at the turn of the century.

There's lots of special pampering, too. A complimentary bottle of wine from the local Alexis Bailly vineyards and snacks of fruits and pastries await guests. Then there are those breakfast baskets.

"People seem to enjoy the morning breakfast baskets more than anything else," Pam told me as we sat in the parlor of her gracious inn. "It has grown into quite a tradition." Once when she mentioned to a repeat couple that she'd been thinking of changing that practice, "They immediately spun around, with dismayed looks on their faces, and said, 'You wouldn't.' I knew right then we could never change."

Lucky for us. The breakfast basket, delivered to the door of your room, is stuffed with platters of fresh fruits, omelets or quiches, pull-apart pastries and rolls, home-baked breads, coffee, juice, and more. As Dick says, "Pace yourself."

How to get there: From LaCrosse, take U.S. 61 north to Hastings; then turn left on Fourth Street and proceed to inn.

Innkeepers: Pam and Dick Thorsen
Address/Telephone: Fourth and Pine; (612) 437–3297
Rooms: 7; all with private bath and air conditioning. Wheelchair access. No smoking inn.
Rates: $87 to $157, single or double, EPB. Can arrange for pet-sitters. Special package rates available.
Open: All year.
Facilities and activities: "Hat box" dinners in your room. Nearby: walking tour of historical area just blocks away. Quaint Mississippi River town with specialty and antiques shops, several good restaurants. Parks and nature trails; also river, streams, lakes, and all sorts of summer and winter sports.

St. Charles House

ST. CHARLES, MISSOURI 63301

Open the door to this re-created 1800s brick building within sight of the lazing Missouri River, and you step back into a setting of nineteenth-century luxury and romance.

The inn sits on Main Street of Missouri's first state capital, a street lined with more than one hundred historic brick buildings dating to the late nineteenth century (and today largely inhabited by arts and antiques shops).

It's a lovingly restored retreat from the bustle of visitors that can overwhelm the tiny hamlet. The replica house looks fit for a prosperous frontier businessman, sporting spacious rooms, fine antiques, and elegant surroundings.

"All of our antiques pre-date 1850," said Patti. Many were purchased in Denver, some right in town. Especially noteworthy is a massive Austrian buffet with intricate hand carving and a 9-foot-tall French walnut armoire.

The house's open floor plan includes a four-columned foyer and a bedchamber complete with oak hardwood floors, queen-sized canopy bed, and original Mary Gregory table lamp.

An elegant sitting area offers oriental-style rugs and a place to relax. There's even a mini-refrigerator in an antique side buffet along with a small wet bar.

Walk downstairs to reach the bath. Behind handsome double doors is a claw-footed tub under a crystal chandelier in a huge room decorated in pink and blues. Just outside is another Victorian-style sitting room. (Insert your own fantasies here.)

The innkeepers also own a guest cottage located a few doors down Main Street. This 1850s house is charming, outfitted in English country antiques that include a Welsh cupboard dating to 1813. Its two rooms offer pencil-post and four-poster cannonball beds, antique claw-footed tubs, and more fabulous antiques.

Hard to believe, but "it took only three days to buy all our pieces," Patti said. "We went on an antique-buying spree, and every place we stopped just happened to have exactly what we wanted."

But it's the St. Charles House's main residence that's best suited for "getting-to-know-you" adventures.

How to get there: From St. Louis or Kansas City, exit I–70 at First Capital Drive, and follow that north, then east to Main Street; turn right and continue to the inn.

Innkeepers: Patricia and Lionel York

Address/Telephone: 338 South Main Street; (314) 946–6221 or (800) 366–2427 via town Tourism Center

Rooms: 1 suite with sitting room, porch overlooking Missouri River, and private bath. One 2-bedroom guest cottage with 2 baths, dining room, small porch. No smoking inn.

Rates: $95 weekdays, $130 Friday and Saturday for suite; $75 weekdays, $90 weekends for each room in cottage; deluxe continental breakfast.

Open: All year.

Facilities and activities: Walk to quaint shops, restaurants, riverboat cruises, tours of the first state capital. A short drive to downtown St. Louis and the Arch, St. Louis Art Museum, restored Union Station, Opera House, Powell Symphony Hall, and Fox Theatre.

The Cambridge Inn

CAMBRIDGE, NEBRASKA 69022

"We always said it'd take a lot to get us out of Colorado," noted Elaine. "But once we stepped inside this house, we knew it had to be ours."

"It" is The Cambridge Inn, a historic 1907 Neoclassical Revival house that's been a landmark in Cambridge for as long as anyone can remember. Built by W. H. and Anna Faling (he helped incorporate the town), the magnificient house retains the elegant features of an era long past.

These include luxurious cherry, oak, and pine woodwork; stained and beveled glass; and hand-grained walls and ceilings created by Danish craftsmen.

Actually, it was Mike who first spotted the house, then for sale, on a return trip from visiting his son's college in Galesburg, Illinois. He drove around the block a few times, then told Elaine about it on his return home to Colorado. They made the five-hour drive from Loveland on a pleasant day in October, walked inside the house, . . . "And that was it," Elaine said.

The innkeepers have fashioned an elegant inn full of Victorian charm and romance. An entrance hall showcases a magnificent oak staircase leading to second-floor guest rooms; above the landing is an incredible stained-glass window original to the house. Memorable breakfasts in the dining room, itself a showplace, with its 10-

foot-tall built-in fruitwood and leaded-glass sideboard, might include French toast stuffed with cream cheese and walnuts, fruit plates, and more. And the parlor features twin oak columns at least 10 feet high.

Among the guest rooms, Ivy Court is my favorite. Originally the home's master bedroom, it retains a high Victorian ambience. Its antique furnishings include a writing desk. There's a sitting room and a bay window gussied up with lace curtains. Its private bath also claims the home's original "water closet"—a claw-footed tub, pedestal sink, and unusual foot bath.

Choose Morningside and you'll get a quilt-covered bed and antique oak armoire (see if you can find the signatures of those Danish workmen who crafted all the house's wood-grain appearances out of common oak). Or opt for the more simple Goldenrod, once the maid's room but now a bright, cozy retreat decorated with patterns of wildflowers.

And make sure to get out and explore the region during your stay here. The inn is located in the heart of the Republican River Valley of the Prairie Lakes region in Southwest Nebraska—a spot noted for boating as well as biking across its gently rolling hills.

How to get there: Take U.S. 6/34 into Cambridge (whose name changes to Nasby Street in town). Follow the road to the intersection of Nasby and Parker; the inn sits on the corner.

Innkeepers: Mike and Elaine Calabro
Address/Telephone: 606 Parker (mailing address: P. O. Box 239); (308) 697–3220
Rooms: 5; 3 with private bath. No smoking inn.
Rates: $35 to $65, single; $50 to $75, double; EPB.
Open: All year.
Facilities and activities: Lunch and dinner available by arrangement. Parlor, library, dining room, front porch. Nearby: golf, museums, antiques stores, Medicine Creek State Recreation Area, hunting, fishing, boating, biking.

The Inn at Chagrin Falls

CHAGRIN FALLS, OHIO 44022

Driving into Chagrin Falls, I thought I'd entered a cinema time warp and arrived at Bedford Falls, home to Jimmy Stewart in the movie *It's a Wonderful Life*. See if you don't get the same feeling when you first arrive.

The inn is an elegant retreat fashioned from the historic Crane's Canary Cottage. Built in 1927, it still sports canary-colored clapboards that give a light and airy touch to the surroundings.

Inside, guests first reach the Gathering Room. It boasts English-style antiques, including my favorite—a plump, King George wing chair. There's also a Victorian round-back sofa fronting the large hearth, whose fire always seems to be going.

Guest rooms are exquisitely fashioned with antique reproductions of fine furniture houses such as Colonial Williamsburg, Drexel, and Baker. Romantics should choose the Crane Suite, with its king-sized bed, Jacuzzi, and a (now gas-burning) fireplace, original to the home, that has a massive hearth; it must measure at least 6 feet long and 4 feet high.

The Philomethian Suite is another beauty, offering a four-poster mahogany bed, plantation-shuttered windows, corner fireplace, and whirlpool.

You can enjoy breakfast in a handsome pine-paneled dining room that features oak refectory tables and highbacked Windsor chairs.

Morning fare usually consists of cereals, seasonal fruits, English muffins with fresh jams, and the inn's specialty—sour cream coffee cake.

Do try dinner at Gamekeeper's Taverne, attached to the inn. Where else might you sample char-grilled blackwing ostrich fillet, black buck antelope, or sautéed elk tenderloin? Other delicious entrees include herb-crusted rib pork chop, cedar-planked salmon, and penne pasta with smoked venison sausage.

Of course, no visit to the inn would be complete without a hand-holding walk among the boutiques of this quaint, picture-perfect village. And why not partake in a village tradition on your visit: Buy and ice cream cone and relax by the falls!

How to get there: From Cleveland, take I–77 south to I–480 east, then follow U.S. 271 north. The first exit on 271 is Chagrin Boulevard; get off and go east 9 miles to reach Chagrin Falls. As you come into town there will be a large hill; before reaching the stoplight at the bottom of the hill, turn right on West Street to the inn. If you pass the stoplight, turn around.

Innkeeper: Mary Beth O'Donnell
Address/Telephone: 87 West Street; (216) 247–1200, fax (216) 247–2122
Rooms: 15, with 4 suites; all with private bath, several with fireplace and whirlpool. No smoking in rooms.
Rates: $105 to $195, double; subtract $10 for single; continental breakfast.
Open: All year.
Facilities and activities: Gathering room with fireplace; Gamekeeper's Taverne for fine dining. Nearby: walk to falls, browse quaint village shops, hike in Western Reserve surroundings. Eastern suburb of Cleveland only a short ride to Rock 'n' Roll Hall of Fame, Jacob's Field, home of the Cleveland Indians; Severance Center, home to Cleveland Orchestra; The Flats, Cleveland's riverfront nightlife; and Sea World.

The Inn at Brandywine Falls

SAGAMORE HILLS, OHIO 44067

There's nothing more romantic than a waterfall. And Brandywine Falls check in at 67 feet. But the hike on the boardwalk to the falls, and then down deep into the gorge itself, seems much greater.

Maybe that's because of the grandeur of nature at Brandywine Falls, part of the massive Cuyahoga Valley National Park. We had been marveling at the natural beauty for miles before we came upon this handsome inn.

The Inn at Brandywine Falls turned out to be among our favorites on our swing through eastern Ohio. Not only does it boast a waterfall, but hiking and biking trails, and expansive grounds perfect for romantic nature walks with your partner.

The inn, a Greek Revival beauty built in 1848 by James Wallace, was the centerpiece of a once-thriving pioneer community with a sawmill and gristmill, thriving businesses along the falls.

Today, all that is left of that village are some mill foundations and the inn. But the inn (and the falls) are more than enough!

Inn suites are among *my* favorites on the Midwest country inn landscape. For a complete, reclusive getaway, the Granary offers towering windows overlooking a hemlock grove and rustic, wide-plank pine floors and hand-hewn wooden beams. Then there are the king-sized bed, wood-burning stove, two-person whirlpool, microwave, and fridge.

Another good choice is the Loft, which began as a small barn in the 1800s; it has been transformed into another rustic wonder with a wall of windows overlooking that hemlock grove, as well as a romantic loft area with bed and oversized whirlpool.

Downstairs, you can marvel at all the country geegaws decorating the suite. There's even a model train that circles the ceiling.

In the main house, the James Wallace Parlor has an elegant double sleigh bed luxuriating on Axminster carpeting, English armoire, hand-painted lamp shades, and an antique chair (oldest original piece of furniture in the house) that came from 1820s Maryland.

But I might opt for Adeline's Retreat, a charming and romantic second-floor room with double sleigh bed, claw-footed tub and the only guest quarters with glimpses of the falls.

Guests take breakfast in the dining room, where a portrait of James Wallace gazes down over the festivities. Goodies might include fruited oatmeal soup, fresh juices, homebaked breads, and hot beverages.

Did I mention that it's a candlelight breakfast?

Most important, however, is that a visit to Brandywine Falls offers you a chance to walk, listen, and marvel at nature. Relax. Visit the falls. Doze in the sun. Breathe in the aroma of wildflowers and the forest.

Just be. Together.

How to get there: From the Ohio Turnpike, take exit 12, then continue on Highway 8 for 1½ miles to Twinsburg Road. Turn west (left) and drive another 1½ miles to a dead end at Brandywine Road. Turn right and cross the bridge. The inn is on the left.

Innkeepers: George and Katie Hoy
Address/Telephone: 8230 Brandywine Road; (216) 467–1812 or 650–4965
Rooms: 6, with 3 suites; all with private bath. No smoking inn. Wheelchair access.
Rates: \$94 to \$185, double; for single, subtract \$5; EPB.
Open: All year.
Facilities and activities: Located on 33,000 acres of parkland known as Cuyahoga Valley National Park. Porch swings, chairs overlooking gorge. Short hike to boardwalk to falls and down into gorge. Bike and hike trails yards away.

Cameo Rose Bed and Breakfast

BELLEVILLE, WISCONSIN 53508

If there is a more attractive Victorian-style inn than this one, let me know about it. But I'll put my money on the Cameo Rose, a hostelry that's blossoming into one of the finest little romantic getaways in the Midwest.

"We built the house specifically for a bed and breakfast," Dawn told me. It was completed in 1991, though it has the Victorian-era complement of ornate gingerbread, slashing gables, and an imposing tower.

Inside, you'll find modern elegance. The "foyer" is two stories high, incredibly decorated to the season, with stairs leading to second-floor guest rooms. But first enjoy the guest parlor, with skylights gracing a cathedral ceiling and looking as if a *House Beautiful* layout has come alive.

Dawn does all the decorating—and it is exquisite. Of course, romantic roses are everywhere, especially in the Tower Room, graced with Cameo Rose wall coverings, Battenburg lace, handsome quilts, and a double whirlpool whose window looks out over the surrounding valley.

Is there a more enticing spot for a romantic rendezvous?

I also loved the Rose Arbor room, with its rococo reproductions (such as that antique fainting couch). And all guest rooms have televisions and VCRs; the inn's film library contains more than 700 titles.

Dawn's breakfasts are elegant too. Served in the formal dining room on antique china with crystal goblets, consider hot breakfast fruit compote, eggs Benedict, berry struesel muffins ("Wild berries grow everywhere around here," Dawn said), and homemade cinnamon rolls—a house specialty.

The inn is located on 120 acres of hills and trees. Part of the renowned Ice Age Trail edges across the property. There are also miles of hiking paths that loop to hilltops, through maple and oak groves, and into the valley. Or relax among Dawn's rose and flower gardens, a blaze of colors in the growing season.

The Cameo Rose is a special place. But don't take my word. See for yourself.

How to get there: The inn is located 5 miles south of Verona, 3 miles north of Belleville (and about 12 miles southwest of Madison) in unincorporated Basco. From madison, take Highway 151 (Verona Road) west and use the Paoli exit. Basco, the town, is basically a sign and a small group of houses at Henry Road along Highway 69 about 1 mile past Paoli, on the way to Belleville. You'll see the Cameo Rose to the left on a hill, a bit more than 1 mile down Henry Road.

Innkeepers: Dawn, Gary, and Jennifer Bahr
Address/Telephone: 1090 Severson Road; (608) 424–6340
Rooms: 5; all with private bath. No smoking inn.
Rates: $79 to $129, single or double, EPB.
Open: All year.
Facilities and activities: Cathedral great room, porches, rose gazebo, flower gardens, 120 acres of hills, woods, hiking trails. Nearby: fifteen minutes from Madison, the University of Wisconsin, the State Capitol, State Street (shops and specialty stores), Dane County Coliseum, golf courses, water sports on Lakes Medota and Monona.

Canoe Bay

CHETEK, WISCONSIN 54728

Staying at Dan and Lisa's inn, one of the "Top Three" country inns in the Midwest, is like waking up in the middle of a romantic dream.

Imagine luxurious cottage suites, featuring Frank Lloyd Wright's signature Prairie-style architecture along with "every possible creature comfort with the ultimate in privacy." (Even Canoe Bay's exterior spaces have received Wright's "organic architecture" treatment, with natural prairie, woodland grasses, and wildflowers designed and installed by a nationally renowned consulting ecologist.)

For example, the Oak Park Suite boasts a 14-foot wall of casement windows overlooking a lake; the Wood Grove Suite allows guests to observe natural surroundings from their platform two-person Jacuzzi through wraparound windows. And you can luxuriate in front of a river-rock fireplace with stereo TV/VCR/CD, wet bar with refrigerator, microwave oven, and huge private deck at hand.

Or how about a dream cottage with a see-through fireplace next to the whirlpool plus lake views?

The main building centerpiece is a great room, with soaring natural-cedar cathedral ceilings, a wall of windows, and a 30-foot-tall, hand-constructed fieldstone fireplace. A perfect spot to whisper sweet nothings in your honey's ear.

Dan (former TV weatherman for WFLD-Channel 32 in Chicago) and Lisa built their inn on the shore of crystal-clear Lake Wahdoon, a fifty-acre spring-fed body of water surrounded by 280 acres of private oak, aspen, and maple forests. The inn provides breathtaking views, incomparable service, and complete privacy besides the many opportunities for outdoor recreation and relaxation, including wildlife watching.

Mornings bring pampering, with breakfast baskets delivered to your room or brought out to the patio overlooking the lake, where you can enjoy scores of chirping songbirds. Canoe Bay also offers dinner featuring gourmet cuisine to guests that would be difficult to beat even when considering Chicago or Minneapolis's best restaurants, thanks to CIA-trained Chef Bruno.

The inn's standout season could be autumn, with its incomparable colors, but holidays receive special treatment, too. Thanksgiving and New Year's Day guests can enjoy guided cross-country ski tours, ice skating, ice fishing, and a 14-foot-tall Christmas tree with all the trimmings. Not to mention a free, personal weather forecast from prognosticator Dan, who's often heard to say, "If there's a better place on Earth, I don't know it."

Forget Earth. This is heaven.

How to get there: Once in Chetek, Highway 53 is named Second Street. Follow that through town, over a bridge, and turn right on County D (there's a cemetery at this intersection); go about 1½ miles to Hogback Road (look for a CANOE BAY sign here); turn left and continue for about 7 miles to the inn.

Innkeepers: Dan and Lisa Dobrowolski
Address/Telephone: W16065 Hogback Road; (715) 924–4594 or (800) 568–1995
E-mail/URL: canoebay@discover-net.net / http://discover-net.net/canoebay
Rooms: 12, including 4 main lodge luxury suites and 4 luxury cottage suites; 3 luxury lodge suites, and 1 "dream cottage"; all with private bath, whirlpool bath, and air conditioning. No smoking inn.
Rates: $160 to $180, single or double, inn; $135 to $165, lodge; $175 to $205, cottages; $245, "dream cottage"; EPB. Gourmet dinners $50 per couple.
Open: All year.
Facilities and activities: Located on private 280 acres: 2 private lakes, hiking paths, nature trails, cross-country ski trails, cross-country rentals, bike rentals, fishing, swimming, canoes, rowboats, and more. Sitting room, video room, library. About 45 minutes west of St. Paul, Minnesota.
Recommended Country Inns® Travelers' Club Benefit: 10 percent discount, subject to availability.

The American Club

KOHLER, WISCONSIN 53044

Just 4 miles from the shoreline of Lake Michigan, amid tall pines, patches of white birch, scrubbed farmhouses, and black soil, is one of Wisconsin's most romantic retreats.

There's an uncommonly European ambience at the elegant American Club. With its Tudor-style appointments of gleaming brass, custom-crafted oak furniture, crystal chandeliers, and quality antique furnishings, it looks like a finely manicured baronial estate. It's also the only five-diamond resort hotel in the Midwest.

Built in 1918 as a temporary home for immigrant workers of the Kohler Company (a renowned plumbing manufacturer, still located across the street), the "boarding house" served as a meeting place where English and citizenship classes were taught—a genuine American Club.

Talk about romance: Some rooms feature a four-poster canopied brass bed and huge marble-lined whirlpool bath. Other suites contain a saunalike environmental enclosure with a push-button choice of weather—from bright sun and gentle breezes to misty rain showers. And consider guest pamperings: fluffy bathrobes, twice-daily maid service, daily newspapers—the list goes on!

The inn's showcase restaurant is The Immigrant, a romantic hideaway where we dined on a four-course gourmet meal that included smoked Irish salmon. The wine list is impressive, too. For dessert we walked to the Greenhouse, in the courtyard. This antique English solarium is a perfect spot for chocolate torte and other Viennese delights.

Not to mention your late-night rendezvous with your special sweetheart.

How to get there: From Chicago, take I–94 north and continue north on I–43, just outside of Milwaukee. Exit on Wisconsin 23 west (exit 53B). Take 23 to County Trunk Y and continue south into Kohler. The inn is on the right.

From the west, take I–94 south to Wisconsin 21 and go east to U.S. 41. Go south on 41 to Wisconsin 23; then head east into Kohler.

Innkeepers: Susan Porter Green, vice-president; Alice Hubbard, general manager
Address/Telephone: Highland Drive; (414) 457–8000 or (800) 344–2838, fax (414) 457–0299
Rooms: 236; all with private whirlpool bath, air conditioning, TV, and phone. Wheelchair access.
Rates: Novermber through April: $130 to $585, single; $160 to $585, double; summer season rates slightly higher. Each child over 10, $15 extra; children 10 and younger free. Two-night minimum on weekends from July through September. Several packages available.
Open: All year.
Facilities and activities: Nine restaurants and full-service dining rooms. Renowned for extravagant buffets, special-event and holiday feasts; large Sunday brunch. Ballroom. Sports Core, a world-class health club. River Wildlife, 500 acres of private woods for hiking, horseback riding, hunting, fishing, trapshooting, canoeing. Cross-country skiing and ice skating. Also Kohler Design Center, shops at Woodlake, Kohler Arts Center, Waelderhaus. Nearby: antiquing, lake charter fishing, Kettle Moraine State Forest, Road America (auto racing).
Business travel: Located 5 minutes from downtown Sheboygan. Corporate rates, conference rooms, fax services.

Victorian Treasure Bed and Breakfast

LODI, WISCONSIN 53555

Kimberly and Todd have done a remarkable job transforming this 1897 Victorian into an elegant, romantic getaway that everyone wants to return to again and again.

Little Wonder. Polished chandeliers, brass door fittings, and natural woodworks harken back to a more elegant era. A grand staircase leads to a wide hallway ushering guests to the bedchambers. Then, there's Kimberly and Todd themselves—two of the most affable and pampering innkeepers around.

What else is special here? How about the Queen Anne's Lace Room, with its queen-sized four-poster canpy bed draped with antique lace panels for privacy? Did I forget to mention its expansive bath featuring a two-person whirlpool?

Then there's the Wild Ginger Room, boasting not only a hand-carved walnut bed but a private porch perfect for coosome-twosome stargazing.

Any room you choose here is bathed in romance—all beds possess cozy down comforters, four pillows, luxurious linens—real European romantic style.

Lovers of food will savor Kimberly's five-course gourmet breakfasts; they might include fresh fruit with ginger syrup, home-baked nut breads and cinnamon rolls, vegetable fritatta, omelets, locally "grown" sausages, and more.

Perhaps you'll even be served the house specialty: pecan cream-cheese stuffed French toast topped with fruit sauces.

There's lots more. Other choices at the Victorian Treasure is whether to overnight at the inn's other property: the Palmer House. This bit of elegance is an 1893 Queen Anne with four additional luxury suites that include whirlpool bath, fireplace, stereo, and wet bar.

A romantic's favoriate is the Angelica suite, perhaps the inn's finest. It boasts three rooms of its own, a mahogany tester bed, double whirlpool—even a private front porch. Imagine the delights.

How to get there: From Chicago and Milwaukee, take I–90/94 to Wisconsin 60 and go west into Lodi. In town take Route 60 (now called Lodi Street) 1 block west, then turn right on Prairie Street. It's the first house on the left.

Innkeepers: Kimberly and Todd Seidl
Address/Telephone: 115 Prairie Street; (608) 592–5199
Rooms: 8, including 4 suites; all with private bath and air conditioning. No smoking inn.
Rates: $65 to $169, single or double, EPB, afternoon wine, cheese, and fruit.
Open: All year.
Facilities and activities: Sitting rooms, porch. Nearby: water activities on Wisconsin River and Lake Wisconsin. Hiking, rock climbing, bird-watching on Baraboo Range. Also nearby: restaurants; downhill and cross-country skiing; Devil's Lake State Park, with 500-foot bluffs; American Players (Shakespearean) Theater in outdoor amphitheater; Taliesin, home of Frank Lloyd Wright; golf; bald eagle watching.
Business travel: Located about 20 miles north of Madison, 20 miles south of Baraboo. Corporate rates, meeting room, fax.
Recommended Country Inns® Travelers' Club Benefit: 20 percent discount, Monday–Thursday.

St. Croix River Inn

OSCEOLA, WISCONSIN 54020

This eighty-plus-year-old stone house is poised high on a bluff overlooking the scenic St. Croix River. It allows unsurpassed, breathtaking views while providing one of the most romantic lodgings in the entire Midwest.

I'm especially fond of a suite with a huge whirlpool bath set in front of windows, allowing you to float visually down the river while pampering yourself in a bubble bath.

"The house was built from limestone quarried near here," Bev said. "It belonged to the owner of the town's pharmacy and remained in his family until a few years ago."

Now let's get right to the rooms (suites, really), which are named for riverboats built in Osceola. Perhaps (and this is a *big* perhaps) Jennie Hays is my all-time favorite inn room. It is simply exquisite, with appointments that remind me of exclusive European hotels. I continue to rave about a magnificent four-poster canopy bed that feels as good as it looks and a decorative tile fireplace that soothes the psyche as well as chilly limbs on crackling-cool autumn or frigid winter nights.

Then there is the view! I'm almost at a loss for words. A huge Palladian window, stretching from floor to ceiling, overlooks the river from the inn's bluff-top perch. It provides a romantic and rewarding setting that would be hard to surpass anywhere in the Midwest. The room has a whirlpool tub, and there's a private balcony with more great river views.

The G. B. Knapp Room is more of the same: a huge suite, with a four-poster canopy bed adorned with a floral quilt, tall armoire, its own working gas fireplace, and a whirlpool tub. Then walk through a door to the enclosed porch (more like a private sitting room), with windows overlooking the river. There are also exquisite stenciling, bull's-eye moldings, and private balconies.

Pampering continues at breakfast, which Bev serves in your room or in bed. It might include fresh fruit and juices, omelets, waffles, French toast, or puff pastries stuffed with ham and cheese, and French bread and pound cake.

Bev also delivers to your room a pot of steaming coffee and the morning paper a half hour before your morning meal. She can recommend a great place for dinner. But you simply may never want to leave your quarters.

Let's face it: This is one of the Midwest's most romantic retreats—pure grace and elegance.

How to get there: From downtown Osceola, turn west on Third Avenue and follow it past a hospital and historic Episcopal church (dating from 1854, with four turreted steeples). The inn is located on the river side of River Street.

Innkeeper: Bev Johnson
Address/Telephone: 305 River Street; (715) 294–4248
Rooms: 7; all with private bath and air conditioning, 2 with TV.
Rates: Friday and Saturday, $100 to $200; Sunday through Thursday, $85 to $150; single or double; EPB. Gift certificates available.
Open: All year.
Facilities and activities: Outdoor porch, sitting room overlooking St. Croix River. Nearby: several area antiques shops, canoeing, fishing, downhill and cross-country skiing at Wild Mountain or Trollhaugen. A short drive to restaurants and Taylors Falls, Minnesota—a lovely little river town with historic-homes tours and cruises on old-fashioned paddle wheelers.

White Lace Inn

STURGEON BAY, WISCONSIN 54235

Bonnie and Dennis Statz call their award-winning inn "a romantic fireside getaway." I can't think of a better place to spend a cozy, pampered weekend for two.

And things have only gotten better since my last visit. Now the White Lace Inn resembles a private Victorian-era park, with three handsome historic buildings connected by a red-brick pathway that winds through landscaped grounds filled with stately trees, wildflower gardens, and a rose garden featuring varieties dating from the 1700s. You will also enjoy the Vixen Hill gazebo, a great place to pause among the inn's many gardens; it is a beauty from Pennsylvania.

The Main House was built for a local lawyer in 1903; what's surprising is the extensive oak woodwork put in for a man of such modest means. Stepping into the entryway, I was surrounded by magnificent hand-carved oak paneling.

Bonnie has a degree in interior design and has created guest rooms with a warm feel, mixing Laura Ashley wallpaper and fabrics with imposing, yet comfortable, antique furnishings like rich oriental rugs and high-back walnut and canopied beds. Fluffy down pillows are provided, handmade comforters and quilts brighten large beds, and lacy curtains adorn tall windows.

The 1880s Garden House has rooms with their own fireplace. They're done in myriad styles, from country elegant to the grand boldness of oversized Empire furniture.

This time my wife and I stayed in the Washburn House, another "old" addition to the White Lace. All rooms here are luxurious; ours had a canopy brass bed with down comforter, fireplace, and two-person whirlpool. It was graced with soft pastel floral chintz fabric and white-on-white Carol Gresco fabrics that tell a story (in fact, some of her work is part of the Smithsonian Design Institution collection). The bath's Ralph Lauren towels are heavenly.

And next time, we want a room in the Hadley House—maybe one with a huge whirlpool, fireplace, and private balcony.

Back in the main house, Bonnie's homemade muffins are the breakfast treat, along with juice, coffee, and delicious Scandinavian fruit soup (a tasty concoction served cold) or old-fashioned rice pudding. Blueberry soup and apple crisps are summer specials. It's a great time to swap Door County stories.

How to get there: From Milwaukee, take U.S. 41 north to Wisconsin 42, toward Sturgeon Bay. Just outside the city, take Business 42/57 and follow it into town, cross the bridge, and you'll come to Michigan Street. Follow Michigan to Fifth Avenue and turn left. White Lace Inn is on the right side of the street. Or you can take the 42/51 bypass across the new bridge to Michigan Street. Turn left on Michigan, go to Fifth Avenue, and take a right on Fifth to the inn.

Innkeepers: Bonnie and Dennis Statz
Address/Telephone: 16 North Fifth Avenue; (414) 743–1105
Rooms: 19, in 4 historic houses; all with private bath and air conditioning, some with fireplace, whirlpool, TV, and wheelchair access.
Rates: $75 to $190, single or double, continental breakfast. Special winter or spring fireside rates and packages available November through May.
Open: All year.
Facilities and activities: Five blocks to bay shore. Nearby: specialty and antiques shops, restaurants, Door County Museum, Miller Art Center; swimming, tennis, and horseback riding. A short drive to Whitefish Dunes and Potawatomi state parks, Peninsula Players Summer Theater, Birch Creek Music Festival. Cross-country skiing and ice skating in winter. Gateway to the peninsula.
Recommended Country Inns® Travelers' Club Benefit: 25 percent discount, Monday–Thursday, November–April, excluding holidays. Not valid with any other offers or reduced rates.

The Southwest

by Eleanor S. Morris

Ah, romance! Who can define it?

Dictionaries try. *Webster's* defines romance as "extraordinary life, not real or familiar," adding "colloquially, to make love." *Thorndike Barnhard* agrees; its definition reads, "a love affair, an interest in adventure and love." *Collins Gem* (a French dictionary) declares it *"poesie"* and *"idylle,"* and *Cassell's New Compact French Dictionary* says romance is not only *"amourette"* and *"aventure"* (love and adventure), it is also *"inventer a plaisir"*: to imagine a pleasure, a delight.

So, is it more of a feeling we bring to a place, or can the place itself be romantic, engendering romantic feelings in us? I think it's both; I like the way the French say that romance means to invent a delight. Imagination inspires us to look for surroundings that will complement and enhance romance.

Herein are twenty-two inns of the Southwest that provide a delightful ambience of *"idylle et poesie."* Although they help keep romance alive, part of their magic comes from what you bring along with you. Whether it's romance amid the opulence of a Victorian mansion, in an eagle's aerie in the mountains, or in the pampered Southern comfort of an antebellum plantation, these inns provide the perfect setting for a wonderful experience of romance.

The rest is up to you.

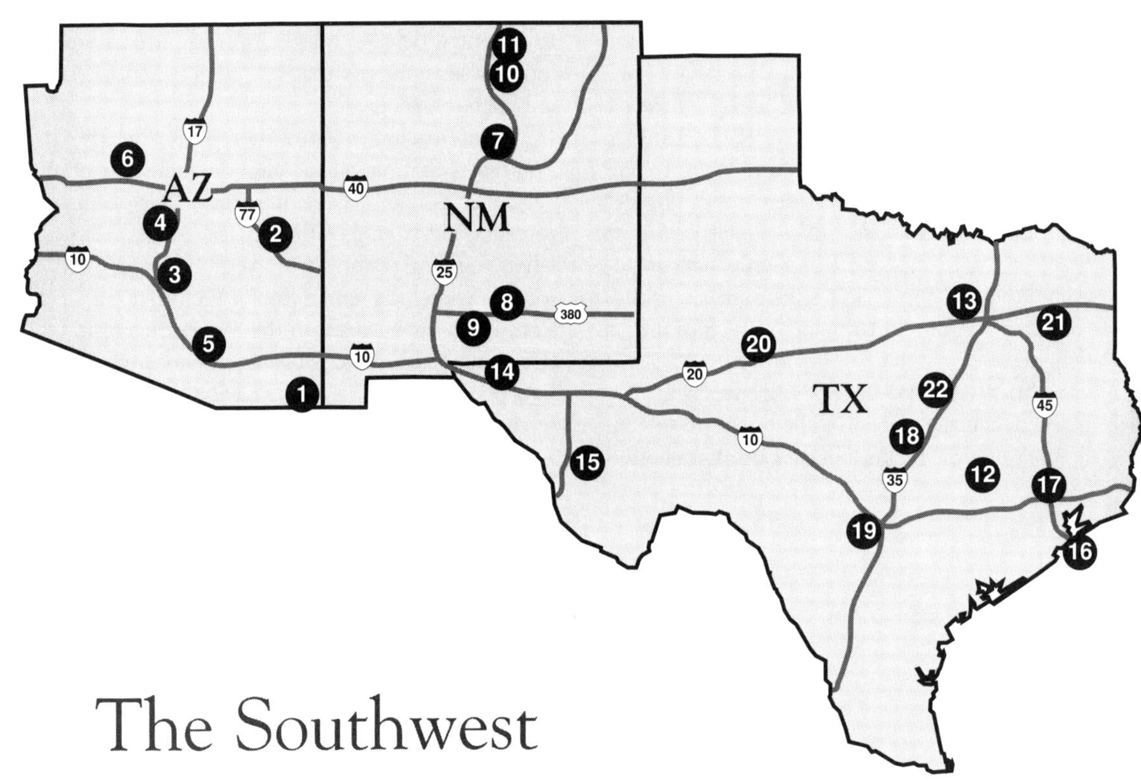

The Southwest

The Southwest

Numbers on map refer to towns numbered below.

Arizona

1. Bisbee, Bisbee Grand Hotel 196
2. Pinetop/Lakeside, The Meadows Inn 198
3. Scottsdale, Inn at the Citadel 200
4. Sedona, Saddle Rock Ranch 202
5. Tucson, The Suncatcher 204
6. Williams, Terry Ranch Inn 206

New Mexico

7. El Prado, Taos, Las Campañas de Taos 208
8. Lincoln, Casa de Patron 210
9. Nogal, Paz de Nogal 212
10. Rancho de Taos, Adobe & Pines Inn 214
11. Taos, Casa Europa 216

Texas

12. Chappell Hill, The Browning Plantation . . . 218
13. Dallas, Hôtel St. Germain 220
14. El Paso, Sunset Heights Inn 222
15. Fort Davis, The Veranda Country Inn 224
16. Galveston, The Gilded Thistle 226
17. Houston, La Colombe d'Or 228
18. New Braunfels, Gruene Mansion 230
19. San Antonio, The Ogé House 232
20. Sweetwater, Mulberry Manor 234
21. Tyler, Charnwood Hill Inn 236
22. Wimberley, The Inn Above Orion Creek . . . 238

Bisbee Grand Hotel

BISBEE, ARIZONA 85603

Opulence, extraordinary almost-out-of-the-world opulence, is what we found at the well-named Bisbee Grand. Grand is a perfect adjective for this inn—so is elegant. From the red-velvet Victorian Suite to the other-worldly Oriental Suite, exotic luxury abounds in this posh, treasure-filled inn.

The modest, small black marquee over the double doors, squeezed in between two store-fronts, hardly prepared us for what awaited as we climbed the red-carpeted stairs leading from the narrow entrance to the second floor and the inn rooms. Once there, faced with an iridescent stuffed peacock at the head of the stairs, I found ourselves in a world we certainly had never expected in the quaint and charming Old West mining town of Bisbee.

Each of the seven guest rooms is a world in itself, full of beautiful furniture and decorative details. "These antiques were collected for thirty years," innkeeper Bill says with justifiable pride. As for the three suites, they are extravaganzas, excitingly imaginative, full of unexpected appointments, such as a working fountain next to a lovely, large flower arrangement in the Garden Suite.

We chose the unashamedly opulent Oriental Suite, with walls covered in black, pink, and gold fabric depicting Chinese scenes. The brass bed is adorned with onyx and alabaster. "It's a unique, one-of-a-kind honeymoon bed," Bill explained. It's wide and high, with an oval mirror and paintings, while bronze dragon vases and black lacquer vie with other choice collectibles in the room.

As for the Victorian Suite, it's dripping with deep-red-velvet hangings, not only on the windows but also making a cozy nest of the canopied bed. The Garden Suite is a bower of flowers; as for the rest of the rooms, like the Coral and the Gray rooms, Deer Springs and Crow Canyon, well, any one is a perfect place for a romantic getaway.

On the main floor, adjacent to the Grand Western Saloon, the inn's old-fashioned Victorian parlor has an antique piano that you may play if you're careful. The saloon's 35-foot bar came from Wyatt Earp's Oriental Bar by way of the Wells Fargo Museum.

Breakfast will satisfy both the most eager gourmet and the health food aficionado. "All our food is from Tucson Cooperative Warehouses," Bill noted, "and we recycle and compost everything." The fruit course consisted of watermelon, cantaloupe, pineapple, and green grapes; the delicious quiche was full of cheese and mushrooms, with ham on the side; the homemade bread was delicious; and for sweets, there were cheese Danish and cinnamon rolls.

"We treat our guests very special, with all the grace and elegance of the best of a Victorian mining town," Bill said. Morning coffee, hot tea, ice tea, and a plateful of ginger snaps, lemon bars, and peanut butter and chocolate chip cookies are available in the saloon practically 'round the clock. And not the least of the pleasures of this small, elegant inn is watching together the sunset, or the rainbow after it rains, over the mountains facing the front balcony.

How to get there: From Highway 80 east take Tombstone Canyon Road for approximately 2½ miles until it becomes Main Street. You can't miss the Bisbee Grand on the left.

Innkeeper: Bill Thomas
Address/Telephone: 61 Main Street (mailing address: P.O. Box 825); (520) 432–5900
Rooms: 11; all with private bath. No smoking inn.
Rates: $52 to $115, double; $15 extra person; EPB.
Open: All year.
Facilities and activities: Grand Western Saloon with complimentary snacks, pool table, large TV screen, and Ladies' Parlor; Murder Mystery weekends. Nearby: Old Bisbee Tour, City Mine Tour, Bisbee Mining and Historical Museum, antiques shops, art galleries.
Recommended Country Inns® Travelers' Club Benefit: 25 percent discount or stay two nights, get third night free, Monday–Thursday, subject to availability.

The Meadows Inn

PINETOP/LAKESIDE, ARIZONA 85935

Here's a wonderful find—a country inn that was built to be a country inn, a charming, small place in a lovely country setting between the small towns of Pinetop and Lakeside, which grew until they grew together. Planned down to the finest detail, the inn is a combination of French country charm and a gourmet restaurant.

Steve was the chef of a Tucson country club, Ruth was employed at a health spa, and Nicole was in a related business.

They really pamper their guests, with tea, sodas, coffee, and homemade cookies around the clock (those chocolate macadamia cookies are to die for)—and nightly turndown service in the evenings, as well as a glass of wine, beer, a cordial, whatever your preference.

The inn is set in the magnificent White Mountains, the wildlife is all around, and these cityfolk innkeepers had a lot to learn about nature.

"Elk migrate here in the spring," Ruth said ruefully. "The first spring here, I planted 250 tulips, all ready for a wedding we were having. Next day the herd came through—and ate all the tulips! I'd never seen an elk, and they are *huge*. I wasn't about to tell them they couldn't!"

The sitting room is two stories high and we looked down from the staircase on a cozy fireplace, soft cushiony sofas, an antique Victrola, an organ, and a rocker. Upstairs, the library offers more than 300 books, as well as a television with a small video library and lots of games and puzzles. It's a pleasant retreat, with white leather sofas, a colorful rug, and an old trunk.

The guest rooms are almost too pretty to describe properly, and all have unusually large and bright bathrooms. The downstairs guest rooms are sunken, which makes for nice high ceilings—you step down a step or two into the room. Bright and fresh are the pretty flower-print quilts and wainscoted decorator wallpaper.

In the restaurant, Steve serves some mighty delicious breakfasts. Would you prefer a Lorraine Omelet (with bacon, onion, and Swiss cheese) or a Geneva Melt (of turkey, tomato, and egg and cheese on English muffins), or perhaps cheese blintzes? Of course, there are fresh fruit, juice, and all the other trimmings.

Dinners are delicious; one of Steve's specialties is duck, and both he and Ruth were delighted when a guest from England had this to say: "I love duck, and wherever I go, I order duck. And, this was the best I've ever had!" The apple toffee tart for dessert is worth raving over, too.

How to get there: The inn is off Woodland Lake Road between the twin towns of Lakeside/Pinetop. Turn south on Woodland Lake Road and take the first road on your left; it's a gravel road, and the inn is at the end of it.

Innkeepers: Ruth and Steve Brayer and Nicole Edgington
Address/Telephone: 453 North Woodland Road (mailing address: P. O. Box 1110); (520) 367–0334, fax (520) 367–8200
Rooms: 7; all with private bath and telephone; wheelchair access to two. No smoking inn.
Rates: \$85 to \$155, double seasonal; \$15 to \$20 extra person; EPB and snacks.
Open: All year.
Facilities: Restaurant, library, games, VCR library. Nearby: Woodland Lake Park with hiking, nature trails, water sports; Apache Indian Reservation; fishing and boating, biking, tennis, golf, horseback riding, skiing and antiques shops.
Recommended Country Inns® Travelers' Club Benefit: 10 percent discount, subject to availability.

The Inn at the Citadel

SCOTTSDALE, ARIZONA 85255

"Everything has family meaning," Kelly Keyes said of this posh, family-built inn in chic Scottsdale, at the foot of outstanding Pinnacle Peak. "It's all been built in threes and fives; those three arches over there are for three daughters—me and my two sisters."

The sentiment goes beyond the immediate family. Kelly pointed out that the brands decorating the Marque Bar are those of everyone who had anything to do with the building of the inn. "Architects, builders, my parents—theirs is the flying double K," she explained.

The inn had a propitious beginning. Built on Hopi Indian land, the Hopis were invited to a blessing of the land. "Everyone, even the children, came. It was a black-tie-and-jeans event, jeans and boots."

This is a pretty sumptuous establishment for the casual Southwest, more like a fine European-style hotel than a country inn, but "we try to put guests at their ease," Adam Wilson said. "Sometimes they're a little taken aback, awed by the location." This is grand country, with Pinnacle Peak just overhead.

Kelly's mother, Anita Keyes, is an interior designer, and each of the eleven rooms is decorated with careful detail, down to the smallest item. Original artwork by such artists as Jonathan Sobel and Armond Laura hang on the walls, and antiques are used extensively. The armoires in six of the rooms were painted by local Arizona artists Liz Henretta, Skip Bennett, Sherry Stewart, and Carolyn Baer.

Rooms have safes, robes, hair dryers, bath amenities, and an honor bar, stocked with not only premium liquors, wine, and champagne, but also playing cards, along with the expected soft drinks, crackers, and candy bars.

Fresh hot coffee comes along with the complimentary newspaper each morning. A massage, facial, or manicure can come to your room, too, if you wish. Each room has cable television with HBO.

The larger rooms are more like suites, with large sitting areas and desks. The king-sized beds are covered with quilted satiny spreads, and the pillow shams match the dust ruffles.

Actually, the Citadel is not just an inn. It's a restaurant and shopping complex in a shady courtyard complete with a pond and a bubbling waterfall. The continental breakfast is served either in The Market or in your room, which we preferred. Fresh-squeezed orange juice is followed by a large serving of seasonal fresh fruit—we had raspberries—and then moist zucchini, bran, or corn muffins, and, of course, coffee or tea.

We surfaced for the market, where you can get anything from blue corn waffles to hamburgers, pastas, salads, and enchiladas, and it's all deliciously fresh and nicely served. The award-winning 8700 at the Citadel really goes all out, with the finest regional American cuisine. One of chef Leonard Rubin's specialties is roast rack of black buck antelope. "It's pretty popular," Adam said. The menu also features 8700 Mixed Grill, poached salmon, and coffee toffee crunch cake, so we wined and dined in great style.

How to get there: From I–17 take Bell Road 30 miles east to Scottsdale Road, then go north 4 miles to Pinnacle Peak Road and east 2 miles to the inn.

Innkeepers: Kelly Keyes, Jane De Beer, and Adam Wilson
Address/Telephone: 8700 East Pinnacle Peak Road; (602) 994–8700 or (800) 927–8367
Rooms: 11; all with private bath; wheelchair accessible. No smoking inn.
Rates: $295, double, continental breakfast.
Open: All year.
Facilities and activities: Two restaurants, piano bar, limo tours of the desert, health and beauty spa facilities, boutiques. Nearby: Hiking to Pinnacle Peak; golf.
Business travel: Located in Scottsdale (not downtown). Desk in room; conference space, boardroom, secretarial services, computer and fax facilities; banking, banquet, and catering facilities.

Saddle Rock Ranch

SEDONA, ARIZONA 86336

This luxurious home is not what you would expect from a place that calls itself a ranch. Today the historic homestead, built in 1926, is on the edge of a residential area. But it sits on three acres of hillside overlooking Sedona, and it has starred in many Old West films.

"I just saw a late-night 'thirties movie, *Angel and the Bad Man*," Dan said, "and there was our whole house! It was a dude ranch back then, and the wife of the owner always played an Indian princess in the films," he added with a laugh.

Fran and Dan, who met while both were employed at a prestigious California hotel, are experts in providing special attention to guests. What we found was the same VIP treatment that they gave to many of the "rich and famous." And before that Dan had a rather adventurous career: My companion recognized his name, because he played football for the Pittsburgh Steelers.

"He's lived every man's fantasy," Fran said. "He also raced with Mario Andretti on the Indy circuit." They moved to Sedona for the climate, and now Dan and Fran are having an adventurous time innkeeping. "Our guests are wonderful, outstanding, and we want them to have the same total experience throughout their visit. It's a point of pride to us that our guests get the best of not only what we have to offer, but also what Sedona has to offer as well," Dan said, and we reveled in full concierge service with restaurant reservations at Sedona's finest—concerts, theater, tours, and anything else we could think of.

Guest rooms are elegantly comfortable, as is the living room. Large Saddle Rock Suite has a country French canopied bed and a rock fireplace; furniture in the Rose Garden Room was Fran's great-great-grandfather's, and the room has its own private, walled rose garden. The Cottage in back, with wood-paneled walls, is surrounded by panoramic vistas as well as having its own private patio. Robes, nightly turndown, chocolates, bottled water, afternoon snacks, guest refrigerator, and microwave oven—we made ourselves right at home in this just-about-perfect inn.

There are cuddly teddy bears everywhere, and it's Dan who collects them! "I was born at home, and the doctor brought a bear when he delivered me—I still have it," he says. It lives in retirement with other teddy bears on a daybed that belonged to his great-great-grandfather.

Breakfast is served in the large and sunny dining room, and specialties are heart-shaped peach waffles and individual Dutch babies (pancakes) filled with apples and vanilla ice cream or yogurt. "I like to use our local Sedona apples, peaches, and pears," Fran says. Orange juice is always fresh-squeezed, and if you prefer tea to coffee, there are sixteen different ones to choose from.

At the rear of the property, a national forest shelters wildlife; deer come to the salt lick, and quail abound. The inn has tamer specimens in Diana and Fergie, miniature schnauzers. "But guest quarters are off-limits to them," Fran said, "unless you particularly request some puppy love!"

How to get there: Take Highway 89A (Airport Drive) to Valley View; go south 1 block to Rock Ridge Drive, left to Forest Circle, and right to Rock Ridge Circle; continue beyond Rock Ridge Drive and take the gravel road on the left up the hill to Saddle Rock.

Innkeepers: Fran and Dan Bruno
Address/Telephone: 255 Rock Ridge Drive; (520) 282–7640, fax (520) 282–6829
Rooms: 3; all with private bath and cable TV with remote. No smoking inn.
Rates: $110 to $140, double; $20 extra person; minus $5 single; EPB and afternoon snacks. Two-night minimum stay; extended stay specials.
Open: All year.
Facilities and activities: Swimming pool and spa, concierge service, Sedona airport transportation. Nearby: restaurants, shops, hiking, fishing, horseback riding, Hopi Mesa tours.
Recommended Country Inns® Travelers' Club Benefit: $10 discount, Monday–Thursday, November 15–February 29, excluding holidays. Complimentary three-hour, four-wheel-drive, high-country tour for two with a five-night stay.

The Suncatcher

TUCSON, ARIZONA 85748

Here's a really romantic retreat, out in the wide open spaces under the sun and the warmth of the desert. Yet there's elegance here, too.

"The Suncatcher has tried to take all the qualities of a first-class hotel and put in the charm of a bed and breakfast," Shirley said of her luxurious inn. "I've kept everything just about the same as it was with the previous owner, David Williams." A sure clue is each guest room's name, that of one of the world's prestigious hotels. There's the Connaught, the Four Seasons, the Regent, and the Oriental.

One guest room opens off the huge airy and spacious common area, two have French doors opening off the pool, and the fourth is around the corner with its own entrance.

The Connaught (London) is furnished with Chippendale-style furniture in gleaming dark mahogany; the Four Seasons with a formal canopied bed; the Regent (Hong Kong) has lovely original Oriental scrolls, and the Oriental (Bangkok), the largest, has its own Jacuzzi among its other splendors. We chose the Oriental—oh, that Jacuzzi!—but all have at least one comfortable chair, writing desks, original artwork, and fresh flowers.

Shirley has kept the inn emblem, little terra-cotta faces that are on the walls and elsewhere. "The inn was named for the desert attractions—the sun, the dry heat, the desert—

and I want to keep it as a retreat, a getaway, a place to catch the sun."

She had a restaurant in New Jersey for fourteen years, "and I was ready for a change," she said. "I began thinking about other things I could do." She'd always come west for vacations, and when she began to look for a house, with plans to open another restaurant, she came across The Suncatcher for sale. With the inn, she says she has the best of both worlds, a home, and looking after people. (And, she confides, she's finding innkeeping much less work than a restaurant!)

The huge common area (70 feet square), with its soaring ceiling, has several focal points. In one corner there's a large copper-hooded fireplace; in another, a mirrored mesquite bar. Display cases show off treasures from Shirley's travels to Thailand and Hong Kong, and she has also collected interesting Southwestern pieces. The entire area—sitting, dining, kitchen—is open, and you can watch the chef prepare breakfast. It's a full hot meal, with Southwestern eggs, or maybe an omelet, mushroom, perhaps, or ham and mozzarella cheese, accompanied by corn muffins, blueberry muffins, cheese pastries, and bagels.

"People can mingle; they hang out in the main house now, since I leave the door open all the time. We sit around and talk and laugh; people talk about things in their lives. It's nice. My pleasure is sitting down and speaking with my guests."

How to get there: The inn is on the edge of Saguaro National Monument. From I–10 and downtown Tucson, take Broadway east, crossing, as a last landmark, Houghton. Continue on to Avenida Javelina, bearing in mind that Avenida Javelina is beyond the DEAD-END sign on Broadway. Turn north on Javelina, and the inn is on the left in the middle of the block.

Innkeeper: Shirley Ranieri
Address/Telephone: 105 North Avenida Javelina; (520) 885–0883 or (800) 835–8012
Rooms: 4; all with private bath, phone, TV, and VCR; wheelchair accessible. No smoking inn.
Rates: $125 to $145, double; $25 extra person; EPB.
Open: All year.
Facilities and activities: Heated pool and spa, bicycle. Nearby: restaurants, tennis and health club, hiking, horseback riding, Saguaro National Monument; 15 minutes to downtown Tucson.

Terry Ranch Inn

WILLIAMS, ARIZONA 86046

There's a romantic reason why this inn calls itself a ranch, and it's not because it really is a working ranch. There has been a Terry Ranch in the Terry family since the 1650s, although back then the locale was Bucks County, Pennsylvania.

"Family tradition dictated that only the eldest son could inherit the family spread, so younger sons went off and created their own Terry Ranch," Del Terry said.

Sheryl said she always wanted a bed-and-breakfast inn, all the while they were raising Brangus cattle (still are).

"I knew I could build it (the inn). I knew I could decorate—but I wasn't certain I could run it," she confessed with a laugh. "I'm a shy person basically. But I was inspired by another Arizona innkeeper, and I've learned how wonderful it is to meet new people."

So Del and Sheryl built the inn from scratch—literally. "We built it ourselves, log by log," Sheryl said as she lovingly stroked one of the smooth wood logs that make up the walls of Terry Ranch Inn.

"We try to offer the same hospitality that Terry Ranches have provided since 1670," the innkeepers say.

Guest rooms and baths are exceptionally roomy. The guest rooms are named for the brides who lived at Terry Ranch during the

1800s, a lovely, romantic theme. A portrait of each bride hangs in her room, and each is decorated in her favorite colors.

Mary Ann's Room is named for the first Utah bride, who helped build the Utah ranch, first living in a dugout, then a stone fort.

Eliza Jane, the second bride, was the youngest—sixteen. She came west as a child, being what in our day we call a "child bride." Hannah Louisa's Room is named for the third bride, who, "at 23, was the oldest," Del says.

Charlotte Malinda helped her husband establish the town of Enterprise, Utah, just south of the Terry Ranch there. She liked baby blue and white, and on the wall of her room hangs a quilt made by Sheryl.

The large dining room table easily seats twelve, and it's covered with a lovely lace cloth made by Del's mother. In the shelves on each side of the fireplace repose grandmother's wedding china. But pretty as it is, it has to share space with Sheryl's collection of twelve individual place setting that she serves breakfast on. Each one has a story.

Speaking of breakfast, the Terrys serve a real hearty ranch breakfast—what else? Begin with fruit topped with yogurt, cream, and sweet crumb sprinkles, then English Floddies, which are grated potato, egg, onion, and crumbled bacon pancakes, along with Amish friendship bread muffins.

The Amish Friendship bread has a history, too—Sheryl makes it from a starter she's had since the late seventies!

How to get there: Take 4th Street north to Railroad Avenue. Turn right (east) and follow it around to Rodeo Drive. Turn left and go a short way to Quarterhorse; the inn is on the corner of Rodeo and Quarterhorse.

Innkeepers: Sheryl and Del Terry
Address/Telephone: 701 Quarterhorse; (520) 635–4171
Rooms: 4; all with private bath, with wheelchair access. No smoking inn.
Rates: $85 to $105, double, seasonally, $15 extra persons; EPB.
Open: All year.
Facilities and activities: Nearby: quaint small town with walking map of shops and restaurants; Grand Canyon, Grand Canyon Railway, Grand Canyon Helicopter tours, 9-hole golf course, hiking, hunting, fishing, skiing.

Las Campañas de Taos

EL PRADO, TAOS, NEW MEXICO 87529

"The Bells of Taos," in the suburb of El Prado north of Taos, takes its name from a more-than-100-year-old bell from the old Ranchos de Taos Presbyterian Mission School, part of the history of the area, and an old Mexican bell, age unknown. You'll see the bells as you enter the gateway of this fantastic luxury adobe mansion.

"This home is too big for one couple," said Quina in a marvel of understatement. Nearly 15,000 square feet of Southwest splendor are incorporated into this inn, sitting on twelve and a half acres of spectacular views. The sagebrush-covered plains of the Taos Valley spread to the Sangre de Cristo Mountains, which rise to 12,000 feet under the blue New Mexico sky.

"It feels good, special, I want to share it. That was in my mind the first time I saw it," says Quina, who hails from the jungles of Panama and whose life is a story in itself. "God has been so good to you, I thought, share it, homestyle, home away from home. People have forgotten how to be pampered."

Not only are guests treated with tenderness, they're treated to fantastic luxury. The huge, elegant Great Room has ceilings 23 feet high, tile floors, silver chandeliers, fireplace, copper-topped bar (stocked with soft drinks), with wonderful handcarved cabinets, leather sofas . . . I could go on and on. The inn is a showplace.

Guest rooms are practically suites, with fireplaces protected by hand-forged screens. Hand-hewned vigas (ceiling beams) and Spanish tile, Mexican light fixtures, little niches, skylights, enormous windows open to the marvelous views, all add to the spacious, gracious ambience of the inn.

The lap pool, 14 x 50 feet, is surrounded by tall windows—you feel like you're swimming outdoors. The spa and exercise equipment area has a changing room, shower, and laundry room, so you don't necessarily have to trek all the way back to your room—this is a very large inn!

Quina becomes enthusiastic just talking about cooking, and the number of guests waiting to be fed does not daunt her in the least.

"I've made as many as nineteen *huevos rancheros*," she says happily. "I do shrimp or seafood omelets, too." With the *huevos rancheros* come potatoes, baked and browned in olive oil, turkey or chicken sausage, and oatmeal with fruit and honey. Other mornings, enchiladas, beans, chorizo, Spanish omelets, and always coffee, cold cereal, and bagels are ready for early skiers.

For dinner, Quina's specialties are *paella* and any other Creole or Spanish dish. The open kitchen is both a chef's dream and pleasing esthetically; the carved doors come from a church in Mexico, "I think Guadalajara, but don't quote me," said Quina.

How to get there: Take Highway 68 north through Taos to blinking light, turn right onto Highway 150. In 2 miles turn left onto Highway 230. The inn will be on your right in another mile.

Innkeepers: Aquilina ("Quina") and Wesley Jackson
Address/Telephone: Highway 230 (mailing address: P.O. Box 24607); phone and fax (505) 776–5777
Rooms: 6; all with private bath and phone, 3 with Jacuzzi; TV/VCR. No smoking inn.
Rates: $200 to $300, double, EPB.
Open: All year.
Facilities and activities: Dinner by reservation; indoor lap pool, spa and exercise equipment; laundry; deck and patios. Nearby: Taos, with its Plaza of shops, art galleries, and restaurants; historic Taos Pueblo; Kit Carson House; Millicent Rogers Museum; Rio Grande Gorge; Taos Ski Valley; hiking; fishing; white-water rafting on Rio Grande; horseback riding; golf.

Casa de Patron

LINCOLN, NEW MEXICO 88338

Innkeepers Cleis (pronounced Cliss) and Jeremy used to camp in nearby Lincoln National Forest, and she fell in love with the little town of Lincoln. We did, too, and could understand when she told us.

"I told Jerry I *had* to live here," Cleis said with a laugh. "He thought I was bananas; this house was a wreck. But it had great charm, and after it was fixed, we decided to share it with others."

The historic nineteenth-century house was the home of Juan Patron, born in 1855. The Jordans decided to name the inn after his family, who lived in the house and kept a store there during the mid-1800s. Young Juan lost his father in an 1873 raid on Lincoln, forerunner of the Lincoln County Wars. Billy the Kid, Sheriff Pat Garrett, murders, and rival mercantile establishments—these are the ingredients of the bloody Lincoln County Wars. We could hardly wait to visit the museums and hear the story; it was pretty wild in Lincoln back then.

But we found plenty of peace and tranquillity in the beautiful forested country, the calm broken only by the festivals and pageants in the tiny town and in nearby Capitan (home of Smokey the Bear) and Ruidoso.

Each guest room in the spanking white adobe-and-viga house is decorated with collectibles and antiques such as the 1800s spinning wheel from Jerry's family back in Deerfield, Illinois. The number 1 Southwestern Room has twin beds and a full bath; number 2 Southwestern Room has a queen-sized bed and washbasin and private bath around the corner; the Old Store has a queen-sized bed, private bath, and outside entry to a patio. We loved the complete privacy of the casitas, and the Jordans are understandably proud of the fact that they built them from scratch. Casa Bonita has a cathedral ceiling in the living area and a spiral staircase winding up to the loft bedroom.

For our breakfast we had Cleis's baked egg soufflé, strawberry walnut muffins, home-fried potatoes, and fresh fruit—in the clear mountain air, appetites are hearty. The huge kitchen has a wonderful collection of washboards, those old-fashioned thingamajigs for scrubbing clothes. Our refreshing evening drinks were enhanced by music, with Cleis at the baby grand in the parlor or at the real live pipe organ in the dining room. The music was professional—Cleis has a master's degree in organ music.

As for dinner, you can drive to La Lorraine in Ruidoso, Chango in Capitan, or Tinnie's Silver Dollar in Tinnie; but, said Cleis with a laugh, "that's one of the reasons why we went into the dinner business (by prior arrangement only): People said, 'What, you mean we have to get in the car and drive 12 miles?'"

A Salon Evening might be a night of ragtime and American cuisine, or German specialties accompanied by suitable music if you're feeling sociable. We went for a walk in the cool mountain air.

How to get there: Casa de Patron is located at the east end of Lincoln on the south side of Highway 380, which runs between Roswell and I–25. The highway is the main and only road through the tiny town.

Innkeepers: Cleis and Jeremy Jordan
Address/Telephone: P.O. Box 27; (505) 653–4676
Rooms: 3, plus 2 two-room casitas; 3 rooms with private bath, casitas with private bath, hide-a-bed, and kitchen; no air conditioning (elevation 5,700 feet). No smoking inn.
Rates: $89, double; $13 extra person, single deduct $10; EPB for main house, continental for casitas; afternoon drinks and snacks.
Open: All year.
Facilities and activities: Dinner by advance reservation. VCR, special entertainment such as German Evenings and musical Salon Evenings. Nearby: Billy the Kid country with state monuments and Heritage Trust museums, Lincoln National Forest, hiking, skiing, horse races at Ruidoso Downs, soap-making and quilting workshops.
Recommended Country Inns® Travelers' Club Benefit: Stay two nights, get third night free, Sunday–Thursday, subject to availability.

Paz de Nogal

NOGAL, NEW MEXICO 88341

Paz de Nogal means "the peace of Nogal," and the name tells all. Situated in an 1856 restored adobe ranch house out in the open country at the edge of the beautiful Sacramento Mountains, with Carrizo Peak in the distance, blue-gray under the wide blue New Mexico sky, the peace is serene and pervasive and romantic.

There's nothing anywhere around but nature—sky, mountains, fields—and horses. Jane boards them on the property, and if you come riding up like cowpokes in a movie, your mount will receive as much friendly hospitality as you will.

The inn was built in the 1880s by Captain Dan Roberts, a Texas Ranger who had a mercantile store in Nogal during gold-mining days. His daughter married Governor Hinkell of New Mexico, and they moved here in the 1930s.

The front door not only is hand-painted, but it also has a turquoise for a doorknob. Common rooms are bright and spacious, with tile floors, oriental rugs, and furnishings both comfortable and eclectic. The Fern Sawyer Room is the sitting room for a two-bedroom suite, and it's named for a woman pioneer on the professional rodeo circuit, who died at 77 with her boots on. (She was All-Around World Cowgirl Champion in 1947.)

The adjoining Crosby Room, named for a 1920s World Champion Cowboy, has shutters decorated with hand-painted bunches of fruit. Open, they decorate the room; closed, they decorate the porch outside.

The Franklin Room has a Franklin stove and a patterned blue-tiled sunken tub. All the lovely tile in the bathrooms was installed by Jane, who bragged, "I'm an expert tiler now!"

The Bunkhouse has a king-sized bed, a kitchen, a blue-and-white tiled bath, and a television/VCR.

Breakfast is hearty: French toast coated with corn flakes is an unusual treat; eggs Benedict, too; sometimes a hearty ranch breakfast of pancakes, bacon and eggs, juice, fruit, zucchini bread, muffins, homemade granola and yogurt, hot cereal of steel cut oats. Another treat is quiche Lorraine with a parmesan cheese crust, fresh garden herbs, broccoli, and zucchini, with tomato slices and a dab of sour cream.

As for dinners, "Southwestern cuisine is my forte!" Jane declared with enthusiasm. Rack of lamb—free range lamb from nearby Circle Bar Ranch—is a specialty. The first course might be African peanut soup with vegetables and sour cream, followed by a fresh garden salad; breaded breast of chicken with garlic, pine nuts, and herbs; wild rice and zucchini; and meringue topped with fresh fruit and whipped or ice cream for a finish.

How to get there: From Ruidoso take Highway 48 north to Highway 37 north to Nogal. The inn is off 37 on the east side of the highway at mile marker 10.

Innkeeper: Jane Kretchman
Address/Telephone: Highway 37 (mailing address: P.O. Box 93); (505) 354–2826
Rooms: 7, including bunkhouse; 5 with private bath, bunkhouse with TV/VCR; pets welcome; smoking permitted.
Rates: $70 to $90, double; $20 extra person; EPB. No credit cards.
Open: All year.
Facilities and activities: Outdoor hot tub, adobe walled courtyard, two sitting rooms, five fireplaces; meals for 12 persons of fewer for special occasions. Nearby: Golfing, skiing at Ski Apache, fishing at Bonito Lake, shopping and dining in Ruidoso, gambling at Inn of the Mountain Gods, gold panning in Nogal Canyon, horseback riding, and, Jane says, "endless national forests for gorgeous hiking."
Recommended Country Inns® Travelers' Club Benefit: 10 percent discount.

Adobe & Pines Inn
RANCHOS DE TAOS, NEW MEXICO 87557

Even the innkeepers admit that if you're not watching for the orange, blue, and turquoise poles that mark the road to the inn, you'll miss the turnoff. But, like us, you can always turn around and look again. And once you find it, you'll get a friendly welcome from Rascal, the cocker-terrier, who, said Charil, "along with our horse Desi, requests no other pets at the inn."

And what an inn; it's full of beauty, beginning with the lovely mural at the end of the 80-foot-long *portale*, a 1950s scene of the famous Taos Pueblo. "We didn't come into this blind," Charil said. "We even hired a consultant who told us what to expect from innkeeping." She laughed. "We've had our eyes opened more ever since."

Like so many happy innkeepers, they were looking for a lifestyle different from their hectic one in San Diego. They sold everything they owned and traveled in Europe for a year. "We didn't know we were doing our homework," Chuck said. They landed in Taos because Chuck had a birthday and Charil surprised him with tickets to the balloon festival in Albuquerque. While there they chanced to look at an advertisement on business opportunities. "Taos was not a plan, but we fell in love, made an offer.

"Then we had three and a half months of intense renovation," Chuck said ruefully of the 150-year-old adobe home on four acres of fruit and pine trees. He brightened up. "But it's all

Charil's decor. She does a dynamite gourmet breakfast, too!"

This was true. It was so gorgeous we left the table to get our cameras for photos before we destroyed the 4-inch-tall puff pastry hiding banana yogurt and the German pancakes smothered with fresh raspberries and golden raisins.

Chuck is no slouch, either, when it comes to muffins. Lemon poppyseed, apple cinnamon . . . "Guests dub them Chuck's killer muffins," Charil said. They've had so many requests for recipes that Chuck has compiled their own Southwest cookbook.

Rooms are beautiful, too. Two open off the portale: Puerta Azul, a blue room with an antique writing desk and a hand-painted kiva fireplace; and Puerta Verde, with green and rust colors and a romantic canopy bed and sitting area by the fireplace. "We utilized the one hundred-year-old 'Dutch' doors," Charil says. They open at the top for a view outside without opening the entire door.

Puerta Rosa, off the courtyard, conceals a surprise under vaulted ceilings: an oversized, sunken bathroom with Mexican tiles surrounding a large cedar sauna (and a separate shower). There's a fireplace to warm the room and another in the bedroom by the sitting area. Puerta Turquesa, a separate guest cottage off the courtyard, has a jet whirlpool bath as well as two fireplaces. There's a kitchen here, too; it was pretty tempting to stay awhile in this romantic hideaway.

During afternoon hors d'oeuvres, we relaxed, eager to hear about the underground tunnel built for escaping from Indians.

How to get there: The inn is off Highway 68 4 miles south of Taos. The turnoff to the inn, which is on the east side of the road, is marked by orange, blue, and turquoise poles 3/10 mile south of St. Francis Plaza and 4 miles north of the Stakeout Grill and Bar. Both landmarks are on the east side of the road.

Innkeepers: Charil and Chuck Fulkerson
Address/Telephone: P.O. Box 837; (505) 751–0947 or (800) 723–8267, fax (505) 758–8423
Rooms: 7; all with private bath, 1 with TV. No smoking inn.
Rates: \$95 to \$150, double; \$20 extra person; EPB and afternoon snacks.
Open: All year.
Facilities and activities: Jet tub. Nearby: Historic St. Francis de Assisi Church; shopping; art galleries; seven minutes from Taos with its historic Plaza, galleries, shops, and restaurants; historic Taos Pueblo; Kit Carson House; Rio Grande Gorge; Taos Ski Valley.
Recommended Country Inns® Travelers' Club Benefit: 10 percent discount, Monday–Thursday.

Casa Europa

TAOS, NEW MEXICO 87571

There's nothing like majestic mountains to bring out the romance in us. Casa Europa, two miles out of town, offers beautiful mountain views in a peaceful country setting. Birds sing, horses graze nearby, silence reigns supreme, and our hosts Rudi and Marcia are very hospitable: Both are used to the public and enjoy entertaining. Before coming to Taos, they were proprietors of a fine restaurant in Boulder, Colorado, for many years.

"But," Rudi said, "I needed to do something with people again."

"He needs to work about eighteen hours a day," Marcia added with a fond laugh.

"Well, we get our guests started, we introduce them, and then they are fine," Rudi explained. We certainly were fine, our only problem being one of indecision at teatime; should we choose the chocolate mousse–filled meringue or the raspberry Bavarian? Or perhaps the Black Forest torte or one of the fresh fruit tarts? (I really wanted one of each, all made by chef Rudi, who was trained at the Grand Hotel in Nuremberg, Germany.)

Breakfast is another such feast prepared by chef Rudi. We had fresh fruit salad, a mushroom-and-asparagus quiche, lean bacon edged in black pepper, home-fried potatoes, and fresh homemade Danish that absolutely melted in my mouth.

The house itself is a treasure, with fourteen skylights and a circular staircase to the gallery above the main salon, displaying the paintings, pottery, and sculpture of local artists, as well as wonderful Navajo rugs. The inn appears deceptively small from the outside; inside, the large common rooms (but very uncommon!), both upstairs and down, lead to six exceptionally spacious and elegant guest rooms. The new large suite in the west wing has five rooms: kitchen, dining room, sitting room, bedroom, and bath, as well as a private hot-tub room and private phone. It's also very comfortable. The wood floors are graced with Oriental rugs; the white stucco walls are hung with original art. The front courtyard is bright with flowers around the Spanish fountain; the European garden in back offers quiet relaxation. The English Room is a departure, with fine antique English furniture. "It goes into a place where people can see it," Marcia said.

Outdoors, there are numerous cats and dogs, and "two horses for petting," said Rudi. "But only outdoors!"

How to get there: Driving into Taos from the south on Highway 68, take Lower Ranchitos Road left at the blinking-light intersection just north of McDonald's and south of Taos Plaza. Go 1½ miles southwest to the intersection of Upper Ranchitos Road, which will be on your right. There's an UPPER RANCHITOS ROAD sign there now, so you'll know it when you see the sign.

Innkeepers: Marcia and Rudi Zwicker
Address/Telephone: 157 Upper Ranchitos Road; (505) 758–9798
Rooms: 6; all with private bath, several with built-in bancos that convert to twin beds; no air conditioning (elevation 7,000 feet). No smoking inn.
Rates: $85 to $135, double; $20 extra person; EPB and afternoon tea.
Open: All year.
Facilities and activities: Swedish sauna, hot tub, three private courtyards. Nearby: historic Taos Plaza with restaurants, shops, and art galleries; hiking, horseback riding, and winter skiing; Taos Indian Pueblo and museums.
Recommended Country Inns® Travelers' Club Benefit: 10 percent discount.

The Browning Plantation

CHAPPELL HILL, TEXAS 77426

We felt like Scarlett O'Hara and Rhett Butler—or maybe Ashley and Melanie—driving up to this beautiful antebellum mansion hidden in the woods. This elegant mansion easily could be awed by its own splendor; but with Dick and Mildred as innkeepers, the spirit of fun rules instead.

"We have a good time," Dick said. "People don't want to hear how the house was put together or how old Browning died. Mildred and I tell them all *our* troubles, and we have a good laugh instead."

Still, the Ganchans have made an entertaining story of the resurrection of the old Browning plantation, which was truly a formidable undertaking. Mildred was looking for a cute little Victorian house to move to their property elsewhere when they made the mistake of stopping by to see a place that "needed a little attention." What they saw was a completely ruined mansion left over from cotton-and-slavery days.

Listed on the National Register of Historic Places, the inn once again has the fake wood graining that was the height of elegance back when the house was built in the 1850s. Daughter Meg Ganchan Rice spent ages practicing the technique as her contribution to the family restoration effort.

Upstairs guest rooms in the big house have 12-foot ceilings and massive windows and are furnished with nineteenth-century antiques, including plantation and tester beds.

Where to relax is a choice that can be difficult: the parlor, the library, or the south veranda, with its beautiful view over the vast acres of green farmland? Or for an even more breathtaking scene, climb three flights to the rooftop widow's walk that crowns the house.

And there is more. One son-in-law is such a train buff that he has built a model railroad on the property, and if he's in residence, you may be able to cajole him into a ride. "He has more rolling stock than the Santa Fe," Dick brags as he proudly shows off the new two-room "depot" he designed, a replica of a Santa Fe original. Guest rooms inside the depot have horizontal pine paneling and blue-striped-ticking curtains and bedspreads.

You'll feel like Scarlett and Rhett all over again at breakfast around the huge dining table, eating dishes like the inn's Eggs Sardou accompanied by a hot fruit compote. But first there's an Orange Julius eye-opener, and maybe there will also be hot biscuits. There's a social hour with snacks before dinner, too.

How to get there: From U.S. Highway 290 east of Brenham, take FM 1155 south until you come to a short jog to the left. Immediately to your right you'll see a dirt road. Turn right onto it; continue south across the cattle guard and under the arch of trees until you reach the plantation house.

Innkeepers: Mildred and Dick Ganchan
Address/Telephone: Route 1, Box 8; (409) 836–6144
Rooms: 6 in main house and Model Railroad Depot; 2 with private bath, 2 with TV. No smoking inn.
Rates: $90 to $120, double; $15 extra person; EPB and evening snacks. No credit cards.
Open: All year.
Facilities and activities: Swimming pool, model train with 1½ miles of track, 220 acres of natural trails, fishing in lakes on property. Nearby: historic sites in Washington-on-the-Brazos and Independence, Star of the Republic Museum, miniature horses at Monastery of St. Clare; good restaurant in Brenham.

Hôtel St. Germain

DALLAS, TEXAS 75201

For sheer luxury, unabashed, unashamed sybaritic living, the small and elegant Hôtel St. Germain takes the prize. Well, it's already taken several prizes, like the *Inn Business Review*'s naming the St. Germain "one of the outstanding inns of 1992."

The inn, a beautiful residence built in 1906, is architecturally imposing. The white, three-story structure has two balconies on the left and two curved porches on the right, with black wrought-iron railings, which also frame two sets of stairs to the curved driveway in front. French doors lead out, and in the stairwell, a huge twenty-four-paned window is crowned with a glass arch.

With its impressive foyer, 14-foot ceilings, sumptuous parlor, stately library, and lavish suites, it takes all the adjectives in *Roget's Thesaurus* to describe this inn adequately. The antique pieces alone are a feast for the eyes.

"My mom was an antique dealer," Claire said, pointing out the Aubusson carpets, the Mallard beds, and huge armoires. "We serve on antique Limoges—my grandmother's heavy gold china—Waterford crystal, and sterling." She alternates eight different sets of china; they're stored in the china cabinet in the small dining room.

The large dining room has bay windows of decorative glass, topped with an extravagant valence over Austrian shades. The crystal chandelier is palatial. Beyond is a romantic New Orleans–style walled courtyard. Breakfast here took on another dimension: The chive and cheese quiche and blueberry muffins tasted like nectar and ambrosia.

Soft classical music played in the library, and there is a grand buffet piano for more personalized music. The original wallpaper is charming, and we enjoyed looking at the before-and-after-renovation photographs in the hall.

Suite One, a huge room decorated in rose and gray, has a rose spread and a high canopy over the bed. Suite Three has what appears to be a larger-than-life king-sized bed, which can be divided into two twins. The sitting room has a lovely antique Belgian sofa, and there's a separate dressing room. Suite Four boasts a Jacuzzi as well as a Mallard bed, a huge armoire, and a sitting area with a sofa and fireplace.

The Dangerous Liaison Suite is 600 square feet of blue, green, and gold. Beside the bed, there's a bed-lounge in the wall, a Cheval mirror, and antique Mallard furniture. In the sitting area are a fireplace and a sparkling chandelier.

The Smith Suite, on the third floor, overlooks downtown Dallas. The Napoleon sleigh bed has a crown canopy, and there is a Victorian sitting area, complete with fireplace. The padded cloth walls are another example of sheer luxury, an atmosphere that the Jacuzzi in the bath does nothing to dispel.

Hôtel St. Germain is really a taste of another world!

How to get there: From Central Expressway exit at Hall Street; turn right to Cole. At Cole turn left onto Cedar Springs, take a left onto Maple Avenue and go half a block. From North Dallas Toll Road, heading south, pass the Wycliff exit and veer to the left as you curve around to the first traffic light, which is Wolf Street. Turn left for 2½ blocks to Maple, turn right, crossing Cedar Springs to the inn, the large white mansion with a curved driveway.

Innkeeper: Claire Heymann
Address/Telephone: 2516 Maple Avenue; (214) 871–2516, fax (214) 871–0740
Rooms: 7; all with private bath, TV, and radio. Smoking permitted except in dining room.
Rates: $225 to $600, double, continental breakfast.
Open: All year.
Facilities and activities: Dinner by reservation only; bar service, room service, valet parking; guest privileges at the Centrum Health Club. Nearby: downtown Dallas, with Dallas Museum of Art, Kennedy Memorial, Old City Park, Reunion Tower, West End Historic District, Farmer's Market, more.
Business travel: Located in downtown Dallas. Phone in all rooms; fax.

Sunset Heights Inn

EL PASO, TEXAS 79902

Built in 1905 up in the high and mighty area of El Paso overlooking downtown, this inn on the National Register of Historic Homes is a three-story corner house of dark-yellow brick surrounded by an iron fence. Tall palm trees wave over it, and we strolled around the large grounds of almost an acre, which are graced by roses blooming much of the year. "Twenty-nine bushes," Richard says, while he confesses that he doesn't take care of it all by himself.

Food, gourmet food, is his specialty, and you won't be able to predict what he'll feed you for breakfast, because he doesn't know himself. "I don't decide what to serve until I look at my guests the evening before," he said, which brought forth a contented groan from an earlier guest, who was recovering from the morning-before feast in a corner of the beautifully decorated parlor.

The five- to seven-course meal was more like a lunch or dinner buffet than a breakfast. It began with prunes in cream and went on to quiche served with kiwi and purple grapes; then came Cordon Bleu chicken on rice with tomato and avocado, and eggs Benedict with papaya and star fruit, followed by angel-food cake with blueberry yogurt. This took us through the day until the champagne and late-night snacks.

Richard, late of the military, raised three daughters by himself and learned to cook in self-defense. "We entertained a lot and couldn't afford a cook, so we all learned to cook. When the girls were small, sometimes we had sit-down dinners for thirty." But he prefers buffet because "people circulate better." Now at Sunset he has a helper in daughter Kim, responsible for many of the gourmet meals they serve.

Roni, who is a practicing physician, displays a second talent in the decorating of the inn. She did most of the pleasing color selections, while much of the furnishings are antiques from Richard's family. The parlor has a Victrola dating from 1919, and it still plays. Although the old table radio is a replica, the kerosene lamp is one Richard studied by when he was a boy on a farm in Oklahoma. "We didn't have electricity," he said. "That old lamp got me through school." But what we admired the most was the wonderful coromandel screen behind the old sewing machine in the parlor. Richard tells the story of how he was able to get it out of China—back when we weren't speaking to China—by shipping it through Panama.

The inn is a decorator's dream, with beautifully coordinated fabrics and wall coverings, mirrored doors, and sybaritic bathrooms. The Oriental Room has another coromandel screen as well as a brass bed. The bathroom, with brass fixtures and a huge bathtub, is on what was once a porch. But not to worry: All the windows are now one-way mirrors.

How to get there: From I–10 West take Porfiro Diaz exit and turn right for 2 blocks to Yandell. Turn right for 6 blocks (count the ones on the right, not the left) to Randolph, and the inn is on the far corner to the left.

Innkeepers: Richard Barnett and Roni Martinez
Address/Telephone: 717 West Yandell; (919) 544–1743 or (800) 767–8513
Rooms: 5; all with private bath, phone, and TV; wheelchair accessible (electric chair lift from first to second floor). No smoking inn.
Rates: \$80 to \$165, double, EPB.
Open: All year.
Facilities and activities: Dinner for minimum of six people; pool and Jacuzzi. Nearby: many museums and historic fort, old Spanish missions, Tigua Indian Reservation, zoo, scenic drive, Ciudad Juárez in Mexico just across the Rio Grande.
Business travel: Located 5 blocks from downtown El Paso. Fax, all rooms have phones.
Recommended Country Inns® Travelers' Club Benefit: 10 percent discount each night; or or stay two nights, get third night free; or stay five separate nights, get sixth night free (for regular travelers); offers not combinable.

The Veranda Country Inn

FORT DAVIS, TEXAS 79734

If you're really serious about getting away, this Texas outpost is the perfect place. Fort Davis is set in the Davis Mountains of far west Texas, and the Wild West ruins of Fort Davis are there to haunt you—in a nice way, of course, by reminding you of more simple times gone by (but more dangerous, too!).

"We find we're sort of a refuge," Kathie Woods said of the very small town. "Professionals from the hectic life actually 'tear up' when they tell us what a pleasant weekend they've had! Many of them work sixteen hours a day, and they really need a place to relax and rest."

The inn was called the Lempert Hotel back in 1883 when it was built by W. S. Lempert, who was a mail guard and scout for the Overland Trail.

"By 1880 the area was considered free of the Indian menace," Kathie said. Evidently so, since in 1884 the new hotel hosted Quannah Parker, son of Comanche Chief Peta Nocona and white captive Cynthia Ann Parker (one of the romantic and colorful episodes in Texas history).

Kathie and Paul have restored many of the features of the old adobe building, preserving the pine floors, the 14-foot-high ceilings, and the transom windows of the original hotel. The adobe walls are 2 feet thick, making air conditioning in the cool mountain air totally unnecessary.

The Veranda of the inn's name is the place to relax. We spent hours out there in the cool of the evening, rocking away and watching the stars—"Our sky here is famous," Kathie said.

But there are also two secluded walled courtyards, with large shade trees, lilac bushes, and irises. The entire grounds take up a city block, and there are roses and other flowering plants, as well as an herb and a vegetable garden. There's even an orchard, with apples and figs, peaches and apricots, as well as grape and blackberry vines.

Much of this good gardening turns up at breakfast. A favorite are Scotch eggs, hard-boiled and wrapped in sausage, rolled in breadcrumbs and then browned. Or Kathie's special German farmer's omelet, which won Kathie a first prize at the Alpine Fair, served at the inn with homemade biscuits and sour cream coffee cake.

There's always fresh fruit—remember the orchard!— yogurt, and both dry and hot cereal for lighter eaters.

Rooms are roomy, and although baths are private to each room, many had to be built across the hall because of the building's age. But thick, soft Egyptian cotton robes are provided for those whose bath is not attached to the room. Half the baths have large "soaking tubs"; the rest have showers, so take your pick. Linens are hung outside to dry in the fresh mountain air—think how deliciously fragrant that makes them!

How to get there: One block west of the Courthouse. (Kathie says, "We do not describe our location in terms of the Overland Trail, because all streets in Fort Davis are unmarked, and people cannot readily locate the Overland Trail.")

Innkeepers: Kathie and Paul Woods
Address/Telephone: 210 Court Avenue (mailing address: P. O. Box 1238), (915) 426–2233
Rooms: 8 in the main house and the Carriage House just behind the main building, all with private bath, plus 3 "extra" for guest use. No smoking inn.
Rates: $54 to $75, double; $10 extra person; EPB.
Open: All year.
Facilities and activities: Courtyards, walled garden, orchards, rocking chairs on the verandas. Nearby: restaurants in the Limpia Hotel and The Drug Store, Fort Davis National Historic Site, Overland Trail Museum, Neill Doll Museum, Davis Mountain State Park, McDonald Observatory, Big Bend National Park.

The Gilded Thistle

GALVESTON, TEXAS 77550

We asked innkeeper Helen Hanemann to explain The Gilded Thistle's name, because it seemed to be a contradiction. Helen, very much into the island's history, said that like native thistle, sturdy Texas pioneer stock sank deep and lasting roots into the sandy island soil, building a Galveston that flowered into a gilded age of culture and wealth.

Her home was part of those people and their times—in the late 1800s Galveston's Strand was known as "the Wall Street of the West"—and The Gilded Thistle is a lovely memorial to Galveston's past.

The beautiful antiques throughout the house make it an exceptionally elegant place to stay, but the atmosphere is so homey that our awe melted away to pure admiration. Helen is on duty at all times, and we joined the other guests in her kitchen, watching her arrange the fresh flowers that fill the rooms.

It wasn't hard to get used to being served on fine china, with coffee or tea from a family silver service. Breakfast, Helen says, is "whenever you want," so we could sleep late and then eat lazily on the L-shaped screened porch around the dining room, especially enjoying Helen's specialty, "nut chewies," and her crispy waffles. Guests might also have Pat's fulsome scrambled eggs, country sausage, spicy baked potatoes, and homemade biscuits. "That'll take them through lunch," he said.

Tea and coffee are available at all times, and we loved it when our morning began with orange juice and a pot of boiling water for coffee or tea at our bedroom door.

The evening snack tray could almost take the place of dinner; there are strawberries and grapes and other fruit in season, ham and cheese and roast beef sandwiches, at least four kinds of cheese, and wine. And if after that you don't feel like going out, Pat will rustle up something gourmet, such as a bowl of his seafood gumbo with special rice and French bread, compliments of the house.

The Gilded Thistle has been gilded horticulturally: In recent years the inn's landscaping has won two prizes, the Springtime Broadway Beauty Contest and an award for a business in a historic building. And now there's a lovely new gazebo. But the climate never makes it easy and has given rise to the Texas saying (borrowed from Mark Twain) that if you don't like the weather, wait a minute, it'll change. "A few years ago we had that bitter winter," Helen said. "Now we've put in lawn sprinklers and wouldn't you know—too much rain."

In the evening we took a leisurely stroll down Broadway, admiring the oleander lining the esplanade, a Galveston landmark.

How to get there: Stay on Highway 45 South, which becomes Broadway as soon as you cross the causeway onto Galveston Island. The inn is just beyond 18th Street, on the right.

Innkeepers: Helen and Pat Hanemann
Address/Telephone: 1805 Broadway; (409) 763–0194 or (800) 654–9380
Rooms: 3; 1 with private bath, all with TV and TTD for hearing impaired. No smoking inn.
Rates: $125 to $175, per room, EPB and snack tray in evening.
Open: All year.
Facilities and activities: Discounted tickets to Galveston Racquetball Club for exercise, tennis, and golf. Nearby: historic Ashton Villa and the Bishop's Palace; the historic Strand, with Galveston Art Center, Galveston County Historical Museum, Railroad Museum, shops and restaurants; the Seawall and Gulf Coast beaches, Moody Gardens Rainforest Pyramid, Texas Seaport Museum.
Business travel: Laptop computer, modem, fax, copier, separate trunk line; cater to small meetings for up to 20; corporate rates.

La Colombe d'Or

HOUSTON, TEXAS 77006

We didn't have to go to France for romance; this very special inn is patterned after one of the same name in St. Paul de Vence, France, where many famous French painters traded their work for lodging. Houston's La Colombe d'Or ("the golden dove") is hung with fine art, too, and each suite has a name I certainly recognized.

We stayed in the Van Gogh Suite, named for one of our favorite Impressionist painters. Others are named for Degas, Cézanne, Monet, and Renoir; the largest suite, up at the top, is called simply The Penthouse. The suites are decorated with fine art, although there are no original works of their namesakes.

But we hardly miss them, so swathed in beauty and luxury were we in this prince of an inn. On our coffee table we found fruit, Perrier water, and wine glasses waiting to be filled from my complimentary bottle of the inn's own imported French wine.

Owner Steve Zimmerman has succeeded in bringing to the La Colombe d'Or the casual elegance of the French Riviera. European and American antiques, as well as his own collection of prominent artists' works, are set in the luxurious house that was once the home of Exxon founder Walter Fondren and his family.

The twenty-one-room mansion, built in 1923, is divided into suites. Each consists of a huge bedroom with a sitting area and a glass-enclosed dining room where Queen Anne furniture, china plates, linen napkins, and cutlery are in readiness for breakfast. As soon as we rang in the morning, a waiter arrived with a tea cart from which he served a very French-style plate of sliced kiwi fruit, raspberries, and strawberries; orange juice; coffee; and croissants with butter and jam. We ate this artistic offering surrounded by the green leafy boughs waving outside our glass room.

You may have luncheon or dinner served in your room, too, but we feasted downstairs on meunière of shrimp and lobster, cream of potato and leek soup, the inn's Caesar salad, and capon Daniel; and as if that weren't enough, we ended with crème brûlée!

If you long to visit France, you may decide you don't have to once you've visited La Colombe d'Or. The inn is a member of *Relais et Châteaux*, a French organization that guarantees excellence, and we absolutely soaked up the hospitality, tranquillity, and luxury.

How to get there: 3410 Montrose is between Westheimer and Alabama, both Houston thoroughfares.

Innkeeper: Steve Zimmerman
Address/Telephone: 3410 Montrose Boulevard; (713) 524–7999
Rooms: 6 suites; all with private bath; wheelchair accessible.
Rates: $195 to $575, per suite, EP.
Open: All year.
Facilities and activities: Restaurant, bar. Nearby: within five minutes, Houston central business district, Houston Museum of Fine Arts, Rice University, and Menil Art Foundation; the Astrodome.
Business travel: Located 5 miles from downtown Houston. Fax, computer, typing, printer available.

Gruene Mansion

NEW BRAUNFELS, TEXAS 78130

Sharon and Bill not only wanted a resort, they wanted one with history. They found it in the Gruene Mansion, set on a historic cotton plantation on the banks of the Guadalupe River.

The inn is located within the Gruene (pronounced "green") Historic District on the northern edge of New Braunfels's city limits. "Bill and I really like the history of Gruene Mansion," Sharon said. "We feel as if we're caretakers of the property, and we try to carry on the tradition of *gemutlich* begun by Henry Gruene back in the mid-1800s."

Gruene Dance Hall, just down the street, is the oldest dance hall in Texas. Sharon spoke of the original owner as though she knew him. "Henry built the hall for the closeness and warmness of his friends. He also had a little house where travelers could come and stay; they just had to replace the logs for the fire. He was kind to strangers, and we wanted to live that way. It's the best way to meet people."

Curious, we wandered down to Gruene Dance Hall for a beer and some Texas two-stepping. We were thrilled to find live music. We dined next door at the Grist Mill Restaurant, housed in the ruins of a hundred-year-old cotton gin beneath a water tower on the banks of the Guadalupe River, with its pretty little rapids and its happy white-water rafters, many floating down from Canyon River when the water's right.

Cottages with little porches overhang the river, and they are furnished with antiques and handmade quilts; each room is different. Sharon had a great time decorating—imagine having seventeen rooms to design!

We loved Fireside Lodge #2 with its slanted ceiling, papered with a pretty flowered wallpaper of pink and blue flowers on a black background. You can imagine the interesting contrast that makes with the rough wood paneling, made from both poplar and yellow pine. The fireplace wall is white stone; the brass bed has a colorful patchwork quilt and a crocheted afghan laid across the foot. (Feet can get chilly on cool Hill Country nights.)

But tempting, too, was Bluebonnet Lodge, with huge bluebonnets painted on the walls, both bedroom and bath. The shower curtain in the bath is an old quilt (protected by a liner, of course) and dolled up with a pointed lace valance—Sharon has many original ideas. Walls in the Grand River Lodge are painted bright blue between the wood strips and stenciled with red and yellow stylized tulips.

New is the "Sunday Haus" with eight rooms decorated in Victorian rustic elegance. King-sized beds, fireplaces, old Victorian bathtubs, and antiques make the *haus* (German for house) a great addition to the inn.

How to get there: From I–35 take exit 191 (Canyon Lake) and go west on Highway 306 for 1½ miles, following the Gruene Historical signs. Turn left into Gruene and go to the end of the road. The inn is on the right as you turn left onto Gruene Road.

Innkeepers: Sharon and Bill McCaskell
Address/Telephone: 1275 Gruene Road; (210) 629–2641 or –8372, fax (210) 629–7375
Rooms: 25, in assorted cottages on the river; all with private bath and TV. No smoking inn.
Rates: $85 to $200, double; $10 extra person; breakfast $5 extra. No credit cards.
Open: All year.
Facilities and activities: Restaurant and bar overlooking the river. Nearby: Grist Mill Restaurant; Gruene Dance Hall; antiques; museums: Hummel, Sophienburg, Handmade Furniture, and Children's; Schlitterbahn Water Park; rafting, tubing, and swimming on Guadalupe and Comal rivers; bicycling; horseback riding; golf; tennis; Natural Bridge Caverns and Wildlife Ranch; Canyon Lake, with fishing, boating, swimming, and waterskiing; discount shopping malls.
Business travel: Located a half hour from downtown San Antonio and San Marcos. Lodge meeting facilities for 300; fax, video, computer setups available; catering.

The Ogé House

SAN ANTONIO, TEXAS 78204

If you're looking for a proper mansion, you have found it. A tall, three-story building squared off by a set of porches top and bottom, the Ogé House looms ahead at the end of the street, looking almost like a misplaced plantation house. But not too misplaced, because it's set on large, lovely grounds ending only at San Antonio's famous river.

The Ogé House (pronounced "oh-jhay"—it's French) is one of the most magnificent homes to be found in San Antonio's historic King William District of fine homes. It was built in 1857 for Louis Ogé, a pioneer cattle rancher and a Texas Ranger.

Like many old beauties, the home had become an apartment house, but it was just waiting for Sharrie and Patrick to find it. They had been looking, driving up the East Coast for six weeks, before they realized that this was where they wanted to be.

"I used to redo old houses back East," Sharrie said. "And we'd been collecting antiques for ten, twelve years." Visiting her father here, they heard that the old house might be available.

The house is huge, with two guest rooms opening off the majestic lobby, which is actually the second floor, since you climb eleven steps up to the front door. Once there you'll admire the antique French set of two settees and two chairs. "They're from a private suite in the Waldorf

Astoria in New York," Patrick says.

The Library, at the rear of the house, is relaxing, with soft-yellow walls, white woodwork, satin-striped sofas, and books (although "there are books all over the house," as Sharrie says). The brass bucket in The Library is filled with menus from the city's many fine eating places.

Upstairs (third floor) the Giles and Mathis suites both open onto the porch across the front of the house, while Riverview, off the landing by the back stairs, is intensely private, with its own porch and view of the river.

Down below, on the main level, the Mitchell Suite has a platform canopy bed. The Bluebonnet Room is done in Texas antiques, with a four-poster rolling-pin bed and the desk of an old Texas judge. But that's all we found of Texas.

"We're not a Texas country inn," Sharrie says. "We have more of the flavor of a small European hotel or an English country manor house."

Sharrie's "Deluxe Continental Breakfast" begins with poached pears and goes on to such delicacies as pecan log roll, apple torte, cherry cheese cake, and fruit pasties.

You can join everyone for breakfast in the dining room, take it out on the front veranda, or go out on the grounds and sit overlooking the river. "We're on one and a half acres, and when all the trees leaf out in the summer, you can't see any of the neighbors. We couldn't believe we were in downtown San Antonio!"

How to get there: From I–35 take 281 south and exit at Durango. Turn right and go through three traffic lights to St. Mary's. Take the first left to Pancoast, and the inn is head on at the end of the street.

Innkeepers: Sharrie and Patrick Magatagan
Address/Telephone: 209 Washington; (210) 223–2353 or (800) 242–2770, fax (210) 226–5812
Rooms: 10; all with private bath and TV. No smoking inn.
Rates: $135 to $195, double, deluxe continental breakfast.
Open: All year.
Facilities and activities: Parking. Nearby: Downtown San Antonio, with The Alamo, La Villita, Convention Center, museums, RiverCenter Mall, El Mercado.
Business travel: Located 5 blocks from downtown San Antonio. Direct-access phone lines, fax, copier, computer hookups, corporate rates.

Mulberry Manor

SWEETWATER, TEXAS 79556

It's a surprise to discover a mansion like Mulberry Manor in a town the size of Sweetwater (about 12,000 population). It was built in 1913 for banker, businessman, and rancher Thomas Trammell—and the architect was John Young, father of movie star Loretta Young.

Which may account for the Hollywood glamor of this showplace. The focal point of the mansion is a glass-domed atrium, filled with green plants and sunshine, in the center of the house. A white, slatted fence encloses this, the heart of the house, and the inn's rooms surround it. The formal French parlor to the right of the entry is furnished in authentic Louis Quinze; the tailored parlor on the left also contains lovely pieces, garnered from all over.

"Just about everything is from estate sales and antiques shops," Beverly said. "We bought everything in this house on weekends." This gave them something to do while the house was being restored.

The house had a checkered life after the Trammells were gone. To give you some idea of the scale, in 1923 it became Sweetwater and Nolan County's only hospital. Then, like many old homes, the 9,800-square-foot house was divided into apartments. Eventually, it somehow became part of the estate of the brother of General Clair Chennault of the famous Flying Tigers.

The house has three downstairs guest rooms plus a vast suite upstairs. The separate barroom has an oversized television screen and a sitting area. The formal dining room is impressive, but so is the so-called breakfast room, with its brocaded French chairs, a beautiful mirrored sideboard, and an oriental rug on the polished wood floor.

But most exotic is the upstairs suite, which Beverly describes as "neo-classical." To give you an idea of the size, originally it was a ballroom. "It was an apartment, and it was horrible," Beverly shudders. Now, on the huge expanse of white carpet, the furniture is gold and black, with green plants (there's even a fern behind the king headboard). A statuary group, busts of classical figures, occupies a corner. The adjoining bath is suitably sybaritic.

Breakfast is as opulent as the manor: fresh fruit compote, eggs Benedict or quiche, hashed browns, sausage or ham, biscuits and gravy, cinnamon raisin biscuits, strawberry cream cheese on croissants. And afternoons there's a big snack tray with the beverage of your choice; our snack was cream puffs filled with ham salad. Who does all this? "Me. I'm the cook!" Beverly says.

Her dinners are spectacular seven-course meals, too.

And to cap it all off, Raymond takes guests for a fun ride in that shiny 1929 Model A Ford out front.

How to get there: Take exit 244 off I–20 and go north 4 blocks to Sam Houston Street and number 1400. There's a sign on the model A Ford out in front.

Innkeepers: Beverly and Raymond Stone
Address/Telephone: 1400 Sam Houston Street; (915) 235–3811 or (800) 235–3811
Rooms: 6; all with private bath, 2 with TV; wheelchair accessible. Pets welcome.
Rates: $60 to $195, double; $7.50 extra person; EPB and afternoon snacks.
Open: All year.
Facilities and activities: Lunch and dinner by reservation, hot tub. Nearby: horseback riding; golf; Pioneer City–County Museum; lakes Sweetwater, Trammell, and Oak Creek Reservoir with fishing, boating, and water sports; World's Largest Rattlesnake Roundup (March).
Business travel: Office available with computer and fax; phones in rooms.

Charnwood Hill Inn

TYLER, TEXAS 75701

We found it pretty romantic to experience the style of living enjoyed by an old-time Texas oilman. Charnwood Hill Inn was built around 1860 by a Professor Hand, who was headmaster of a school for girls. The mansion passed through several hands until it was purchased by H. L. Hunt in the early 1930s.

"The Hunt family extensively remodeled and redecorated," Don said as we wandered through the tall-ceilinged rooms full of opulent furniture.

We weren't sure what sort of furnishings the Hunts had when this gorgeous mansion was their home, but it would have to be something to equal Patsy and Don's collection. "We spent seventeen years collecting and didn't want to get rid of it," Don said. They needed to find a place worthy of such beautiful antiques, and Charnwood Hill shows them off to perfection. Patsy and Don bought the home in 1978.

We were in a mansion, all right. Common areas of the inn include the formal living room, library, television room, the Great Hall on the first floor and the Lodge on the second floor, the Garden Room, the Gathering Hall, the front and east balconies, screened swing porch, front porches, the arbor, and the beautiful east and west gardens. "Tyler's famous Azalea Trail starts right outside of this house," Don said.

Tyler considers itself "Rose Capital of the

World," and the annual Texas Rose Festival is an important local event. Margaret Hunt was Rose Queen in 1935; and JoAnne Miller, daughter of the then-owner of the home, was Rose Queen in 1954. Both times the Queen's Tea was held in the gardens.

A pair of curved steps leads up to the white-columned entrance. The large foyer and living room are stately. The dining room is impressive, with a handmade table and ten chairs of solid pecan, a Chinoiserie breakfront displaying antique Meissen china, an oriental rug, and a delicate chandelier. It makes a contrast to the bright breakfast room, although even that, in its way, is formal, with its glass tables, chairs covered with summery floral fabric, bricked floor, and branched chandelier.

The 1,500-square-foot Art Deco Suite on the third floor was constructed for the two Hunt daughters; the gray carpet makes a perfect foil for the Chinoiserie pieces and the print fabric on a black background. The second-floor sleeping porch and one bedroom were converted into what is now called The Lodge, which has a bar, television, and lots of room for meetings.

Breakfast on weekends is a full gourmet feast. Eggs Benedict is served with an inn specialty—a tasty breakfast potato casserole—and a mèlange of mixed fruits, and juices, coffee, and tea. If you wish, at 4:00 P.M. Patsy will serve a Lemon Tea of cheesecake with fresh fruit.

Dinners are as you like, also, with Texas steak a specialty.

How to get there: From I–20 take Highway 69 south to North Broadway, which becomes South Broadway at Tyler Square. Continue south 4 blocks to Charnwood and turn left. The inn is on the right, and there's a sign.

Innkeepers: Patsy and Don Walker; and Andy Walker
Address/Telephone: 223 East Charnwood; (903) 597–3980, fax (903) 592–6473
Rooms: 7, including 1 suite; all with private bath, 5 with TV. No smoking inn.
Rates: $95 to $270, double; $15 extra person, single $15 less; EPB weekends; a lighter meal is served on weekdays.
Open: All year.
Facilities and activities: Tea and dinner by reservation, elevator, gift shop. Nearby: Municipal Rose Garden & Museum, Brookshire's World of Wildlife Museum and Country Store, Hudnall Planetarium, Caldwell Zoo, Azalea Trail, Texas Rose Festival, East Texas State Fair.
Business travel: Located near downtown Tyler; The Lodge for meetings. Corporate rates; fax.

The Inn Above Onion Creek

WIMBERLEY, TEXAS 78676

This inn is a true retreat, set on five-hundred acres of the Texas Hill Country, 5 miles away from the nearest town: tiny Kyle, once the home of novelist Katherine Ann Porter.

Janie and John knew exactly what they wanted, but it took longer to find than they expected. "Looking at land was a lot of fun," Janie said. "We wanted to be no more than 30 miles from Austin, yet off a picturesque road that made you feel you were going back in time."

While the setting is rural, the accommodations are not. Each room is large, with room for a sitting area of sofa, love seat, or chaise in front of a stone fireplace. Shelves to put things on are built on one side of each fireplace, and there is room to move around the bed and bedside tables.

And the bathrooms are to rave about. John, into major hydrotherapy, said, "Shoot the budget on bathrooms!" The results are stupendous. Four of them have huge Jacuzzis, several have large, two-party showers enclosed in glass bricks, and for light, several have French doors opening onto small wrought-iron balconies.

The exterior is rustic. "We were really trying to find an old ranch house to save, but they turned out to be scarce," Janie said. So they built their own old ranch house out of cedar and Hill Country stone; upstairs porch railings, of rough cedar posts, are very early-homestead evoking!

Breakfast is a delicious torta of venison sausage ("My son and my husband are the mighty hunters," Janie said), eggs, parmesan and cheddar cheese, with O'Brien potatoes and homemade biscuits, all prefaced by Rio Star grapefruit, the *crème de la crème* of the famous Texas Ruby Red.

For dinner—"supper" in these parts—we had chicken *enchiladas suizas*, black beans, corn dip Olé, and Oreo cheesecake.

The wide porches in the rear look out over miles and miles of Hill Country, with not a sign of civilization in sight. The Capt. Fergus Kyle Room, downstairs, is both wheelchair accessible and wheelchair prepared, with railings and a wheel-in shower.

The Jack Hayes Room upstairs, in a rust-and-gray color scheme, has a king-sized bed and a chaise lounge in front of its stone fireplace.

Both the Hayes Room and the Michaelis Room next door open onto a porch with a wonderful north view. Convenient, too: There are back stairs leading down to the swimming pool.

The Michaelis Room's accent wall is a medium blue, very pleasant. All rooms have wonderful huge armoires, and I wondered how Janie had found so many. "I haunted antiques and garage sales—and watched the ads like crazy!" She also found an artisan who could build her some of the rustic-looking pieces she wanted, such as the tables and chairs in the large dining room.

How to get there: From I–35 take exit 213, Kyle, and go west on Kyle's main Center Street to the stop sign at FM 150. Take FM 150 and go 5³⁄₁₀ miles to the inn gate on the right—there is a sign. Turn in at the gate and go 1 mile, slowly, on a narrow, curved road until you reach the inn.

Innkeepers: Janie and John Orr, Suzanne Johnson

Address/Telephone: 4444 Highway 150 West (mailing address: P.O. Box 2230); (512) 268–1617, fax (512) 268–1090

Rooms: 6; all with private bath, telephone, and TV, 1 with wheelchair access. No smoking inn.

Rates: $125 to $225, double; $30 extra person; EPB.

Open: All year.

Facilities and activities: Lunch and dinner; meeting room; swimming pool; 5 miles of trails in the Hill Country, leading to an overlook of Onion Creek; cooking, art class, and musical weekends. Nearby; San Marcos: with outlet shopping mall; canoeing, tubing, and swimming on the San Marcos River; galleries, restaurants and shops in Wimberley and Gruene.

Business travel: Meeting room for 15 persons, meals served upon request.

Rocky Mountain Region

by Doris Kennedy

In an attempt to select the most romantic inns from the many hundreds I have visited, I first asked myself what I would look for when choosing such an accommodation for my husband and myself. Next I interviewed friends and colleagues, questioning them as to the qualities they would seek in their ideal hideaway for two.

I discovered most of us pretty much thought the same, with the main difference being in the order of preference.

As for me, I would look for a secluded place, private, with soothing sounds in the form of birdsong, the steady chirp of crickets, the rush of a river, or the distant call of coyotes at dusk.

Luxurious or rustic, either would be fine; but if a turret room were available, I would absolutely have to have it, for here we would leisurely sip morning coffee and take turns reading aloud. I would like a fireplace and perhaps a four-poster canopied in ruffles and lace, or one made of rough-hewn logs and covered with billowy quilts.

No phones, please. And if a television must be present, let it be hidden away in an armoire.

Blessed is the innkeeper who is attentive yet discreet. Guests seeking a romantic rendezvous want to be greeted warmly, then graciously left alone. Let the innkeeper spin his or her magic by leaving treats and morning coffee outside the door and, while we are out, a fresh rose on the bed, a pitcher of ice water spiked with floating fresh strawberries, and a love poem or a sachet of potpourri under the pillows.

Flowers, candles, adjustable soft lighting, and a nearby wood or a park for wandering hand in hand would be nice.

Most of all, let it be peaceful, where hushed conversations proceed without interruption, where secrets are shared and promises made, and where cherished memories have their beginnings.

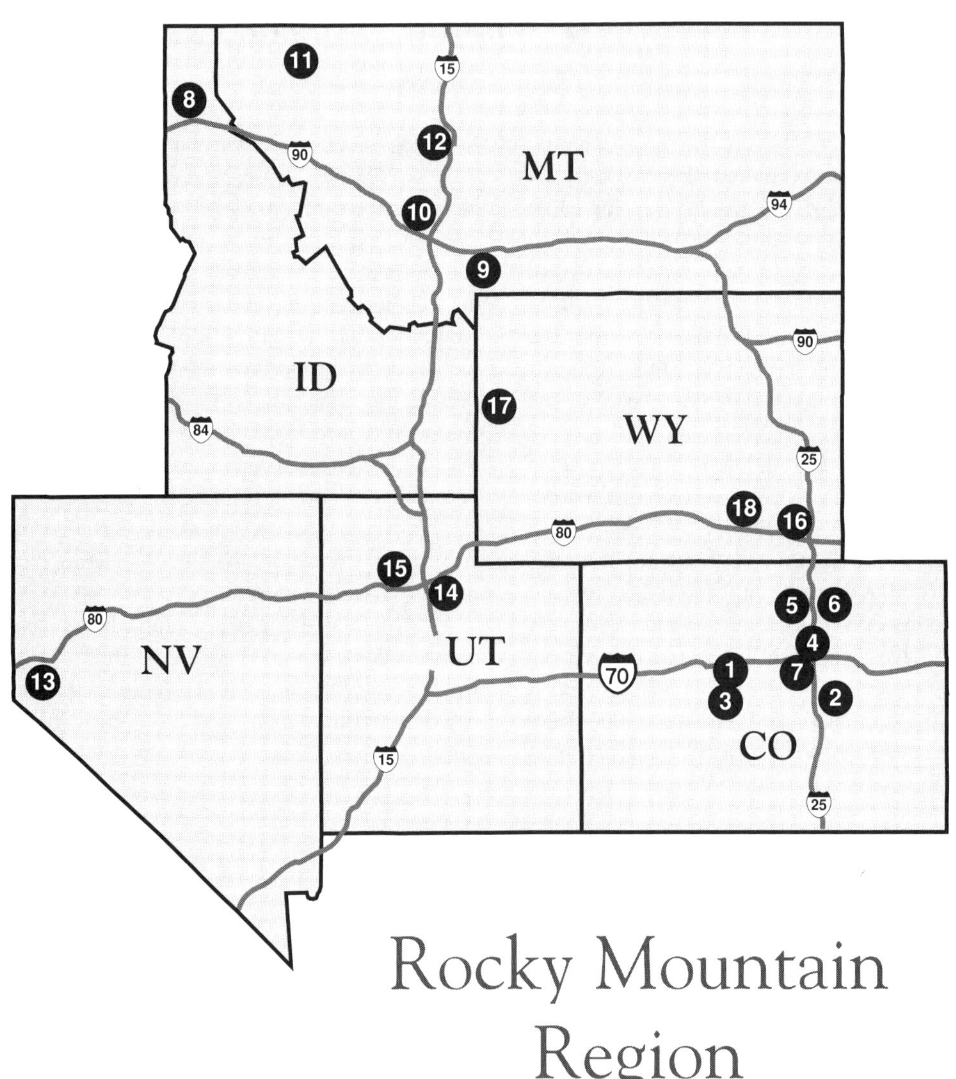

Rocky Mountain Region

Rocky Mountain Region

Numbers on map refer to towns numbered below.

Colorado

1. Aspen, Sardy House 244
2. Colorado Springs, Chyenne Cañon Inn 246
3. Crested Butte, Crested Butte Club Victorian Hotel & Spa 248
4. Denver,
   Castle Marne 250
   The Lumber Baron Inn 252
   Queen Anne Inn 254
5. Estes Park, River Song Inn 256
6. Loveland, The Lovelander Bed & Breakfast Inn 258
7. Pine, Meadow Creek Bed & Breakfast Inn . . 260

Idaho

8. Coeur d'Alene,
   The Blackwell House Bed & Breakfast 262
   Gregory's McFarland House 264

Montana

9. Bozeman, The Voss Inn 266
10. Butte, Copper King Mansion Bed & Breakfast 268
11. Essex, Izaak Walton Inn 270
12. Helena, The Sanders-Helena's Bed & Breakfast 272

Nevada

13. Gold Hill, Gold Hill Hotel 274

Utah

14. Park City, Washington School Inn 276
15. Salt Lake City, Pinecrest Bed & Breakfast Inn 278

Wyoming

16. Cheyenne, Rainsford Inn 280
17. Jackson,
    Davy Jackson Inn 282
    The Wildflower Inn 284
18. Medicine Bow, The Historic Virginian Hotel 286

Sardy House

ASPEN, COLORADO 81611

If your ideal romantic getaway leans toward turreted, Victorian mansions, perhaps this is the inn for you: a red-brick masterpiece with original oak staircases and sliding parlor doors, round reading rooms tucked away in a turret, gourmet breakfast set upon pearl gray linen centered with fresh flowers, and fine dining in the evenings as well.

Soft plum carpeting with pale pink roses, made in Ireland especially for the Sardy, is used throughout the building, and wallpaper of subdued gray cloaks the walls. The guest rooms have thick terry his and her robes, heated towel racks, down comforters with Laura Ashley duvets, and televisions hidden in walls or armoires. Except for two units with antique tubs, all have whirlpool baths.

We have a thing about carriage houses, and that is where we chose to stay, in a beautifully appointed complement to the main mansion. Our room had a vaulted, many-angled ceiling; natural wicker table, chairs, and writing desk; a cherry-wood, high-off-the-floor bed with feather-filled comforter and five fluffy pillows; and a bay window that looked out on Aspen Mountain and the ski slopes. The almond-scented lotion, shampoo, and bath gel were another nice touch. If you add just a few drops of bath gel to your whirlpool bath, you'll both disappear into a myriad of boundless bubbles!

Our breakfast was a Sardy Frittata, with eggs, Brie cheese, scallions, and *pico de gallo;* a granish of fresh fruite; coffee; and orange juice.

For dinner, we chose an appetizer of lobster crabcakes with red pepper chili aoili; a warm spinach salad with mushrooms, onion, eggs, and applewood smoked bacon dressing; and grilled Rocky Mountain rainbow trout stuffed with shiitake mushrooms, leeks, and fresh chives. Alas. Depsite the wonderful dessert selections, I sadly had to decline.

For those who prefer the privacy of their room, the Sardy House will serve either or both breakfast and dinner in your guest room.

The Sardy House is a popular place for small weddings, receptions, and private dinners. It has been awarded the Mobil 4 Star rating: "Outstanding . . . worth a special trip."

How to get there: Sardy House is on the corner of Main and Aspen streets in downtown Aspen.

Innkeeper: Jayne Poss
Address/Telephone: 128 East Main Street; (970) 920–2525 or (800) 321–3457
Rooms: 20, including 6 suites; all with private bath and TV, most with whirlpool bath, suites with VCR, stereo, and dry bar. No air conditioning (elevation 7,908 feet).
Rates: $95 to $749, single or double, depeneding on choice of room and season; EPB. Best to phone for current rates. Romance packages available during off-season.
Open: All year.
Facilities and activities: Dining room open to public for breakfast, dinner, and Sunday brunch. Concierge service, room service. Bar, heated outdoor pool, sauna, Jacuzzi. Nearby: restaurants, shopping, art galleries, free ski shuttle, all within walking distance; summer music festivals, hiking, fly-fishing, river rafting, downhill skiing (Aspen Mountain, Snowmass, Aspen Highlands, and Buttermilk), cross-country skiing, ice skating.

Cheyenne Cañon Inn

COLORADO SPRINGS, COLORADO 80906

A terraced garden and fountain greet guests as they approach this beautifully restored, Mission-style mansion. Inside the spacious Great Room, cozy library, and formal dining room await. The grand staircase leads to an open foyer with vintage wood-burning stove, seven luxurious bed chambers, and a redwood spa boasting spectacular views of Cheyenne Mountain and the Will Rogers Shrine to the Sun.

Guests can choose to stay in the Italian-style Villa, with canopied, queen-size brass bed; the Hut, blessed with a fireplace, bamboo twin beds and an African motif; the Swiss Chalet, a corner room with a king-size, lodgepole pine bed and fireplace; the tropical Cabana, enhanced by mosquito netting daintily draped over a queen-size bed; or the Hacienda, featuring a private sitting alcove, king-size, hand-carved sunburst bed with matching trastero and chest, and a whirlpool tub-for-two.

Le Petit Chateau, the inn's new, romantic cottage, provides couples with just about anything they could wish for, including complete privacy (the morning repast will be brought to their door or they can join other guests in the main dining room), a handmade, king-size metal designer bed, a marble bathroom with a shower-for-two, a television, a VCR, a breakfast nook, and a wet bar. Twosomes staying in this honey-moon haven can hold hands and whisper promises before the wood-burning, rock fireplace and soak under a canopy of stars in their own hot tub on their private redwood deck.

And then there is the Lodge, with aspen canopy bed, fireplace, Jacuzzi, and sitting area; or the exquisite Tea House, dressed in hues of soft peach and green, with king-size, wrought-iron canopy bed and priceless treasures from the Orient, including an inlaid-pearl-and-lacquer screen, a hand-carved, camphor wood chest and superb artwork.

As guests indulge in breakfast entrees of oven-baked apple pancakes or, perhaps, crab quiche before a crackling fire in the Great Room, 7-foot-high windows reveal the crests of Cheyenne and Almagre mountains awash in glowing shades of rose and amber. This is truly an elegant inn.

How to get there: Traveling from Denver south on I–25, take exit 141. Go west on U.S. Highway 24 to 8th Street, turn left, and proceed to Cheyenne Boulevard. Turn right onto Cheyenne and watch for inn's sign on right. Proceed 100 yards past sign to driveway leading to upper parking lot.

Innkeepers: John and Barbara Starr
Address/Telephone: 2030 West Cheyenne Boulevard; (719) 633–0625, (800) 633–0625
Rooms: 8, including 1 cottage; all with private bath, TV, and phone, 4 with fireplace, 3 with whirlpool tub. No smoking inn.
Rates: $75 to $130, double; EPB and afternoon refreshments. Cottage: $175, double; EPB and afternoon refreshments. Seniors, 10 percent discount.
Open: All year.
Facilities and activities: Indoor spa with mountain view, library, rock garden, and patio. Nearby: Pikes Peak, Seven Falls, Pikes Peak Cog Railway, Garden of the Gods, Starsmore Discovery Center, Cave of the Winds, Cheyenne Mountain Zoo, Broadmoor World Arena (ice skating), Will Rogers Shrine of the Sun, U.S. Olympic Complex, Miramont Castle, Air Force Academy, hiking, biking, fishing, golf, horseback riding, cross-country skiing (30 miles away).
Recommended Country Inns® Travelers' Club Benefit: 10 percent discount, Monday–Thursday, October–April.

Crested Butte Club Victorian Hotel & Spa

CRESTED BUTTE, COLORADO 81224

A stay at the Crested Butte Club is a taste of luxury that everyone should experience at least once and, preferably, many, many times. All the guest rooms are beauties, but the romantic elegance of the Presidential Suite is nonpareil. I had decided on this room, sight unseen, when making a reservation by phone. I couldn't have made a better choice.

As I opened the door, I caught my breath—it was that overwhelming. A rich royal blue carpet, strewn with peach and yellow roses and gold curlicues, spread before me. A French Provincial four-poster, which I later discovered to be an exceptionally comfortable waveless waterbed, stood against the far wall. Fresh flowers graced the coffee table in front of a white brocade love seat.

Ah, but there was even more opulence to discover. In the bathroom, dark wood wainscoting met cream-colored wallpaper sprinkled with tiny blue flowers; twin pedestal sinks, imported from Italy, sat beneath oak cabinets; an oak pull-chain commode hid in one corner; and, best of all, a sloped-to-fit copper tub with hammered-brass feet beckoned me to break out the bubble bath. Later, imagine lying in bed and watching the flickering firelight glimmer against the brass and candlestick chandelier.

Other rooms feature oak or white-iron–brass beds; televisions hide in armoires or above fireplace mantels; two rooms have decks; and all chambers have gas fireplaces and copper tubs.

The Crested Butte Club has a first-class spa with complimentary use for inn guests. It also is open to the public, but guests have private after-hours privileges.

Honeymooners and anniversary couples receive champagne, with a choice of labels. In addition, newlyweds are given a gift copy of the *Colorado Cookbook*, with a personal note of congratulations and best wishes. Horse and carriage rides from the hotel to one of many romantic restaurants can be arranged by the innkeeper.

Depending on the season, couple can opt for a thrilling hot-air balloon ride, stroll hand-in-hand amid meadows of wildflowers, hike through forests of golden aspen, or cross-country ski over virgin snow. And then there's always the temptation to do nothing but sip a glass of wine by candlelight or snuggle before the fire.

How to get there: From Gunnison, about 220 miles southwest of Denver, take Highway 135 north to Crested Butte. When you reach Crested Butte, take Elk Avenue into town. Turn left onto Second Street. The inn is on the left.

Innkeeper: Joe Rous
Address/Telephone: 512 Second Street (mailing address: P.O. Box 309); (970) 349–6655
Rooms: 7, including 1 suite; all with private bath, cable TV, phone, and working fireplace. No air conditioning (elevation 9,000 feet). No smoking inn.
Rates: $75 to $225, double, depending on room and season, continental breakfast and Happy Hour. Seniors, 10 percent discount. Spa packages available.
Open: All year.
Facilities and activities: Sports Pub, weight gym, lap pool, three whirlpools, two steam baths, two massage rooms, climbing wall, "Pilates" instruction, personal weight trainers. Nearby: restaurants, shopping, shuttle to ski slopes, hiking, mountain biking, wildflower meadows, championship golf course, tennis, horseback riding, jeep tours, downhill and cross-country skiing, Aerial Weekend (hot-air ballooning, skydiving, hang gliding, stunt pilots), Chamber Music Festival, Slavic Harvest Festival, wildflower and photography workshops.

Castle Marne

DENVER, COLORADO 80206

For those of us not lucky enough to grow up in a castle amidst opulence and grandeur, the Castle Marne provides a wee glimpse of what we missed. The exterior is stunning. For years, passersby have paused to admire the medieval-looking rusticated stone structure. Now they come to spend the night.

Inside, one can't help but marvel at the glowing woodwork, original fireplaces, and exquisitely decorated rooms. The parlor, blessed with a baby grand piano and treasured family antiques, lends itself nicely to the intimate Victorian tea served each afternoon on heirloom porcelain china and silver.

There's something hopelessly romantic about climbing the stately oak staircase, past the resplendent beveled-crystal and stained-glass Peacock Window, to your guest room. Our favorite chamber is the Presidential Suite, an elegant affair featuring a king-sized brass–white-iron tester bed with rose bed cover peeping through ecru lace. This room is further enhanced by a tiny fireplace, an antique gentleman's dresser, and a cozy turret room surrounded by five lace-paneled windows. French doors lead to a private solarium with a large whirlpool tub and a balcony overlooking downtown Denver.

The Conservatory also caught our fancy. This light and airy room has a queen-sized bed, a wicker armoire and love seat, and creamy walls sprinkled with cabbage roses.

Imagine a private candlelight dinner in the Castle Marne's formal dining room amid the gracious ambience of days long past. Soft music accompanies your conversation, and you scarcely notice the striking of the wall clock as you dine on chilled marinated shrimp and Cornish game hen with apricot glaze and fruit and nut stuffing, followed by chocolate mousse and café au lait. Later you climb that wonderful oak staircase, soak in the oversized Jacuzzi with balcony doors open to the stars and, eventually, sip a cup of wine or tea in your own tiny turret hideaway. Every couple should have just such an evening at least once in their lifetime. Hopefully, many, many times.

Extraordinarily good breakfasts come from Jim and Diane's kitchen, too. A fresh fruit plate is followed by wonderful homemade breads, muffins, and cinnamon sticky buns. Perhaps you will choose one of their many waffle varieties with real maple syrup, an innovative quiche, or a hot-from-the-oven breakfast casserole.

How to get there: From East Colfax Avenue, turn north onto Race Street. Proceed for almost 1 block. Inn is on southeast corner of Race Street and Sixteenth Avenue.

Innkeepers: Jim and Diane Peiker
Address/Telephone: 1572 Race Street; (303) 331–0621
Rooms: 10; all with private bath and phone; 3 with jetted whirlpool tubs for two on private balconies. No air conditioning (not needed; walls are 20 inches of solid stone). No smoking inn.
Rates: $90 to $200, double, EPB plus Victorian tea.
Open: All year.
Facilities and activities: Concierge service; Victorian luncheons and candlelight dinners available with prior arrangement; game room with pool table and exercise equipment; gift shop. Nearby: Elitch Gardens Amusement Park, Coors Field, Bronco Stadium, McNichols Arena, business and financial districts, Colorado State Capitol, U.S. Mint, Center for the Performing Arts, restaurants, convention center, museums, recreation centers, shopping facilities, professional sporting events, golf, tennis, hiking, fishing, biking; downhill and cross-country skiing approximately 50 miles away.
Recommended Country Inns® Travelers' Club Benefit: 5 percent discount, Sunday–Thursday. Please mention when making reservation.

The Lumber Baron Inn

DENVER, COLORADO 80211

Located in Denver's historic Highland neighborhood, only five minutes from midtown, this luxurious, three-story, red-brick mansion is the recipient of many honors, including the prestigious "Great American Home Award," presented by the National Trust for Historic Preservation. The inn took second place overall in the national category for bed and breakfast inns. And rightly so.

Innkeepers Maureen and Walter Keller spent more than two long years laboriously tearing down and replacing walls and ceilings, repairing, refinishing, scouring, painting and polishing, all the while convinced that they could transform the dilapidated, thirty-five-room apartment building back to its original grandeur. And they did exactly that.

Built in 1890 for John Mouat (a Scottish immigrant and building-supplies merchant), his wife, Amelia, and their five children, the turreted masterpiece was a designer's showcase incorporating superior hardwoods, with custom-carved details and the most exclusive building materials available at the time.

A sweeping front porch, a handsome foyer, and a grand staircase greet arriving guests. The front and back parlors are enhanced by exquisite period wallpapers by Bradbury & Bradbury, fireplaces, and elegant, one-of-a-kind antiques. As was the case when the house was first built, the striking, 1,600-square-foot, third-floor ballroom accommodates weddings and receptions.

The John and Amelia Mouat Honeymoon Suite features Neo-classical wallpaper in shades of pale peach, soft blue, and vanilla, an antique queen-size bed, and a luxurious dressing room with a whirlpool tub-for-two tucked away in the turret.

The Margaret Valentine Suite honors a Mouat daughter who was born and raised in the mansion. An antique, king-size canopy bed from Java, an in-room claw-footed bathtub, and walls sheathed in deep shades of red lend an air of romance to this chamber.

A circa-1840, four-poster canopy bed, a whirlpool tub-for-two, and a pair of faux-marble pillars separating the bedroom from the open bathroom enrich the John and Marguerite Gaffney Suite, named for Maureen's maternal grandparents. The Helen Keller Suite pays homage to Walter's famous, though distant relative. One of the largest chambers, it boasts an antique, hand-carved, queen-size bed, and an oversized whirlpool tub.

A breakfast basket, containing fresh-ground coffee; orange juice; a selection of scones, muffins, pastries, and croissants; fresh fruit; and a hot entree, is brought to each room. Guests can enjoy these breakfast delights in the dining room, on the porch, in the garden, or all snug in bed. A special Sunday brunch buffet is available to Saturday-night guests and, with reservations, to the general public.

How to get there: The inn is located in West Denver, on the corner of Bryant Street and 37th Avenue.

Innkeepers: Walter and Maureen Keller
Address/Telephone: 2555 West 37th Avenue; (303) 477–8205 or (800) 697–6552
Rooms: 5, including 3 suites with whirlpool tubs; all with private bath and phone. No smoking inn.
Rates: $125 to $185, single or double, EPB.
Open: All year.
Facilities and activities: Ballroom, catered events, garden and landscaped grounds. Nearby: business and financial districts, Colorado State Capitol, U.S. Mint, Center for the Performing Arts, restaurants, micro-breweries, shopping, convention center, museums, recreation centers, professional sporting events, hiking, biking, cross-country and downhill skiing (approximately 50 miles away).
Recommended Country Inns® Travelers' Club Benefit: 10 percent discount, Monday–Thursday.

Queen Anne Bed & Breakfast Inn

DENVER, COLORADO 80205

The two side-by-side Victorians that make up the exceptionally romantic Queen Anne Inn reign amid a row of lovely old homes in downtown Denver's Clements Historic District. While you relax in the beautifully appointed parlor, you are apt to witness a breathless couple arriving by horse and carriage, she still in her long, white wedding dress, he nervously trying to avoid stepping on same. Or the newest arrivals might be a middle-aged pair, with bottle of champagne in hand, bent on escaping their lawn-mowing, car-polishing neighbors for a romantic weekend getaway. They've come to the right place.

Every guest room is different, and each one is special in its own way. The Fountain Room, overlooking Benedict Fountain Park, boasts a four-poster with frilly, white-ruffled arched canopy, soft peach walls, a blue-and-peach love seat, and a black-tiled sunken tub tucked away in one corner. A more romantic room would be hard to find.

While the Tower Room, with European carved king-sized bed and bay window love seat, is exceptionally inviting, the Aspen Room is definitely the most unusual. Located in the turret, it features a hand-painted, wraparound mural of an aspen grove. If you lie on the bed and look up at the ceiling, you will gradually see the forest come alive until the aspen leaves seem to quake in the alpenglow.

The grounds are positively lovely. A series of latticework arbors leads to an enclosed backyard garden bordered by brick and flagstone planters filled with flowers and greenery. Ornate, white iron tables and chairs and a center fountain beckon couples to linger awhile.

According to Tom, "This inn is known for providing 'White Lace Romance.' The Queen Anne hosts an average of two honeymoon couples, two anniversary couples and three couples on a 'getaway' per week." When I asked him what he thinks makes his inn so romantic, he replied, "The fresh flowers, chamber music, champagne upon arrival, candlelight dinners, antique brass beds and canopied four posters, claw-footed tubs and soaker tubs-for-two, lights on dimmer switches, direct-dial phones to call friends with happy news, and late checkout. And then there's the private garden, perfect for a secluded breakfast or evening glass of wine."

Numerous publications, including *Bride's* magazine, *Romantic Hideaways*, *Bridal Guide*, *Country Inns*, *Travel Holiday*, and *Vacations* agree. All have raved about the Queen Anne's romantic qualities.

How to get there: From East Colfax Avenue, take Logan Street north to 20th Avenue. Turn left onto 20th Avenue and then immediately right onto Tremont Place.

Innkeeper: Tom King and Chris King

Address/Telephone: 2147-51 Tremont Place; (303) 296–6666 for information; (800) 432–INNS for reservations, fax: (303) 296–2151

Rooms: 14; all with private bath, phone, air conditioning, and stereo chamber music. No smoking inn.

Rates: $75 to $165, single or double; EPB and evening wine and cider. Special rates for travel agents, entertainers, and members of AAA. Inquire about rates for Romance Package.

Open: All year.

Facilities and activities: Innkeeper will arrange horse-and-carriage rides, catered candlelight dinners, musicians for private serenading, tours of Denver and Colorado, reservations for restaurants and other inns, and just about anything else your imagination (or his) can come up with. Nearby: Colorado State Capitol, U.S. Mint, Center for the Performing Arts, Elitch Gardens Amusement Park, Coors Field, Bronco Stadium, McNichols Arena, museums, shopping, restaurants (several five-star), all within walking distance; hiking, fishing, biking; downhill and cross-country skiing approximately 50 miles away.

River Song Inn

ESTES PARK, COLORADO 80517

If planning a formal wedding is not to your liking, you may want to check out the River Song's three-night Elopement Package. Included are a full breakfast each morning, one therapeutic massage per person, a gourmet picnic lunch, and a candlelight dinner for two. The bride and groom can take their vows, performed by innkeeper Gary Mansfield, either at the inn or, during winter, on snowshoes amongst breathtakingly beautiful surroundings in Rocky Mountain National Park.

The River Song recently added a wonderfully secluded two-unit cottage, with guest quarters separated by a foot-and-a-half-thick wall to ensure privacy. Named "Wood Nymph" and "Meadow Bright," the two chambers are nestled on the mountainside (easily accessible) near a rushing stream and tranquil, trout-filled pond, with a spectacular view of the snow-capped peaks of Rocky Mountain National Park. Both have fireplaces, canopied beds (Wood Nymph's is handmade of river birches, and Meadow Bright's is a massive hand-hewn log affair), decks, and radiant-heated floors. Wood Nymph has a Jacuzzi whirlpool tub and Meadow Bright features a fireside jetted tub and a waterfall shower. Both rooms have wheelchair access.

But, if you are looking for something unique and also romantic, you really should ask for the River Song's most requested accommodation:

Indian Paintbrush. A charming cottage sequestered among tall pine trees, it is tastefully done in Southwestern decor and features a love seat, handwoven Navajo wall hangings, an oversized bathtub, and, best of all, a swinging, queen-sized bed suspended from the ceiling by heavy white chains in front of a rose-tiled fireplace.

Sue is an excellent cook and makes many delectables such as apple pandowdy, blueberry cobbler served with vanilla yogurt, and corn fritters topped with genuine Vermont maple syrup.

Elegant candlelight dinners, served in style with heirloom silver, crystal, and china, are available with prior notice. A typical repast might begin with Avocado RiverSong, followed by Oriental soup with shrimp and shiitake mushrooms, basil chicken, rice pilaf, Japanese eggplant, and amaretto torte.

Plush off-white couches and a soft blue carpet add luxuriance to the living room, where one entire side is a window with a magnificent view of tall pines and mountains. Books line two walls, a warm fire crackles in the fireplace, and the grandfather clock periodically chimes the hour. All's well at River Song.

How to get there: Going west on Elkhorn Avenue, Estes Park's main street, turn left onto Moraine Avenue and proceed 4 blocks. At first stop sign, turn right onto Highway 36. At stoplight (1²⁄10 miles) turn left onto Mary's Lake Road. Watch for River Song Inn mailbox just across bridge. Turn right and proceed for ⁸⁄10 mile. The road ends at River Song.

Innkeepers: Gary and Sue Mansfield
Address/Telephone: Mary's Lake Road (mailing address: P.O. Box 1910); (970) 586–4666
Rooms: 4 in main inn, 1 carriage house suite, 4 deluxe cottages; all with private bath. Three with whirlpool tubs; 3 with wheelchair access. No air conditioning (elevation 7,522 feet). No smoking inn.
Rates: $135 to $225, double, EPB. Inquire about rates for three-night Elopement Package.
Open: All year.
Facilities and activities: Candlelight dinner and box lunches by reservation. Wedding performed on-site by RiverSong's own "Marrying Sam." Romance, honeymoon and elopement packages available. Located on twenty-seven acres of land with easy hiking trails. Nearby: Rocky Mountain National Park, restaurants, shopping, hiking, fishing, sailing, mountain climbing, golf, tennis, wildlife seminars, cross-country skiing, snowshoeing.

The Lovelander Bed & Breakfast Inn

LOVELAND, COLORADO 80537

Loveland, Colorado, is known nationwide as the Sweetheart City, where one can send his or her valentines to be postmarked by hand and mailed from "Loveland." What better way to impress that special someone?

The Lovelander Bed and Breakfast Inn fits right into the scheme. Its Victorian elegance definitely lends itself to romance. Here guests whisper sweet promises in the garden, sip sherry on the porch, and take a tea tray to the privacy of their room. Want more? How about a soak in an antique footed tub filled to the brim with passion fruit–scented bubbles?

A wide veranda wraps around the front and one side of this lovely circa-1902 inn; inside, gleaming woodwork, an ornate organ from the late 1800s, a corner fireplace, and plush overstuffed furniture add to the inviting glow of the parlor.

Lace-curtained bay windows spread soft light into the dining room, where one can always find coffee or tea and genuine, homemade Victorian vinegar cookies on the sideboard. Breakfast is served either at tables set for two or at the large oval dining room table.

And the two of you are in for a treat when you come down to breakfast. Baked eggs Florentine, cinnamon-raisin breakfast pudding, stuffed French toast with fruit sauce, almond scones, banana-oatmeal pancakes, gingered melon with honey, and strawberry-banana smoothies are only a few of the specialties Marilyn cooks up in her kitchen.

The private and secluded guest rooms are tucked away in downstairs corners and upstairs gables. Sloped ceilings and lots of nooks and crannies, along with antique writing desks, armoires, carved walnut and oak and brass and iron beds, and claw-footed bathtubs, add to the charm of these chambers.

Our favorite is the Columbine, with king-sized bed and elegant bath with 6-foot whirlpool tub.

The Lovelander dedicates the entire month of February to romance. The chef creates gourmet candlelight dinners, musicians entertain, and lovers receive commemorative valentines and complimentary boxes of chocolates. Throughout the year, guests staying over either Friday or Saturday night can partake of four-course, prix fixe gourmet dinners served in the Hearthside at the Lovelander dining room, located in a late-Victorian home across the street from the inn. Menu items might include velvety pumpkin soup with a hint of ginger, mixed greens with pears, toasted walnuts, and dried cranberry vinaigrette, roast pork tenderloin, and bread pudding served with apple slices in a carmel-pecan sauce, topped with carmel gossamer, and pooled in creme anglaise. Dinner is available to inn guests and their friends, only, and reservations must be made at least 24 hours in advance.

How to get there: From I–25, turn west onto Highway 34 to Garfield Avenue. Turn left onto Garfield to West 4th Street. Turn right onto West 4th Street. Inn is on the right.

Innkeepers: Marilyn and Bob Wiltgen
Address/Telephone: 217 West 4th Street; (970) 669–0798
Rooms: 11; all with private bath, air conditioning, and phone, some with whirlpool bath. No smoking inn.
Rates: $85 to $125, double, EPB and beverages and snacks. Dinner available on Friday and Saturday evenings, with 24-hour advance reservations. Approximately $28 per person, depending upon menu items served.
Open: All year.
Facilities and activities: Meeting and reception center. Nearby: restaurants, shopping, art galleries, museums, concerts, performing arts, lectures, theater, outdoor and indoor swimming pools, outdoor and indoor Jacuzzis, golf, tennis, hiking, biking, fishing, boating, cross-country skiing, llama farm, Rocky Mountain National Park.

Meadow Creek Bed & Breakfast Inn

PINE, COLORADO 80470

Our idea of a perfect couple of days would be to hide away in this inn's Room in the Meadow, a delightful cottage set in a grassy meadow and blessed with a fireplace, Jacuzzi for two, brass king-sized bed, private deck, microwave, and fridge. We would spend time outdoors, too, wandering through the woods in search of wildflowers and forest critters, listening to the wind rustle through the aspen, fir, and pine, and having afternoon lemonade in the gazebo, all the while absorbing the peace and quiet of the countryside.

Or your choice might be the new Colorado Sunshine Suite, a dream-come-true love nest with a king-sized bed, see-through, double-hearthed fireplace, private hot tub, sauna, and patio. From above, skylights spread moonbeams and stardust over all.

This inn was once the summer home of a prince, and in my opinion it's still fit for a king and queen. The two-and-a-half-story stone structure was built in 1929 for Prince Balthasar Gialma Odescalchi, a descendant of nobility from the Holy Roman Empire. When the prince left Colorado in 1947, the residence was absorbed into a 250-acre ranch; more recently, it has been transformed into a lovely country inn.

Among other guest accommodations are the Wild Rose Room, where a lop-eared cousin of Flopsy, Mopsy, and Cottontail, dressed in pink taffeta, sits on a queen-sized bed covered with white lace, and the cheery Sun Room, featuring a white wicker bed and love seat.

I recommend that you make dinner reservations at the time you book your room. The night we were there, the fare was marinated, grilled chicken with mandarin orange sauce, homemade bread, tossed green salad, pecan pie, ice cream turtle pie, and, an inn specialty, mountain mud slide, a cookie crust filled with layers of cream cheese and chocolate mousse, whipped cream, and chocolate bits.

A full breakfast is provided at the inn, or a couple may take a continental-style repast of homemade pastries, fruit, and juice to their room the night before if they don't care to come down to the inn for breakfast in the morning.

How to get there: Take Highway 285 (Hampden Avenue) south from Denver to Conifer. From the traffic light at Conifer, continue on Highway 285 for exactly 5³⁄10 miles. Turn left, follow road past school and take next left onto Douglas Drive at Douglas Ranch. Turn right onto Berry Hill Lane and continue to inn.

Innkeepers: Pat and Dennis Carnahan, Judy and Don Otis
Address/Telephone: 13438 U.S. Highway 285 (Barry Hill Lane at Douglas Ranch); (303) 838–4167 or (303) 838–4899
Rooms: 7, including 1 luxury cottage; all with private bath, 3 with private hot tub, fireplace, king-sized bed and private entry. Limited wheelchair access. Air conditioning in Grandma's Attic and Colorado Sunshine Suite (elevation 8,200 feet).
Rates: $89 to $180, double, EPB. Two-night minimum stay on weekends preferred.
Open: All year.
Facilities and activities: Dinner available, with 24-hour advance reservation, Friday and Saturday evenings, $18 per person. Outdoor hot tub, sauna, gazebo, gift shop, picnic table, fire pit in old brick silo for marshmallow roasts, thirty-five acres of woods to roam, toboggan hill. Nearby: restaurants, mountain towns, shopping, hiking, fishing, golf, cross-country skiing, one hour to downhill skiing.

The Blackwell House Bed & Breakfast

COEUR D' ALENE, IDAHO 83814

People passing by with no intention of spending the night cannot resist ringing the doorbell and asking if they can see the interior of this stately mansion. From the attractively appointed parlor to the music room with its antique grand piano, from the sweeping staircase to the upper floors of absolutely picture-perfect guest rooms, this inn is a designer's showcase—the perfect place for a wedding. And wouldn't you just know—there's a minister on call to perform the ceremony!

Built by F. A. Blackwell in 1904 as a wedding gift for his son, this magnificent, three-story structure was allowed to deteriorate over the years to the point that, when Kathleen bought it in 1982, it took nine months, one hundred gallons of paint remover, 282 rolls of wallpaper, nineteen tons of sod, and unmeasured amounts of laughter and tears to help bring it around to the masterpiece it is today.

The morning repast is served in the Breakfast Room, where French doors open out onto the patio and spacious lawns. A fire in the fireplace removes the early-morning chill, fresh-ground Irish cream coffee warms the tummy, bowls of fruit center the round, cloth-covered tables, and baskets of huckleberry muffins soon appear hot from the oven.

The second-floor Blackwell Suite is a pink-and-white dream with oak-spool bed; white wicker settee, table, and chairs; white ruffled curtains with pink tiebacks; white eyelet-trimmed comforter and bed ruffle; pink floral wallpaper; dusty rose carpet; and claw-footed bathtub sequestered in its own little alcove.

But, before you decide on this one, you must also see the former servants' quarters and children's playroom on the third floor. Smaller but ever so cozy, the three rooms share a sitting area with love seat, and they, like the others, are exquisitely decorated.

The hospitality here even extends to your friends, who are welcome to join you for late-afternoon tea and cookies or wine and munchies. If you haven't yet tried staying at country inns, The Blackwell House would be a great place to start.

How to get there: From city center, go east on Sherman Avenue (main street) for approximately 5 blocks. Inn is on the right.

Innkeepers: Kathleen Sims and Margaret Hoy
Address/Telephone: 820 Sherman Avenue; (208) 664–0656
Rooms: 8, including 3 suites; 6 with private bath.
Rates: $85 to $135, double, EPB and late-afternoon refreshments; champagne in room for special occasions.
Open: All year.
Facilities and activities: Catered luncheons and dinners for six or more guests; weddings, and receptions. Minister on staff. Music room with grand piano, large yard with gazebo and barbecue, within walking distance to downtown. Nearby: Lake Coeur d'Alene, "World's Longest Floating Boardwalk," Tubb's Hill nature trails, shopping, restaurants, hiking, fishing, boating, bicycling, downhill and cross-country skiing, snowmobiling.

Gregory's McFarland House

COEUR D'ALENE, IDAHO 83814

This inn hosts many weddings and receptions, due to its lovely facilities and attentive innkeepers. Warm and hospitable, Win and Stephen clearly enjoy seeing to it that brides and grooms have a memorable wedding day. And, year after year, many couples return to celebrate their anniversaries.

The McFarland House just keeps getting better and better, with the addition of more and more quality antiques. Guests have the use of all the common areas, including the more casual family room with its regulation oak-wood pool table, television, VCR, and stereo.

And then there's the pretty-as-a-wedding-cake conservatory. Looking out onto the beautifully landscaped backyard, it features pink wicker chairs padded with pink floral cushions, pink tablecloths, place mats, and napkins; and pots and pots of pink geraniums. I am convinced that, even on a cloudy day, this room must glow with cheerfulness.

The conservatory is where we had breakfast, and it was gourmet to the last crumb. A frothy fruit drink made of blended fresh fruits and skim milk and served in stemmed glassware began the affair. Next came a fresh fruit cup, muffin, and Irish cream coffee. A light and fluffy egg dish garnished with spears of fresh asparagus and slices of wheat toast completed this extraordinarily delicious meal.

Many of the antiques throughout the inn are from Win's family. My room had a circa-1860 bed with a pink-on-white bed cover, ecru eyelet ruffled skirt, and piles of eyelet-trimmed pillows. Later, when I returned from dinner, Win had left a mint surprise, Stephen brought ice water to my room, the ceiling fan circulated the cool evening air filtering through the imported lace curtains, and the floral-upholstered love seat beckoned me to read awhile. It feels very good here.

I have another reason for especially liking this inn. The Gregorys' three kitty cats, Sweet Boy, Valentino, and Lil Darlin', gave me my "cat fix" for the day. It surely helped for the moment, but, three days later, I was happy as usual to get home to my own cream Persian, Murphy, my bluepoint Himalyan, Frosty, and my calico, Garfy the Wonder Cat.

How to get there: Located 7 blocks from Coeur d'Alene Lake. From midtown, go east on Sherman (Coeur d'Alene's main street) to 6th Street. Go north on 6th Street to Foster. Inn is on the northeast corner.

Innkeepers: Winifred, Carol, and Stephen Gregory
Address/Telephone: 601 Foster Avenue; (208) 667–1232
Rooms: 5; all with private bath. No smoking inn.
Rates: $85 to $135, double, EPB and complimentary afternoon wine, tea, coffee, and cookies. Reduced off-season rates available. Special packages available for skiers and wedding parties.
Open: All year.
Facilities and activities: Landscaped grounds, piano. Private entrance and area for weddings; minister and photographer on staff. Nearby: Lake Coeur d'Alene, "World's Longest Floating Boardwalk," Tubb's Hill nature trails, restaurants, shopping, hiking, fishing, horseback riding, golf, swimming, waterskiing, sailing, snowmobiling, downhill and cross-country skiing.

The Voss Inn

BOZEMAN, MONTANA 59715

Often referred to as one of Montana's most romantic bed and breakfasts, The Voss Inn is located in Bozeman's historic district. Many a couple, bent on a blissful weekend, walks hand in hand through this inn's English cottage perennial garden, up the steps, past Victorian wicker furniture on a porch ablaze with geraniums, and into the lovely parlor. And it only gets better from here.

As meticulously scrubbed, starched, pressed, and polished as an Easter-morning Sunday School class, The Voss Inn exudes perfection. Antique beds, private sitting areas, breakfast nooks, and bay windows all add to the charm of this stalwart, red-brick Victorian. Every room we peeked into was captivating. The Sartain Room on the main floor features a provocative tub and bathing alcove; the front parlor is graced with an ornate, etched-glass chandelier; the Chisholm Room, a favorite with honeymooners, boasts a magnificent 9-foot brass headboard with an antique brass lamp hanging from it, a claw-footed bathtub, and an antique gas fireplace.

Flowered wallpaper banks the staircase leading to the immaculate upstairs guest rooms. We entered our favorite, Robert's Roost, by descending three steps into a bright and cheerful garden of white wicker, deep green walls sprinkled with tiny white blossoms, white ruffled curtains, and a private balcony. The bed, brass and iron, has a white eyelet spread and is embellished with dark green, rose-flowered pillows. A miniature bottle of liqueur and two small glasses waited on the bedside table.

Frankee tiptoes upstairs and leaves early morning coffee and tea in the hallway. Then, a little later, she brings fresh fruit, orange juice, homemade cinnamon rolls and muffins, and wonderful egg-soufflé dishes to the hall buffet. Breakfast is taken to tiny tables in the guest rooms, and that's a definite plus because you'll want to spend as much time as possible in your newfound hideaway.

Or, if you prefer, you can enjoy the morning repast in the company of other guests in the parlor where breakfast is served on hand-crocheted tablecloths from Zimbabwe, accented with heirloom silver and fine china.

According to Frankee, "We endeavor to provide personal service without disturbing our guests' privacy. They may join the other guests for tea and conversation if they like, or they can choose to have no interaction at all. The choice is entirely theirs." If you are celebrating a honeymoon or anniversary, let her know in advance so she can have champagne or wine in your room awaiting your arrival.

Bruce and Frankee's courtship is proof that love will find a way. While Frankee was on a photo safari in Africa, she met Bruce in Botswana where he was working at the time. He visited her in Los Angeles, and she later revisited him in Botswana. They subsequently married and tried to live in L.A. but eventually decided that Bozeman, Montana, near Yellowstone National Park, was where they wanted to operate a bed and breakfast and raise their family. Another "happily ever after" story.

How to get there: From I–90, take exit 306 into Bozeman. Turn south onto North 7th Avenue, left onto Main Street, and proceed to South Willson. Go south on Willson for approximately 3½ blocks to the inn.

Innkeepers: Bruce and Frankee Muller
Address/Telephone: 319 South Willson; (406) 587–0982
Rooms: 6; all with private bath, some with air conditioning, fans available for others.
Rates: $80 to $95, double, EPB, a traditional English tea, and nightcap.
Open: All year.
Facilities and activities: During winter, transportation to ski slopes for nominal charge. Nearby: Lewis and Clark Caverns, Museum of the Rockies, Bridger Bowl and Big Sky ski areas, restaurants, shopping, hiking, fishing in blue-ribbon trout stream, downhill and cross-country skiing; personalized daytrips into Yellowstone National Park and other points of interest, including gourmet breakfast and picnic lunch.
Recommended Country Inns® Travelers' Club Benefit: 10 percent discount.

Copper King Mansion Bed & Breakfast

BUTTE, MONTANA 59701

"A mile high, a mile deep, and always on the level," was the motto in Butte, Montana (elevation 5,280 feet) when its nineteenth-century copper mines burrowed an equal depth underground. The man most noted for the extraction of ore from the region was William Andrews Clark, better known as the "Copper King," who later became a U.S. senator.

Clark built this mansion in 1884 at a cost of $250,000—a mere half day's wages at the height of his earnings (estimated at $17 million a month). He spared no expense to procure the best craftsmanship and quality. German woodcarvers chiseled ornate figures in the Philippine mahogany fireplace. Rosewood, cherry, and oak are among the nine different woods that adorn the house, including the hand-carved central staircase and parquet floors. Frescoed ceilings and jeweled Tiffany stained-glass windows are part of the opulent decor.

While the building attests to Clark's wealth and taste, the preservation and renovation of the home reflect the resourcefulness of two women, the great-grandmother and grandmother of the current innkeeper, Maria Wagner. They acquired the building, stripped of its appointments, in 1953, and filled it with period pieces dating from 1880 to 1930, the era when the copper magnate and U.S. senator called Butte home. Today, twenty original items from the Clark family are among the priceless furnishings.

Guests seeking a romantic interlude can pamper themselves regally with a stay in the Master Suite, with adjoining sitting room and private bath. A carved headboard stands sentinel over the satin and hand-crocheted bed covers. Overhead, a fresco of nudes has been restored—a group of nuns, former occupants, had discreetly painted over it. Perfume bottles and an ivory manicure-and-comb set leave the impression that Clark and his wife still use this room.

No matter which quarters one chooses, there's no need to fear missing anything at this inn. Overnight lodging includes a tour of the mansion as well as a delicious breakfast of French toast, quiche, or omelet served on Limoges china with silver service. Tasteful elegance reigns in the dining room under a gold-embossed leather ceiling hung with a crystal chandelier.

How to get there: From I–90, take Montana Street exit. Turn left onto Montana and proceed to West Granite Street. Turn left onto West Granite and go 1 block to Idaho Street. Inn is on the corner of West Granite and Idaho streets.

Innkeeper: John Thompson and Erin and Pat Sigl
Address/Telephone: 219 West Granite Street; (406) 782–7580
Rooms: 5; 2 with private bath, 1 with TV. Pets allowed with prior approval. No air conditioning (elevation 5,280 feet).
Rates: $45 to $95, double, EPB, wine or beer, and tour of the mansion.
Open: All year. Mansion tours for public occur between 9:00 A.M. and 5:00 P.M., May through October. During this season, bed and breakfast guests check in between 5:00 and 9:00 P.M. and must check out by 9:00 A.M.
Facilities and activities: Robes for shared bath, bottled water. Nearby: World Museum of Mining, Arts Chateau Gallery, historic walking tour, ghost towns, hiking, fishing, horseback riding, snowmobiling, downhill and cross-country skiing.

Izaak Walton Inn

ESSEX, MONTANA 59916

For couples seeking seclusion and total privacy, a stay in one of this inn's cozy "little red cabooses" would be a great choice. Genuine Great Northern cabooses, now resting on the hillside overlooking the inn, have been totally remodeled with pine interior and accented with blue-and-white pinstripe bedding and red pillows and include a mini-kitchen, private bath, and deck. If you prefer complete isolation, you can forego the meals offered in the inn's dining room by requesting, in advance and for an additional fee, that your tiny cupboard and fridge be stocked in anticipation of your arrival.

I recommend that you, on at least one of your nights here, first pamper yourselves in the Finnish-style sauna and, later indulge in a moonlit dinner on your caboose's private deck. As Larry and Lynda proclaim, "At our inn, time stands still and lets you catch up." Allow a couple extra days here, and there even will be time to "catch up" on a little old-fashioned courting.

Built in 1939 to accommodate service crews for the Great Northern Railway, whose enormous task it was to keep the mountain track open during winter, the inn is still very much involved in the railroad business. It is here that "helper" engines hook onto lengthy freight trains and help push them over the Continental Divide. The inn is also a designated flag stop, with Amtrak passing through daily. If you decide to arrive via Amtrak, inn personnel will meet you at the platform to help with luggage.

Fifteen to twenty freight trains pass by the front door of the inn each day; and, whether resting in one of the charming guest rooms, playing volleyball in the playfield, or downing a few in the Flag Stop Bar, one is hard-pressed to keep from running outdoors like a kid to watch as the massive trains chug by.

The Izaak Walton is packed with signal lanterns, vintage photographs, and all sorts of train memorabilia. In the Dining Car Restaurant, you may be seated next to a striped-capped engineer from the train waiting out on the tracks or sharing a meal and spirited conversation with members of an international rail fan club.

Highlights of our stay at the Izaak Walton: lovely accommodations, light and fluffy breakfast crepes filled to overflowing with huckleberries; a dinner of honey-glazed chicken sautéed with orange slices and onions; the sighting of whole families of shaggy, beautiful mountain goats zigzagging their way down the hillside to a salt lick; and spotting a yearling bear cub peacefully munching his way along the side of the road.

Wildlife photographers can have the time of their lives here: black bears, mountain lions, mountain goats, spawning salmon, and, from early October to early November, a sometimes large migration of bald eagles.

How to get there: Inn is ½ mile off of Highway 2, on southern rim of Glacier National Park between East and West Glacier. Watch for sign for Essex turnoff.

Innkeepers: Larry and Lynda Vielleux

Address/Telephone: Off Highway 2 (mailing address: P.O. Box 653); (406) 888–5700, fax (406) 888–5200

Rooms: 31, plus 2 suites and 4 cabooses; all with private bath, 1 with gas fireplace. No air conditioning (elevation 3,860 feet).

Rates: $92 to $142, double, EP. Cabooses: 425 for 3 nights; $800 for 7 nights, based on 4-person occupancy; EP. Three-, five- and seven-day packages, including meals, available. Personal checks preferred.

Open: All year.

Facilities and activities: Full-service dining room, bar, sauna, laundromat, ski shop, gift shop with Montana-made items; Amtrak flag stop # E.S.M., train activity, train memorabilia; mountain bike rentals and tours, antique "jammer" bus tours over the "Going-to-the-Sun Highway" in Glacier Park, cross-country ski rentals, snowshoe rentals, guided cross-country ski tours into Glacier National Park, guided snowshoe treks. Nearby: Glacier National Park and Bob Marshall Wilderness Area, constituting more than a million acres of wilderness; fishing, hiking, horseback riding, rafting, wildlife viewing, photography, cross-country skiing.

The Sanders - Helena's Bed & Breakfast

HELENA, MONTANA 59601

Montana Senator Wilbur Sanders and his wife, Harriet, built this Queen Anne home in 1875, at the beginning of his political career. An important figure in Helena, Sanders also founded the Montana Historical Society and was its president for twenty-six years.

Innkeepers Bobbi Uecker and Rock Ringling realized the importance of preserving as much of this landmark structure as possible when they undertook the restoration of the mansion. A museum in its own right, the inn still houses most of the original furnishings belonging to its first family. Today, as then, rich wooden paneling, gleaming oak floors, and priceless antiques add elegance throughout the inn.

The luxurious Colonel's Room features the Sanderses' 8-foot-high headboard of bird's-eye maple, matching dressers (one with a marble top), and a bay window. Modern amenities are tastefully hidden away in armoires and dressers.

The sleep chamber called Teddy's Buckaroo, named in honor of Bobbi's cattleman father, appeals to honeymooners. A four-poster brass bed, draped with a canopy of mosquito netting, dominates this room. The adjoining bathroom, however, is the drawing card. A 5 x 5-foot tile enclosure with dual shower heads invites guests to linger amid lush potted plants.

Lest the inn showcase only the Sanderses' past, some items modestly pay homage to Rock's family. A portrait of his great-grandfather Alf T. Ringling, one of the five brothers who began the famed Ringling Bros. Circus, hangs prominently in the Colonel's Room. Above the upper stairway is a bust of "Chili Bean," a roping steer who performed at Madison Square Garden and spent his old age at the Ringling Ranch.

Come morning, both Bobbi and Rock appear in chef's hats. Bobbi's concoction of orange soufflé and the Sanderses' recipe for cream cheese–filled French toast delight guests. The huckleberry pancakes, mushroom crepes, and Grand Marnier French toast also receive raves from visitors.

How to get there: From I–90, take the Capitol Area exit and follow Prospect Street west to Montana Street. Turn left onto Montana Street and proceed to 6th Avenue. Turn right onto 6th Avenue and right again onto North Ewing. Inn is on the left.

Innkeepers: Bobbi Uecker and Rock Ringling
Address/Telephone: 328 North Ewing; (406) 442–3309
Rooms: 7; all with private bath, phone, TV, and air conditioning. No smoking inn.
Rates: $90 to $110, double; EPB, snacks, and beverages.
Open: All year.
Facilities and activities: On National Register of Historic Places, flower gardens. Nearby: St. Helena's Cathedral, Holter Museum, Myrna Loy Theater, historic governor's mansion, state capitol building, Historical Museum, cultural center, fishing, down hill and cross-country skiing.

Gold Hill Hotel

GOLD HILL, NEVADA 89440

Not many years ago, this luxurious country inn was nothing more than a decaying six-room, one-bath hotel and bar. Built during the gold rush to the Comstock Lode in 1859, the hotel served a bustling community that received as many as fifty scheduled trains a day, hauling commodities in and ore out. The stone section of the building still stands, and a new wooden addition has been added to replace that which disappeared sometime before 1890. It is the oldest operating hotel in Nevada.

A walk through this comfortably elegant hotel reveals quality antiques and a genteel ambience unexpected in this rather remote section of Nevada.

The guest rooms boast period furnishings and lovely decor, but our choice, and often that of newlyweds, was Room 6, with a private balcony; stone fireplace; a beautiful circa-1850 half-tester bed; marble-topped dresser and bedside tables; wet bar; fine-print blue wallpaper; and an extra-large bath. The pink-draped corner windows look out to the Sierra Nevada mountain range.

In the hotel's Crown Point Restaurant, the tables are clad with white linen and set with crystal stemware and fine china. Soft rose drapes and upholstered chairs, sea green carpet, and an antique sideboard contribute to the elegance of this room. Chef Herb Richardson serves a wide range of French and Continental cuisine. Although the dining room exudes elegance, casual dress in keeping with Nevada's informality is most acceptable.

The cozy, stone-walled bar has a large corner fireplace and is home to an extensive wine list, an astonishing number of old whiskies from Scotland and Ireland, imported cognacs and brandies, and more than fifty imported and domestic bottled beers.

The former mining metropolis of Gold Hill is now a small village surrounded by historic sites and adjacent to the rollicking former mining town of Virginia City. Area hiking includes trails along old mining roads and abandoned rail lines.

For a glimpse into the Old West, browse the Gold Hill Hotel's bookstore and gift shop to see more than 2,000 titles describing the history of the western United States. Upon request, you may view a videotape of more than 200 historical photos dating from the 1860s to the present.

How to get there: From Reno, take Highway 395 south to Highway 341 turnoff to Virginia City. At Virginia City, continue south for 1 mile to Gold Hill. Hotel is on the right.

Innkeepers: Carol and Bill Fain
Address/Telephone: Highway 342 (mailing address: P.O. Box 304, Virginia City, NV 89440); (702) 847–0111
Rooms: 11, plus 2 guest houses; 9 rooms and guest houses with private bath. Second-floor guest rooms with wheelchair access.
Rates: $45 to $135, double, rate depends on choice of room and season; continental breakfast.
Open: All year except January.
Facilities and activities: Full-service dining room with wheelchair access, closed Mondays and Tuesdays; Great Room lounge; saloon, lectures by local historians. Nearby: restaurants, gambling casinos, excursion train, mine tours, hiking, fishing, exploring; downhill and cross-country skiing at Lake Tahoe, approximately 35 miles away.

Washington School Inn

PARK CITY, UTAH 84060

Although the perfect hideaway for grown up childhood sweethearts, there's no more "readin', 'ritin', and 'rithmetic" at the old Washington School. The three Rs now more accurately stand for "romance," "rendezvous," and "resplendent." Built in 1889, the structure served as a public school for forty-two years, became a social hall during the '30s, and lay vacant from the '50s until 1984. The hammered-limestone exterior, bell tower, dormer and classroom windows, and curved entry porticos have been retained, thus qualifying the inn for the National Register of Historic Places.

The entry hall still has the feeling of an old-fashioned schoolhouse, with exposed original timbers supporting the three-story bell tower. A library/mezzanine overlooks the elegant living room, where complimentary beverages await your arrival and refreshments are served during the afternoons.

Each morning an antique sideboard in the formal dining room is lavishly spread with breakfast items such as eggs Florentine or cheese strata served with bacon, ham, or sausage; fresh fruit and lemon-nut bread; homestead pumpkin bread; Grandma Anderson's brown bread; or, perhaps, Utah beer bread.

During winter, apré's-ski refreshments bring crabcakes, fondues, or baked Brie with raspberries, along with hot cider and wine. Afternoon tea, with fresh-baked cookies or chocolate-dipped strawberries, is served in the summertime.

All guest rooms are elaborately custom-decorated and bear the names of former school teachers. "Miss Thatcher" has a brick fireplace, king-sized bed, rose carpet, and, heavens to mercy!, a pink-flowered love seat and a wet bar. "Miss Thompson" has a green iron-and-brass bed, fireplace with round windows on either side, and, also, a love seat and wet bar. Our favorite room was "Miss Urie." Bright and sunny, it has pink and blue flowers sprinkled on yellow wallpaper, a chatting corner, a writing alcove, and a four-poster pine bed. An antique book acts as doorstop.

Couples especially enjoy the lower level of the inn, which features a wine cellar and a luxurious whirlpool spa with stone floor, bent-willow furniture, dry sauna, and steam showers. Wouldn't the Misses Thatcher, Thompson, and Urie have loved this as their "Teacher's Room"?

Some comments I gleaned from the guest book that I would like to share with you: "Long live our marriage, thanks to our first night at the Washington School Inn." "A wonderful honeymoon retreat." "Just like another honeymoon." "Great place for newlyweds." "Beautiful, charming place to spend a romantic weekend."

How to get there: From I–80, take Highway 224 south to Park City; 224 turns into Park Avenue at Park City. Inn is on the right side of street.

Innkeepers: Nancy Beaufait and Delphine Covington
Address/Telephone: 543 Park Avenue (mailing address: P.O. Box 536); (801) 649–3800 or (800) 824–1672
Rooms: 15, including 3 suites; all with private bath. Wheelchair access. No air conditioning (elevation 7,000 feet).
Rates: $100 to $300, single or double, depending on season; EPB and afternoon refreshments. Seniors, 65 and over, 10 percent discount.
Open: All year.
Facilities and activities: Lunch for groups of ten or more. Hot tub, Jacuzzi, sauna, steam showers, concierge services. Nearby: restaurants, golf, tennis, hiking, fishing, horseback riding, sailboarding, sailing, waterskiing, Park City Ski Area, Park West Ski Area, Deer Valley Ski Resort, downhill and cross-country skiing.

Pinecrest Bed & Breakfast Inn

SALT LAKE CITY, UTAH 84108

Just 6 miles up Emigration Canyon, the same canyon from which Brigham Young and his followers first entered what was to become Salt Lake City, the Pinecrest Bed & Breakfast Inn stands sedately amid acres of tall pines and blue spruce, wildflowers and forest paths, and meticulously landscaped formal gardens. The large iron gates leading to the inn were installed in the '30s by David Henderson, a Hollywood actor who owned the estate at the time and who bought the gates from Paramount Studios.

The spacious living and dining area features rich cherry-wood paneling and woodwork, a large stone fireplace, red-wine velvet couches, and a splendid grand piano. A wall of windows looks out onto the garden area.

Guest rooms are exceptionally well situated to ensure privacy. The Jamaican Jacuzzi Room is accessed by a wrought-iron, circular staircase that leads to the lower level from one corner of the living room. This very private chamber has a king-size bed, a sauna, and a sunken Jacuzzi. The Library is on the main floor and features a king-size bed and a 1930s radio that Phil has rigged to play Glenn Miller and George Burns and Gracie Allen tapes, in addition to many other old-time favorites. The Oriental Suite takes the entire upper story and has a king-size bed, private balcony, Jacuzzi, Ming silk couches, and an exquisite coromandel screen from mainland China.

Phil and Donnetta have added a lovely new room with Southwestern decor and a fireplace and Jacuzzi.

The guest house is comfortably rustic and has had as guests the likes of Robert Redford.

Phil prepares a continental-plus breakfast of perhaps sour-cream–banana pancakes or fresh-raspberry crepes, fruit coffee cake, juice, and coffee or tea. There are several good restaurants close by. Phil recommends the Santa Fe for lunch, dinner, or Sunday brunch. He also tells me that Crompton's, a favorite with locals, probably makes the best hamburgers and sandwiches in all of Salt Lake City.

This is a restful place with plenty of room to wander about outdoors, breathe the good fresh air, and listen to the birds sing. There's even a chance you might see raccoons, porcupines, squirrels, and three gigantic moose that live in the canyon. Keep your camera handy.

How to get there: Go east on 800 south, past Research Park on your left and the zoo on your right, to Emigration Canyon Road. Proceed on Emigration Canyon Road for approximately 6 miles past zoo. Inn is on your left.

Innkeepers: Phil and Donnetta Davis
Address/Telephone: 6211 Emigration Canyon Road; (801) 583–6663 or (800) 359–6663
*E-mail:*pdj27@aol.com
Rooms: 6 in inn, plus 1 guest house; all with private bath, 3 with fireplace and Jacuzzi.
Rates: $75 to $185, single or double, EPB.
Open: All year.
Facilities and activities: Sauna; 6 acres of formal gardens, landscaped and natural grounds. Nearby: Temple Square, Great Salt Lake State Park, state capitol, University of Utah, LDS Genealogical Library, museums, restaurants, shopping, hiking, fishing, swimming, downhill and cross-country skiing.
Recommended Country Inns® Travelers' Club Benefit: 10 percent discount, Monday–Thursday.

Rainsford Inn

CHEYENNE, WYOMING 82001

The hospitality here is first class, with a friendly greeting upon arrival and, quite possibly, a bear hug when you leave.

This outstanding, turn-of-the-century inn sits in a quiet, tree-shaded neighborhood within walking distance of downtown Cheyenne. A gracious ambience greets guests as they enter the antiques-filled parlor. Here lace curtains filter the afternoon sunlight, wood floors gleam, a player piano awaits would-be musicians, and a vintage rocking chair begs travelers to come sit awhile.

From the entryway, an oak staircase leads to four guest rooms on the second and third floors. The School Room is particularly enticing with its red, navy, and cream-colored patchwork quilt displaying old-fashioned school houses. Here, tiny classroom chairs, rag dolls on an antique bench, a framed "Teacher's Rules," and a braided rug present a nostalgic glimpse of long-ago school days.

While any one of the lovely, individually decorated rooms is sure to invite special moments, perhaps the most romantic of all is the Moonlight and Roses Suite. Blessed with lace-covered bow windows, an ornate, antique bed with matching armoire and marble-topped dresser, oak floors, ceiling fans, whirlpool tub, sitting corner, and gas fireplace, this chamber is just as popular with not-so-newlyweds as it is with newlyweds. A small table set in the bay window alcove allows for a romantic, private breakfast for two.

The first-floor guest room is designed for those with special needs. Light and airy with a bay window, it features a heart motif quilt on the queen-size antique bed, a matching dresser, and roll-in shower with bench, handrails, and hand-held shower head.

In addition to homemade breads, jams, and granola, breakfast might include sausage and cheese casserole or waffles and bacon. For the health-minded, she will prepare poached eggs and dry toast or an entree using egg substitute. Whatever your needs or wants might be, you won't go away hungry.

One more thing: Be sure to ask Nancy to show you the hidden staircase she discovered during the renovation of the house.

How to get there: Located in Cheyenne on the corner of 18th and House streets in the Rainsford Historic District, east of downtown area.

Innkeepers: Nancy Drege
Address/Telephone: 219 East 18th Street; (307) 638–2337; fax (307) 634–4506
Rooms: 7; all with private bath, cable TV, phone jack with private line, and air conditioning, 4 with whirlpool tub. Wheelchair accessible; 1 room with roll-in shower designed for handicapped. No smoking inn.
Rates: $60 to $100, single or double, EPB, snacks and beverages. Seniors and military, 10 percent discount.
Open: All year.
Facilities and activities: Player piano, sunporch, patio. Nearby: restaurants, microbrewery, antique shops, state museum, Old West Museum, Vedauwoo Park, Curt Gowdy State Park, Cheyenne Frontier Days, Wyoming–Colorado Railroad excursions (45 miles, at Laramie), rock climbing, fishing.

Davy Jackson Inn

JACKSON, WYOMING 83001

This lovely Victorian-style inn, a masterpiece in design, invites guests to read before the fireplace, wander the hallways to admire the antiques, and sit down at the grand piano in the parlor. (Go ahead and play, even if you are not an accomplished pianist. Good-natured Kay is quick to assure you that she herself plays the radio better than she can play the piano.)

Located in a quiet neighborhood, only a few blocks from the Town Square, this inn has twelve guest rooms, each one impeccably furnished.

Among my favorite chambers is the Tower Room (Number 302), with a king-size, four-poster bed enhanced by a dainty, hand-tied, cotton-thread canopy, an antique Victorian fainting couch, a whirlpool tub, a steam shower, and a gas-log fireplace.

Room 303 is another of my favorites. A king-size four-poster and a white-wicker love seat, chair, lamp, and table enhance this chamber. A steam shower and Jacuzzi await in the bathroom, and the private balcony provides the perfect place for an early morning cup of coffee.

All chambers have down comforters and solid maple beds, night stands, and armoires made by the renowned Hitchcock Chair Company.

More than twenty years ago, while driving across the country, Kay and Gordon fell in love with the small town of Jackson, Wyoming, and the massive mountains that surround it. Years passed, during which time they owned and operated a bed and breakfast in Suffield, Connecticut, before finally opting to move west. Connecticut's loss is Wyoming's gain.

Kay's breakfasts begin with fresh-squeezed orange juice, fruit, and her grandmother's recipe for homemade cinnamon rolls. Or perhaps she will have baked her sour-cream coffee cake or apple dumplings for this morning's repast. Special sourdough pancakes might follow or, maybe, potato pancakes, eggs, and sausage.

For guests staying over during Christmas, Kay prepares a traditional family-style feast of turkey, ham, mashed potatoes and gravy, sweet potatoes, and pumpkin pie. She also serves a buffet on Christmas Eve and New Year's Eve.

Each afternoon a formal tea of cookies, cakes, or scones and wee sandwiches is available in the formal dining room. Under a crystal teardrop chandelier, on tables sheathed with cutwork-linen tablecloths, tea is poured from a silver service into antique teacups. Alas, the elegance of days long past.

How to get there: From the Town Square go north on North Cache Street to Perry Avenue. Turn left onto Perry Avenue. Inn is on the right.

Innkeepers: Kay and Gordon Minns
Address/Telephone: 85 Perry Avenue (mailing address: P.O. Box 20147); (307) 739–2294 or (800) 584–0532, fax (307) 733–9704
E-mail: kminns@wyo.com
Rooms: 12; all with private bath, cable TV, and direct-dial phone, 3 with fireplace, 3 with Jacuzzi tub and steam shower. One room especially designed for physically challenged persons. Rooms available for nonsmokers.
Rates: Summer: $185 to $215, single or double; Winter: $155 to $185, single or double. Low season (spring and late fall): $129 to $149, single or double. EPB and afternoon tea year-round. Christmas dinner at additional charge. No charge for Christmas Eve and New Year's Eve buffets.
Open: All year.
Facilities and activities: Outdoor hot tub, turn-down service. Nearby: Snow King Ski Resort, Yellowstone National Park, Grand Teton National Park, National Elk Refuge, Jackson Hole Ski Resort, restaurants, shopping, art galleries, wildlife viewing, hiking, fishing, downhill and cross-country skiing.
Recommended Country Inns® Travelers' Club Benefit: 20 percent discount when booked direct, subject to availability.

The Wildflower Inn

JACKSON, WYOMING 83002

Sherrie confided to us that she and Ken dream of one day saving an evening just for themselves. They plan to choose their favorite guest room, pack the well-used champagne bucket with ice, take along the crystal glasses etched with wildflowers, gaze at the stars from the private deck, and hear nothing but the melancholy vocalizing of happy frogs. Now how could you go wrong with romantic innkeepers like these?

Made of glowing lodgepole pine inside and out, with balconies, gables, and, everywhere, wildflowers, this inn is at once both elegant and country. In the expansive sitting room, Native American rugs hang on log walls, a freestanding wood stove stands before a massive river-rock wall, and the polished wood floor is centered with a colorful braided rug. This room, along with the solarium and dining room, looks out onto a wooded three acres of aspen and cottonwood trees, a creek-fed pond, and a meadow where horses graze. Just the day before we visited, a mama duck and her baby ducklings had paddled into the pond, lingered a while, and then ventured on downstream.

The guest rooms have a secluded feeling, and all five are beautifully decorated. Indian Paint Brush has a cathedral ceiling and private deck. The queen-sized hand-hewn pine-log bed, made by Ken, sports a bed ruffle made of blue-and-white ticking and a red print down comforter. Red-and-white checked curtains flank the windows, and red plaid Ralph Lauren towels brighten the private bath.

Sherrie is a master of spontaneous, creative cooking and serves a full outdoorsman's breakfast, including homemade granola, fresh fruit, oatmeal muffins, and either buttermilk pancakes, French toast, or an egg dish. She will see to it that you don't leave hungry.

Besides appealing to romantics, this inn is popular with outdoor enthusiasts. Ken is a ski instructor and climbing guide, and both he and Sherrie are authorities on the many interesting things to do in the Jackson Hole area.

After a day of hiking or skiing, put your sports gear in the separate storage area, pile into the hot tub, relax, and watch the day fade to twilight over misty fields and distant mountains.

How to get there: From Jackson, go west on Highway 22 toward Wilson. Before the town of Wilson, turn right onto Teton Village Road. Turn left onto first road past Jackson Hole Racquet Club (also called The Aspens). Inn is at end of roadway.

Innkeepers: Sherrie, Ken, and Jessica Jern
Address/Telephone: Off Teton Village Road (mailing address: P.O. Box 11000); (307) 733–4710, fax (307) 739–0914
E-mail: 102744.2104@compuserve.com
Rooms: 5; all with private bath and TV. No air conditioning (elevation 6,200 feet). No smoking inn.
Rates: Summer: $140 to $150, double; winter: $120 to $130, double, EPB. Inquire about off-season rates.
Open: All year.
Facilities and activities: Solarium, hot tub, deck. Nearby: Yellowstone National Park, Grand Teton National Park, National Elk Refuge, restaurants, art galleries, artist studios, museums, Old West Days, Mountain Man Rendezvous, Jackson Hole Arts Festival, Grand Teton Music Festival, Dancers Workshop, summer theater, acting workshops, rodeo, chuckwagon dinner shows, stagecoach rides, covered wagon trips, photography, wildlife viewing, hiking, fishing, biking, golf, tennis, climbing, horseback riding, llama treks, rafting, ice skating, sleigh rides, snowmobiling, dog sledding; downhill, helicopter, snowcat, and cross-country skiing.

The Historic Virginian Hotel

MEDICINE BOW, WYOMING 82329

If Medicine Bow, Wyoming, is not on your route, you might consider adding it to your itinerary, because you may never have a better chance to experience a truer example of an elegant Old West hotel.

As we sat on a red velvet settee in the Virginian's upstairs parlor, I wished for a long skirt, ruffled blouse, and high-top shoes to replace my jeans and Nikes. A visiting gentleman paused to ask incredulously, "Can you really *stay* here? Do they actually take in *guests*?" That's how authentic the furnishings and decor are in this 1911, National Historic Landmark hotel. It's like a "hands-on" museum where you can not only touch but actually sleep in the beautiful, many-pillowed beds, bathe in one of the oversized claw-footed tubs, sip a cup of tea in a plush parlor, and feel like wealthy turn-of-the-century honeymooners.

The three-story building is named after Owen Wister's 1902 novel *The Virginian*, of "When you call me that—smile" fame. The walls of the Shiloh Saloon are covered with memorabilia from the novel and the movie of the same name; and signed photographs of Wister and his best friend, Theodore Roosevelt, who encouraged the author to write such a story, are in several rooms.

The Owen Wister Suite features a lace-canopied bed and a sitting room, enhanced by a matching, ornately carved, red velvet settee, rocker, and chair set, all in mint condition. This is a chamber meant for fantasizing, where it's easy to imagine that you are the heroine of a romance novel, an adored bride recently wed to a cattle baron or to the owner of a rich gold-producing mine. Such a room must have witnessed many a scene like this; these walls, could they talk, would have wonderful stories to tell.

An abundance of doilies, pillows, quilts, and comforters contributes to the inn's cozy feeling, and an original sign in Room 30 advertises OATS FOR HORSE 1 CENT A GALLON. HORSES STABLED FREE. LIQUOR 6¼ CENTS A GLASS, WINE 25 CENTS A GALLON.

The Eating House serves light lunches, and The Owen Wister Dining Room offers plentiful fare, such as 16-ounce steaks. Less hearty meals of chops and seafood are also available.

This hotel sits out on the "lone prairie" where, indeed, the antelope still roam, and it is a must for anyone wanting a true glimpse of Old West elegance.

How to get there: From I–80 at Laramie, take Highway 30 north. Or, from I–25 at Casper, take Highway 220 south to Highway 487, then drive south on 487 to Medicine Bow. Hotel is on the main street.

Innkeepers: Vernon and Vickie Scott
Address/Telephone: Main Street of Medicine Bow (mailing address: P.O. Box 127); (307) 379–2377
Rooms: 21; 4 suites with private bath, 17 rooms share baths. Pets permitted with prior arrangements. No air conditioning (elevation 6,563 feet).
Rates: $22 to $35, double; $65 to $70, suite; EP.
Open: All year.
Facilities and activities: Full-service restaurant, saloon, ice water brought to rooms in antique pitchers. Nearby: museum, tours of world's largest wind generator, world's largest dinosaur find; Fossil Cabin, said to be the oldest building on earth; ghost town; hiking, fishing, downhill and cross-country skiing.

West Coast

by Julianne Belote

I once facetiously told a friend that the secret of my forty-plus years of marriage to the same man was never to have a meaningful conversation. I now concede there *is* another factor: frequent visits to romantic country inns.

Who can deny the spell cast by precisely the right ambience? Some couples will be delighted with a heart-shaped Jacuzzi tub and champagne breakfast in bed. Others prefer romantic weekends in elegant surroundings with sophisticated food and glamourous big-city attractions. I can go for that.

The West Coast has plenty of inns where you can indulge those yens. But it is our dramatic 2,000-mile-long coastline that offers some of the most beguiling lodgings. It's hard to beat walks above a windswept surf and intimate candlelight dinners in a cozy's inn's dining room.

This collection reflects a range of lodging from simple to splendid. If you claim even a faint ember of romance still glowing, *something* in these selections will fan it. That old Rogers and Hart song says, "My romance doesn't need a castle rising in Spain." Right. I don't need a castle either. But you do have to have a companion for a romantic idyll. And just to encourage a perhaps reluctant partner, it is worth noting that these West Coast inns are undoubtedly a lot more comfortable than most castles. If Jacuzzis, great food, or crashing waves don't pique a partner's interest, promises of comfort just may win the day.

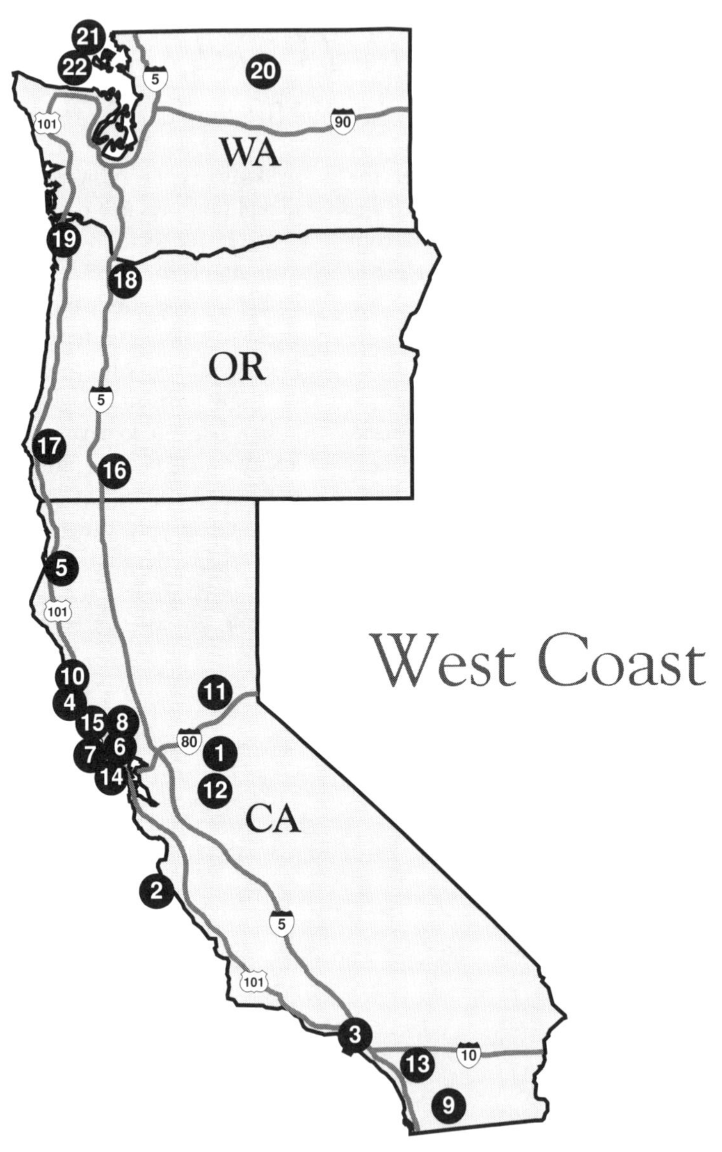
West Coast
WA
OR
CA
21
22
20
19
18
17
16
5
10
11
4
15
8
6
7
14
1
12
2
3
13
9
5
90
101
80
10

West Coast

Numbers on map refer to towns numbered below.

California

1. Amador City, Imperial Hotel 292
2. Big Sur, Ventana Inn 294
3. Dana Point, Blue Lantern Inn 296
4. Elk, Harbor House 298
5. Eureka, Hotel Carter 300
6. Glen Ellen, Gaige House 302
7. Guerneville, Applewood, An Estate Inn . . . 304
8. Healdsburg, Madrona Manor 306
9. Julian, Orchard Hill Country Inn 308
10. Mendocino, Agate Cove Inn 310
11. Nevada City, The Red Castle Inn 312
12. Oakhurst, The Estate by the Elderberries . . . 314
13. Palm Springs, Villa Royale 316
14. Sausalito, Casa Madrona Hotel 318
15. Timbercove, Timberhill Ranch 320

Oregon

16. Ashland, Mt. Ashland Inn 322
17. Gold Beach, Tu Tú Tun Lodge 324
18. Portland, Heron Haus 326
19. Seaside, Gilbert Inn 328

Washington

20. Leavenworth, Run of the River 330
21. Lopez Island, Edenwild Inn 332
22. Orcas Island, Turtleback Farm 334

Imperial Hotel

AMADOR CITY, CALIFORNIA 95601

I am smitten with this addition to gold country lodgings. The 1879 red-brick building with a painted white balcony stretching across the top story sits at the end of the main street running through tiny Amador City, population about 179 citizens. The scene awakens gold rush nostalgia; it's old, authentic, and redolent of romance.

The outside of this venerable hotel is thoroughly old-fashioned, but inside you'll find it has been stylishly renovated with all the modern amenities and a first-class restaurant. First stop should be the beautiful, old full bar, not a reproduction but the real McCoy. In addition to the usual spirits, they stock a large selection of beers and California wines. The low-key, friendly service here is one aspect of a romantic atmosphere throughout the inn.

The dining room has a certain touch of elegance with high ceilings, white tablecloths, and fresh flowers, yet it is welcoming and casual. The intimate room (seats fifty-five) has a changing display of local artwork that stands out beautifully against white walls. Dine in your traveling clothes, by all means, but you won't feel out of place if you want to dress for a special occasion, either.

The dinner chefs offer a menu that is both continental and California fresh. The appetizers are so good that it takes careful planning to save room for the entree. Roasted garlic with Brie and polenta crostini topped with prosciutto were the two we chose. The main event was a roast pork loin in prune sauce followed by an excellent salad with a house dressing I wish I could duplicate. The pastry chef had several hard-to-pass offerings and after all her work, how could we skip a poppy-seed butter-cream tart with fresh raspberries? Eating it seemed the only kind thing to do.

Six bedrooms upstairs are not large, but unexpectably comfortable and whimsically decorated. One has an art deco feeling with Maxfield Parrish prints and a ceiling fan. One has a vivid hand-painted headboard over the king bed and bright folk art on the walls. Rooms One and Two are slightly larger than the others and open onto the front balcony. (The traffic going by does fade away by 10:30 or 11:00.) Each room has a radio and a sparkling white tile bathroom that sports a hair dryer and heated towel bar.

Two balconies are upstairs, one at the back and one at the front of the hotel. A small library is at one end of the hall, with a desk, telephone, and door opening out to the balcony.

In the morning the innkeepers place coffee and newspapers in the hallway outside the guest rooms for early risers. Breakfast is a full, fresh meal prepared with the same skill as the dinner menu. Guests have the option of eating in their rooms, on the second-floor balcony, or downstairs in the dining room.

How to get there: Amador City is 2½ hours from San Francisco on Highway 49.

Innkeepers: Bruce Sherrill and Dale Martin
Address/Telephone: Highway 49 (mailing address: P.O. Box 195); (209) 267–9172
fax (209) 267–9249
Rooms: 6; all with private bath, air conditioning. No smoking in rooms.
Rates: $80 to $90, double occupancy, full breakfast. Two-night minimum when Saturday is involved, lower midweek rates. Singles deduct $5.
Open: All year.
Facilities and activities: Full bar, restaurant; serves dinner every night and Sunday brunch. Wheelchair access to dining room. Nearby: antiques and specialty shops in town; attractive opportunities for photographers in town and nearby mines; many wineries; seasonal events include fall Miwok Big Time Days at Indian Grinding Rock State Park, Daffodil Hill's spring blooms, Amador City's Calico Christmas.

Ventana Inn

BIG SUR, CALIFORNIA 93920

The Big Sur coast has always welcomed the offbeat, and even this sybaritic paradise was designed as a "different" kind of place: no tennis, no golf, no conventions, no Muzak, no disco delights.

What it does offer is a window (*ventana* means "window" in Spanish) toward both the Santa Lucia Mountains and the Pacific Ocean from a redwood and cedar lodge on a magnificent slope. This is the ultimate hideaway, a tasteful, expensive world of its own harmonizing with the wilderness surrounding it. For activity there are two 75-foot pools (heated all year) and two separate bathhouses with luxurious Japanese hot tubs, one of them with saunas. And there are walks over grassy slopes, through the woods, or on the beach. From every point your eyes go to the spectacular Big Sur coast, where boulders send white foam spraying into the air.

Some rooms in the cottages clustered around the lodge look down into a canyon of trees; others face the ocean. Their uncluttered blend of natural fabric and design makes each room seem to be the best one. Every detail—folk baskets holding kindling, window seats, quilts handmade in Nova Scotia, private terraces—has been carefully conceived.

A gravel path leads to the Mobil 4-star restaurant, with the opportunity of seeing native wildflowers and an occasional deer or bobcat on the way. The food is colorful California cuisine: fresh fish, veal, chicken, creative pastas, and a good wine list. The place to be at lunch is the expansive terrace with its 50-mile view of the coast. Dinner inside is a candlelight-and-linen affair. If you've walked over the hills enough, indulge in one of the many desserts from the in-house bakery.

A continental breakfast buffet, accompanied by baroque music, is spread in the lodge lobby by the rock fireplace: platters of melons, papayas, strawberries—whatever is fresh—pastries and breads baked in the Ventana kitchen, honey and preserves, yogurt and homemade granola. An afternoon wine-and-cheese buffet has an incredible array of domestic and imported cheeses.

The Ventana Store near the restaurant (books, baskets, original-design clothing, handmade knives, bird whistles) is as intriguing as its staff—all of whom seemed to be bilingual and have fascinating histories.

If "trickle-down economics" has dropped a little gold your way, this is the place to liberate your plastic for a romantic splash.

How to get there: On State Highway One, Ventana is 311 miles (about a six-and-a-half-hour drive) north of Los Angeles. The inn's sign is on the right. From San Francisco, the inn is 152 miles, 28 miles south of Carmel.

Innkeeper: Robert E. Bussinger
Address/Telephone: Big Sur; (408) 667–2331 or (800) 628–6500
Rooms: 60; all with private bath and TV, most with fireplace, some with private hot tub on deck.
Rates: $195 to $260 for standard guest rooms; $475 to $970 for suites with fireplace and hot tub; double occupancy, continental breakfast and afternoon wine-and-cheese buffet.
Open: All year.
Facilities and activities: Restaurant serves lunch, dinner; cocktail lounge; The Ventana Store. Hot tubs, saunas, swimming pool. Guided nature walks, massages, and facials available. Nearby: hiking, picnicking.

Blue Lantern Inn

DANA POINT, CALIFORNIA 92629

Dana Point is one of those picturesque little beach towns that epitomize the glamour of Southern California's coast—except that it's even better than most of them. Not as crowded as Newport and Balboa, not as rowdy as Santa Monica and Venice, not as nose-in-the-air exclusive as Malibu.

Blue Lantern Inn has a prime location atop Dana Point bluffs. When he stopped along this coast in 1834, Richard Henry Dana wrote in his journal, which was to become *Two Years Before the Mast,* "High table-land running boldly to the shore, and breaking off in a steep hill, at the foot of which the waters of the Pacific are constantly dashing."

Sound romantic? You bet it is—and gorgeous, too. Ask for a balcony room so that, in the morning, you can look down on a sparkling harbor, a 121-foot replica of Dana's brigantine *Pilgrim,* and, beyond the harbor breakwall, on a clear day, a view of the curve of Catalina Island.

For an inn so splendidly situated, the Blue Lantern more than lives up to its promise of comfort. Looking rather Cape Cod in style, the ambience inside is serene, understated, and luxurious. The lobby/sitting room has overstuffed couches and a massive stone fireplace that blazes a welcome at the slightest hint of a chill. A lavish and beautiful breakfast buffet is served at one end of this area, where you help yourself and sit at tables for two or four. On our visit breakfast included juices, melon slices, strawberries, blueberries, granola, cheese quiche, and muffins. The friendly help kept coffee cups filled and tables cleared.

An adjacent library features bleached oak paneling and more comfortable, cushy chairs. Afternoon tea and wine, with fresh fruit, cheese, and raw vegetable platter, are served here.

Our room had a fireplace, a small balcony large enough to sit on, and a huge bathroom featuring a separate shower and Jacuzzi tub-for-two, with a shutter door to fold back and watch the living room fire while you soak.

Every guest room is spacious, and some, like the Tower Suite, are downright lavish. Soft, muted colors like seafoam, lavender, periwinkle blue, and beige; traditional furniture; original art, and printed wall coverings combine for a romantic setting. Refrigerators and terry robes are just part of the scene.

The most unexpected aspect of your stay may be the warmth of your welcome and the genuine hospitality of the staff. It may sound cynical, but at an upscale Orange County beach inn, I almost expected a certain amount of slickness. How pleasant to be surprised.

How to get there: From Los Angeles, take 405 Freeway south to the 5 Freeway south. Exit at Pacific Coast Highway and veer to the right. Continue on PCH for 2½ miles to Street of the Blue Lantern. Turn left; inn is on the right.

Innkeeper: Lin McMahon
Address/Telephone: 34343 Street of the Blue Lantern; (714) 661–1304 or (800) 950–1236
Rooms: 29; all with private bath, Jacuzzi tub, wet bar, telephone, color television, and fireplace, most with panoramic ocean views. Handicapped facilities.
Rates: $135 to $350, double occupancy, buffet breakfast and afternoon tea, wine, and hors d'oeuvres. Special celebration packages.
Open: All year.
Facilities and activities: Library, exercise room, facilities for weddings and private events. Nearby: Dana Point Yacht Harbor; shops, galleries, and cafés of Dana Point and neighboring Laguna Beach.
Business travel: Located twenty minutes south of Orange County Airport. All rooms with private telephone, work space, good lighting; conference room; corporate guest program.
Recommended Country Inns® Travelers' Club Benefit: 25 percent discount, Sunday–Thursday, October–May, excluding holidays and special events, subject to availability, not combinable with other discounts, expires 12/31/97.

Harbor House

ELK, CALIFORNIA 95432

The windswept solitude of this stretch of Northern California's shore is one of nature's tens. And for an inn on the bluffs above the rocky coast, Harbor House has it all: a dramatic location, unique architecture, fresh decor, and fine food.

The house was built in 1916 entirely of virgin redwood by the Goodyear Redwood Lumber Company as a place to lodge and entertain its executives and guests. In the 1930s the house was converted to an inn, and it then variously faded and flourished over the years. The inn's present owners are warm hosts who understand exactly what a spell this inn can cast.

The large living room, completely paneled in redwood with a high-beamed open ceiling, sets the tone: quiet and unpretentious. Comfortable sofas and a piano are grouped on a rich Persian rug before a huge fireplace, with books and a stereo nearby. (Christmas here sounds wonderful—the redwood room glowing in firelight, a giant tree, roasting chestnuts, festive dinners, and music by local musicians.) Bedrooms and cottages are freshly decorated, many with pastel watercolor prints by a local artist of flowers and birds indigenous to the area.

Ocean views from the dining room are breathtaking. On blustery North Coast days, some guests choose to spend the day in this redwood-paneled room watching the churning surf. It's comforting to know that you don't have to leave this warm atmosphere to find a restaurant; wonderful food is in store for you here. Plan on candlelight and wine and long romantic dinners.

The Turners subscribe to that old verity of California cooking: Use only the freshest, best ingredients possible, and keep it simple. Many ingredients are plucked right from the inn's own garden. What they don't grow, they purchase from the finest local sources, like baby potatoes and the locally raised lamb. Fresh fish is often featured, prepared with Harbor House nuances. All the breads and breakfast pastries are homemade. Desserts also tend to reflect whatever is fresh. Typical are poached pears with raspberry sauce, or a sweet flaky pastry stuffed with apricots and cream. A fine California wine list and a good selection of beers are offered. Dinner is a fixed menu, changing every night, but with advance notice, they'll try to accommodate any special dietary needs.

Mendocino's attractions are only twenty minutes farther north, but I'm all for staying right here. Walking on the beach, discovering the secluded patios and paths—one leads to a waterfall and grotto—these are the quiet seductions of the inn. If you're in during the day, a bottle of local wine and a cheese platter from the kitchen are available to hold body and soul together until dinner.

How to get there: From the Bay Area, take Highway 101 to Cloverdale, then Highway 128 west to Highway One. The inn is 6 miles south on the ocean side of Highway One.

Innkeepers: Helen and Dean Turner

Address/Telephone: 5600 South Highway One (mailing address: Box 369); (707) 877–3203

Rooms: 10, including 4 cottages; all with private bath, 5 with private deck, 9 with fireplace.

Rates: $135 to $205, double occupancy, Sunday through Thursday, January through March, breakfast and dinner; $170 to $255, weekends; $175 to $265, April to winter, breakfast and dinner. No credit cards.

Open: All year.

Facilities and activities: Dinner by reservation. Private beach, fishing, ocean kayaking with guide. Nearby: Mendocino shops, galleries, restaurants, forest walks, local wineries; golf, tennis, horseback riding.

Hotel Carter

EUREKA, CALIFORNIA 95501

In the charmingly restored Old Town district of Eureka, the Hotel Carter brings an old Rodgers and Hart song to my mind—"There's a Small Hotel." I've always thought of that song, and small hotels, as the quinessence of sophisticated romance. More cosmopolitan than a homespun B&B, more warmly inviting than a sleek grand hotel, the Hotel Carter is everything you could want in the romantic lodging category. It's the perfect rendezvous—intimate, glamorous, and serving some of the best food and wines available north of San Francisco.

Most first-time visitors assume that Mark Carter restored the yellow Victorian-style building, but it is newly constructed, modeled after a nineteenth-century Eureka hotel. It blends the exterior look and ambience of the past era with today's luxurious conveniences, all done with Carter's impeccable taste in detailings and furnishings. (He also built from scratch the magnificent Victorian-style B&B across the street.)

You may very well fall in love with the hotel the minute you step into the lobby. Despite the Old World elegance of 14-foot-high ceilings here and in the adjoining dining room, even casually dressed travelers will feel at home in an atmosphere both chic and inviting. Plump sofas and chairs are grouped around the room and the work of local Humboldt County potters and painters is showcased brilliantly against the salmon-colored walls. Regional wine and hors d'oeuvres are set out in front of the lobby's marble fireplace in the late afternoon. You may enjoy a look at the hotel's wine shop (The 301 Wine Shop) with its excellent selection of rare and hard-to-find wines for sale. The restaurant's list won a "Best of Awards of Excellence" from the *Wine Spectator* in 1995.

Guest rooms are decorated in pale earth colors, with peach and white linens. They are furnished with handsome antique pine furniture combined with appointments we appreciate—reading lights, telephones, remote-controlled televisions hiding in wardrobes, and whirlpool tubs. Our suite on the second floor, with a fireplace, and a window-seat view of Humboldt Bay, was a spot we would love to return to often.

Breakfast and dinner in the intimate dining room bring some outstanding taste treats. Since the days when Christi Carter, while also managing two babies, cooked at their B&B across the street what came to be known as the famous Carter Breakfast, she has taken the lead in searching for the best chefs, the finest ingredients, and true cutting-edge cuisine. The Hotel Carter has become the right place to see that concern for excellent cooking come to fruition.

Our dinner one night began with baby greens dressed with a strawberry vinaigrette, fresh grilled swordfish with lemon butter, three perfect vegetables grown in the Carters' garden, a new small grain (something akin to couscous), and crusty baguettes. A local chardonnay and a pinot noir *had* to be sampled. A scrumptious apple walnut tart served with homemade ice cream and coffee saw us off to our room impressed with the quiet service and fine food.

If it weren't that the Carters are such nice people, I'd say, "Keep this delightful hideaway a secret."

How to get there: From Highway 101 in downtown Eureka, proceed west on L Street to the hotel.

Innkeepers: Mark and Christi Carter
Address/Telephone: 301 L Street; (707) 444–8062 or (800) 404–1390
URL: http://www.humboldt1.com/-carter52/Welcome.html
Rooms: 19 rooms, 4 suites; all with private bath, TV, telephone; 8 with whirlpool baths, suites with fireplace. Smoking in lobby only.
Rates: $89 to $300, including full breakfast, evening wine and hors d'oeuvres.
Open: All year.
Facilities and activities: Restaurant serves dinner every night. Lobby and dining room showcase of contemporary art. Tours of kitchen gardens available. Nearby: walk along brick pathway bordering marina, through restored Old Town with specialty shops, restaurants; hundreds of restored Victorian homes, many art galleries in town.

Gaige House

GLEN ELLEN, CALIFORNIA 95442

The Sonoma California wine region is an idyllic destination I return to over and over. Its shady country roads and rolling hills of lush vineyards are two never-fail ingredients for a romantic getaway. All you need is the perfect inn: Gaige House.

The name *Rouas* is well known around Northern California for fabulous lodgings and California cutting-edge cuisine. You've heard of Auberge du Soleil in Napa? One of the designers and partners of that highly acclaimed inn, Ardath Rouas, has now turned her skills to a more intimate country inn, this 1890 Italianate Queen Anne called Gaige House.

The immense Victorian has been completely restored with the finest modern conveniences while keeping its romantic ambience. First and foremost, the guest rooms are of unsurpassed comfort: down comforters and bed linens of Egyptian cotton (one full-time person is employed to do nothing but iron them); huge tiled bathrooms and first-class lighting; fresh floral bouquets; and inviting, cushy furniture.

The entire mansion is filled with fine furniture and riveting art that Rouas has collected from around the world. She displays it not just in the common rooms but throughout the house. Just one of the pieces that caught my eye is an enormous armoire from Bali that dominates the drawing room. Despite the elegance of polished oak floors, Persian rugs, and red velour sofas, this is an inviting room.

Each of the nine guest rooms is uniquely decorated. The largest (the Gaige Suite) could be called the "oh, wow!" room, since that's a frequent reaction on first seeing it. A huge four-poster canopy bed, puffy sofa in the sitting area, private deck overlooking the lawn, pool, and wooded hills, and a gorgeous tiled bath with a large Jacuzzi tub make it a favorite honeymoon suite. For a less expensive choice, consider one of the garden rooms facing the pool. They're smaller but still stylish, with queen-sized beds and private entrances.

Breakfast is served in the dining room or on the deck at tables for two or four. It includes fresh-squeezed juices and local seasonal produce (some of which is grown at the inn), and perhaps ham and eggs or oatmeal waffles. I realize you don't go to country inns with kitchens on your mind. Nevertheless, take a look at this one. Sensational!

When you've had enough sporting in the 40-foot pool, lounging on the great deck built over Calabezas Creek, strolling around the beautiful grounds, and exploring this elegant house, there is much more in the surrounding countryside to discover. The little hamlet of Glen Ellen that Jack London made famous is one of the most beguiling settings in the Sonoma wine region. Not smothered with tourists, abundantly picturesque, the Sonoma Valley is at the heart of Northern California's history. Historic landmarks and museums are nearby as well as dozens of premium wineries, fine restaurants, and local galleries. Not to be missed is the museum of London memorabilia and the remains of Wolf House, his private residence claimed by a fire before it was completed.

How to get there: From Highway 101, take the Napa/Vallejo exit (Highway 37), for 7½ miles. Turn left on Highway 121 for 6½ miles, to Highway 116, to Glen Ellen/Petaluma for 1½ miles. Continue for 8¼ miles straight to Arnold Drive through Glen Ellen to inn on the left.

Innkeeper: Ardath Rouas
Address/Telephone: 13540 Arnold Drive; (707) 935–0237
Rooms: 9, including 2 suites; all with private bath and air conditioning, 2 with fireplace. Television, radio, telephone available on request. No smoking inn.
Rates: $125 to $245, double occupancy, full breakfast and afternoon wine and cheese.
Open: All year.
Facilities and activities: Swimming pool, beautiful grounds and decks. Accommodates weddings and special events. Nearby: Jack London State Historic Park; wineries in Glen Ellen, Kenwood.

Applewood, An Estate Inn

GUERNEVILLE, CALIFORNIA 95446

Applewood, formerly called The Estate, is an unexpected taste of romantic glamour in the forested hills hugging the Russian River. As it twists through the Guerneville area, the river's beautiful natural setting has long been a popular choice for "resorts," cabins, cottages, and campgrounds. But . . . this is something quite different.

Handsome surroundings don't always mean a relaxig atmosphere, but that's not the case in this Mission Revival–style house. It was built as a private residence in 1922, and it remains an inviting country home, more comfortable and attractive than ever. On the main floor a large rock fireplace divides the living room from a many-windowed solarium that is now being used as a glamorous dining room. Bedrooms are on this floor as well as on the lower level; there they open to another comfortable sitting room.

I call the decor *Architectural Digest*—with warmth. Darryl studied design in San Francisco, and the house shows it. There's no one "look" but, rather, an understated chic. He's designed stylish slipcovers for some of the chairs and smart duvet covers for the beds. There are fine antiques among some just comfortable furniture. Both he and Jim are always looking for interesting pieces, but they admit that as much as they've bought, it seems to disappear in the large house.

Bedrooms are wonderfully romantic, and there's not a Laura Ashley in the lot. Billowing cotton draperies at an expansive bow of casement windows graced Number 4, my room. But every room, from smallest to grandest, has style, comfortable seating, and good reading lights. The luxury you'll find isn't in ostentation, it's in quality, such as down pillows and comforters, fine linen, and fresh bouquets.

Across the courtyard with splashing fountain the owner/innkeepers have added a second building to the property, a handsome Mediterranean villa that amazingly matches the first house. The new "piccola casa" has seven suites over three floors, with the penthouse being a spacious honeymoon suite with rooftop sun deck and stunning views. The other luxury rooms here have private verandas or patios, personally controlled heat and air conditioning, showers for two, and oversized Egyptian cotton towels.

But it's not just ambience that you're buying at Applewood. The food is quite special. I've breakfasted on a terrace by the pool and dined by the fire in the solarium. The innkeepers' four-course, prix fixe dinner offers several entree choices and a wide selection of local wines.

The ultimate romantic country inn experience, in my opinion, is staying in for dinner, as you can here at Applewood. A relaxing day exploring the Sonoma Coast, visiting wineries, or reading and napping at the inn can be capped off with a leisurely, candlelit dinner right here.

The innkeepers have succeeded in making this classic house a class-act inn by applying a simple philosophy: only the best of everything.

How to get there: From 101 north, take River Road/Guerneville exit just past Santa Rosa; go west 14 miles to Guerneville. At the stop sign at Highway 116 and River Road, turn left, and cross the bridge over River Road. The inn is ½ mile farther on the left. Local airport pickup.

Innkeepers: Darryl Notter and Jim Caron
Address/Telephone: 13555 Highway 116; (707) 869–9093
Rooms: 16 including 7 suites; all with private bath, TV, and telephone, some with fireplace, Jacuzzi tub, and private patio. Complete handicapped access. No smoking inn.
Rates: \$125 to \$250, single or double occupancy, full breakfast; two-night minimum on weekends.
Open: All year.
Facilities and activities: Fixed-price dinner Tuesday through Saturday; reservations required. Swimming pool, spa; facilities for private parties, small business seminars. Nearby: restaurants, golf, tennis, horseback riding; canoeing and other river activities; Guerneville shops; many local wineries; Sonoma Coast beaches. Armstrong Redwood State Reserve.
Recommended Country Inns® Travelers' Club Benefit: Stay two nights, get third night free, November–March, excluding holidays.

Madrona Manor

HEALDSBURG, CALIFORNIA 95448

Country inns continue to spring up in Northern California faster than yuppies are going out of style, but Madrona Manor stands alone. First, it is a truly dramatic Victorian mansion sitting in the midst of landscaped grounds and eight wooded acres. But even more notable is its outstanding California restaurant, the only one in Sonoma County rated three stars by *Chronicle* food critic Patricia Unterman.

The inn's romantic atmosphere begins even as you approach up the shaded driveway and the Italianate mansion first comes into view. Elegant accommodations await inside: antique furnishings, period wallpapers and rugs, and rooms with original plumbing and lighting fixtures. The third floor has renovated rooms with fireplaces, queen-sized beds, and antique reproduction furniture from Portugal. Less opulent but more modern rooms are in two other outbuildings and the Carriage House. Suite 400 in the Carriage House has French contemporary motif with a bath tiled in marble from Greece, a Jacuzzi tub, a fireplace, and a private deck.

Gourmet and *Travel and Leisure* are just two magazines whose critics have raved about the extraordinary food served here. Check out the fabulous kitchen and you'll see a professional staff at work in modern surroundings (contrasting with the rest of the 1881 setting) complete with a mesquite grill and a smokehouse in back that produces smoked trout, chickens, and meats. The gardens produce all the flowers for the dining room and guest rooms as well as herbs and specialty produce for the kitchen.

You shouldn't miss dining here during your stay . . . it's always a culinary treat. The menu lists four- and five-course prix-fixe dinners, at $40 and $50 respectively, at this writing. But smaller appetites are also taken into account. Both of the prix-fixe menus list prices for each course so that one can order à la carte.

My first course of individual goat-cheese soufflé was perfectly crusty on top, with a softly oozing middle. Every element of the meal, down to dessert of amaretto-soaked cake with chocolate-ricotta filling, was meticulously prepared.

The wine list is both extensive and reasonably priced, which, even though this is the heart of the wine country, is not always true up here. Some selections from small local wineries are offered at near-retail prices on a regular basis.

Breakfast for guests is as carefully done as dinner. It includes the wonderful house bread, toasted; a perfectly timed soft-boiled egg; loads of seasonal fruit; oatmeal and granola; ripe, room-temperature cheeses; and house-smoked meats. When the weather allows, take this meal outside on the palm terrace.

What a beautiful place for a special celebration.

How to get there: From San Francisco, drive north on Highway 101, 12 miles north of Santa Rosa; take the Central Healdsburg exit; follow Healdsburg Avenue north to Mill Street, turn left, and it becomes Westside Road. Inn is ¾ mile on the right. From the north, take Westside Road exit from Highway 101; turn right. Inn is ½ mile on the right.

Innkeepers: John and Carol Muir
Address/Telephone: 1001 Westside Road (mailing address: Box 818); (707) 433–4231 or (800) 258–4003, fax (707) 433–0703
Rooms: 18 and 3 suites; all with private bath, telephone, and air conditioning, 18 with fireplace. Wheelchair access.
Rates: $180 to195 in the Mansion; $140 to $170 in the Carriage House; $240 in Suite 400; $170 to $190 in Meadow Wood Complex; $210 in Garden Cottage; double occupancy, full breakfast. Half-price special rate January, February, March.
Open: All year.
Facilities and activities: Dinner nightly, Sunday brunch. Swimming pool. Nearby: golf, tennis, hiking, canoeing, fishing, winery tours, picnics, bicycling, Redwood State Park.
Business travel: Meeting space for up to forty; fax; food service.
Recommended Country Inns® Travelers' Club Benefit: 10 percent discount, Monday–Thursday.

Orchard Hill Country Inn

JULIAN, CALIFORNIA 92036-0425

Julian, Calfornia, may not be a romantic destination that leaps to your mind, but I urge you to reconsider. A new inn—architecturally inspiring, luxuriously comfortable, and staffed with well-trained, amiable people—is waiting to welcome you to a special experience.

Julian is high in the pine- and oak-covered hills of San Diego County's rugged backcountry. A well-preserved 1800s gold-mining boomtown, it is 60 miles northeast of San Diego and has about 500 inhabitants.

On a hilltop in Julian, four 1,200-square-foot cottages, each containing three plush suites, and, still higher on the hill, a magnificent lodge with nine more guest rooms, a great room, and the dining room constitute the inn. All the buildings reflect that noble design style so popular in the 1930s called California Craftsman. Pat Straube has stunningly decorated all the rooms—she's a pro, but that's obvious when you see her work.

The suites are named for local apple varieties. I was in the Cortland, done in a romantic blue toile fabric and wallcovering, with a private patio through French doors and a whirlpool tub. Suites also include fireplaces, sitting rooms with television and VCR, and private wraparound porches. Some, like the Roxbury, are especially spacious and come with a love seat that converts into a twin bed.

Up at the lodge, with its 180-degree view of

the town and surrounding hills, the nine guest rooms are somewhat smaller than cottage suites. They are, therefore, less expensive, and to my eye, just as thoughtfully appointed and beautiful as the suites.

The lodge's common areas are the awesome great room and a dining room. Large sofas and fine upholstered chairs are grouped around the great room and in front of a stone fireplace. Brilliant rugs on the adobe tile floor, elegant antique pieces, and a small wine bar in one corner only begin to define a remarkable space. French doors, from the dining room also, open to a stone terrace enveloping the lodge. Sit out here for breakfast and watch hawks circle in the smog-free sky, or take a glass of wine out for sunset.

Privacy and quiet are here. So clever is the inn's design, it's surprising to gather for breakfast in the lodge and see other guests. But never, never miss a meal at Orchard Hill. Their food will astonish you with its quality and sophistication. I had a dinner that included a rice vegetable soup, fresh salad greens with gorgonzola cheese and toasted walnuts, a gorgeous pork ragout, and the inn's trademark bread pudding with lemon sauce. This . . . is eating.

How to get there: From Highway 15 east and north of San Diego, exit east on Poway Road; proceed through the towns of Poway and Ramona to Julian. Cross Main Street and continue up the hill; inn is on your left.

Innkeepers: Darrell and Patricia Straube, owners
Address/Telephone: P.O. Box 425; (619) 765–1700
Rooms: 12 suites in 4 separate cottages, 9 rooms in main lodge; all with private bath, TV, VCR, telephone, some with whirlpool tub, fireplace, and private patio. Special accommodations for physically challenged. No smoking inn.
Rates: $110 to $124 for lodge rooms midweek; $130 to $145 weekends; Cottage suites $124 to $132 midweek; $145 to $155 weekends; double occupancy; 2-night minimum on weekends. Full breakfast; afternoon wine and hors d'oeuvres. Ask about special packages, off-season discounts.
Open: All year except brief closing in January.
Facilities and activities: Dinners served (to house guests only) usually 3 nights a week and additionally by arrangement; wine, beer, bar; large tape library; terraces, gardens, hammocks. Nearby: walk to downtown Julian for museums, restaurants, antiques, horse-drawn carriage ride to countryside; walk to gold mine; dinner theater; unlimited hiking, horse, and bike trails; local seasonal events.
Business travel: Conference room accommodates 25; fax, VCR, telephones; food service available.
Recommended Country Inns® Travelers' Club Benefit: Stay two consecutive nights, get second night free, Monday–Thursday, excluding holidays and special events, reservations required, expires 12/31/97.

Agate Cove Inn

MENDOCINO, CALIFORNIA 95460

A friend of mine who pursues a lively romantic life insisted that she had discovered a jewel in Mendocino that I had missed. "Fabulous views," she raved. "Best breakfast I ever had at an inn," she went on. "So low key . . . so fresh." Naturally, I had to check it out immediately—besides, traveling the Northern California coast is hardly a tough assignment. As it was an election year, I was ready to forgive a little exaggeration, but I was also prepared to be underwhelmed. Score one for my friend.

Agate Cove Inn is indeed a jewel. Sitting above and behind Mendocino Village on a bluff above the ocean, it appears to be an old farmhouse. That is just what the main house is, built in the 1860s by Mathias Brinzing, who established the first Mendocino brewery. Scattered through the grounds are the cozy cottages, each (except for one room where you have to make do with *only* a lovely garden view) with ocean views, a fireplace, a decanter of sherry, and a private deck for serious sea watches.

But nothing gives a lift to an already inviting inn more than new owners. Scott and Betsy are new proprietors here, but they are experienced innkeepers. They're gradually improving, refreshing, and updating every room. First finished is Obsidian, a large, pleasant room in whitewashed pine, with a colorful floral fabric on the king-sized bed, a gas fireplace, and a sitting area with big overstuffed, comfy furniture.

Other rooms have king- or queen-sized four-poster or canopied beds, handmade quilts, and country decor that goes for comfort rather than excessive cuteness. The luxury cottages have a large double shower or oversize tub, and considering California's water problems, it would be a crime to use one of them alone.

The main house has a spacious living room for guests to enjoy. A red-brick fireplace, bright wingback chairs, love seats, quilts, antiques, and books all bring a country warmth. The room is open to the breakfast room and stunning ocean vistas.

For some of us, breakfast really begins with the morning San Francisco newspaper on the doorstep—and that's the way they do it at Agate Cove, too—then a short walk on a flagstone path through the garden to the main house. Select your juice and fresh fruit and choose a table, already set with fresh, home-baked bread and jams. You must divide your view between your entree being cooked on an antique wood stove nearby and the drama out the window of crashing waves on the rocks below.

Mendocino is an enchanting seaside village, but it is not undiscovered. Agate Cove puts you close to all the village attractions—I walk rather than take the car—but just enough removed to feel that you're in a very special, romantic hideaway. For quiet, uncrowded—some say the most beautiful times—come during the winter season.

How to get there: About a three-hour drive from San Francisco via highways 101 and 128. When you reach the coast, a 10-mile drive north will take you to Mendocino. Upon entering Mendocino's Main Street, turn right on Lansing Street immediately after the traffic light. Continue about ½ mile north of the village to the inn.

Innkeepers: Scott and Betsy Buckwald

Address/Telephone: 11201 North Lansing Street (mailing address: P.O. Box 1150); (707) 937–0551; in Northern California, (800) 527–3111

Rooms: 10; all with private bath, and cable television, all but 1 with fireplace and ocean view. No smoking in rooms.

Rates: \$89 to \$225, weekdays; \$99 to \$250, weekends and July through October; double occupancy, \$25 for additional person; full country breakfast.

Open: All year.

Facilities and activities: Accommodations for weddings and special-occasion parties. Nearby: short walk to Mendocino Village galleries, Art Center, restaurants, specialty shops; hiking, canoeing, horseback riding, tennis, golf accessible.

The Red Castle Inn

NEVADA CITY, CALIFORNIA 95959

It's little wonder the own love with this red brick Victorian mansion the first time they saw it. Looking for all the world like the cover background for a Victorian roamnce novel, it has an undeniably romantic appeal. The thought of ever owning it was mere fantasy, but when at last the Weavers bought the inn, Mary Louise says, it was a case of a dream coming true.

Hanging on a hillside and nestled among dense trees, The Red Castle is an impressive sight from many places around Nevada City. The Gothic Revival mansion is wrapped in rows of white, painted verandas and lavished with gingerbread trim at roofline and gables. From the private parking area, walk around a veranda, with stylish canvas draperies tied back at each pillar, to the front of the house, where you can survey the historic mining town's rooftops and church steeples.

Since it was built in 1857, the castle has had a succession of caring owners who have maintained it without compromising its elegant period character. The Weavers have brought not only their respective professional skills in architecture and design but also some impressive art, including several Bufano sculpture pieces, and fine furniture. Seven guest rooms and suites range over the four floors, each one of them a vibrantly decorated, tasteful delight. Most furnishings are Victorian, but not fragile or frilly. An explosion of color from wallpapers, fabrics, and rugs has an engaging effect in combination with the dramatic architecture. The two-bedroom Garret Suite, on the fourth floor, has a sitting room, bath, and balcony. It was from here that the original owner's son used to serenade the town with impromptu trumpet concerts.

A cozy sitting room/parlor off the entry hall has gradually taken on a more authentic nineteenth-century form with the addition of a pair of upholstered Bar Harbor wicker armchairs and a handsome John Jelliff settee; Jelliff was a noted designer of parlor furniture of the time. Here, also, is a large and inviting collection of gold rush history and art books. We helped ourselves to an elegant tea spread here and took it outside. Three small terraced gardens, one with a fountain and pond, are idyllic sitting and strolling areas. A path through cascading vines leads down to Nevada City's main street.

The Weavers are proud of their vintage inn and are enthusiastic about Nevada City. They'll arrange a horse-drawn carriage tour through the town's historic district, and they always have good suggestions for restaurants and local events. Especially popular are the conversations you can have with Mark Twain and Lola Montez when these famous "guests" turn up at teatime. The Inn's own Victorian Christmas celebration is a truly memorable feast, one for which you should book well ahead of time.

The lavish breakfast buffet is a splendid sight—all of it homemade. Ours was typical, but the menu varies every day: juice, poached pears, glazed fresh strawberries, a baked egg curry with pear chutney, cheese croissants, banana bread, jams, Mary Louise's grandmother's bread pudding (what a treat!) with a pitcher of cream, and, of course, great coffee.

How to get there: From Highway 49 at Nevada City, take Sacramento Street exit to the Chevron station; turn right and immediately left onto Prospect Street. The driveway takes you to the back of the house. Walk around the veranda to the front door.

Innkeepers: Mary Louise and Conley Weaver
Address/Telephone: 109 Prospect; (916) 265–5135 or (800) 761–4766
Rooms: 7, including 3 suites; all with private bath. Third- and fourth-floor rooms air conditioned. No smoking inn.
Rates: $70 to $140, double occupancy, full breakfast and afternoon tea. Two-night minimum Saturdays April 1–December 31.
Open: All year.
Facilities and activities: Prix-fixe dinners served *en suite* by special arrangement; Saturday morning carriage rides, historical narratives and poetry readings, Victorian Christmas dinner and entertainment, picnic baskets by advance request. Nearby: walking path to downtown shops, restaurants, antiques; local theater, musical events; swimming in mountain creek; cross-country skiing twenty minutes away.

The Estate by the Elderberries

OAKHURST, CALIFORNIA 93644

Does a fairy tale castle in wooded mountain foothills, holding beautiful treasures and every luxury you can desire sound promising as a romantic idyll? I can tell you about such a place; you must provide an appropriate companion.

A nine-room castle/hotel called Château du Sureau (translates to "Castle by the Elderberry") and an extraordinary restaurant called Erna's Elderberry House comprise this remarkable inn. There is simply nothing else like it on the West Coast inn scene.

Both of the white-stucco, turreted, and red-tile-roofed buildings are the result of Erna Kubin-Clanin's dream to create an outstanding restaurant and then a small, very personal auberge in the California mountains. The astounding thing is that this uncommonly elegant lodging and sophisticated restaurant are in Oakhurst, a nondescript little town nestling in the rocky foothills of the Sierra Nevada, 20 miles from the south entrance of Yosemite National Park.

Plenty of people (especially her bankers) called her mad, but Erna opened her restaurant, Elderberry House, in 1984. Remote it may be, but Craig Claiborne of the *New York Times* found it, was captivated with the food, and stayed three days—sometimes helping Erna in the kitchen. Rave reviews in *Gourmet* and other publications followed, and Elderberry House was on the map.

Erna turned her sights next to building an accommodation as splendid as was required by guests who made their way to Oakhurst for her food. Château du Sureau opened in 1991, a $2 million, nine–guest room inn reminiscent of Erna's native Austria or a luxurious hillside estate in Provence. Don't give a thought to perhaps feeling ill at ease in an atmosphere this elegant. Just the opposite is true. I've rarely seen service of this caliber combined with such genuine warmth and hospitality.

On arrival, tour the castle, from the tiny chapel to the kitchen. Everything you see speaks of luxury and comfort: antique tiles, oriental rugs, tapestries, magnificent furniture, fresh flowers, and sumptuous bathrooms. The Grand Salon soars to an 18-foot beamed ceiling, with an 1870 piano from Paris the focus of attention two steps up in the circular Music Tower. We were still trying to absorb the splendor of our guest room surroundings when a chambermaid tapped at our door with tea and gourmet snacks.

That evening we walked through the lighted garden to Elderberry House for a leisurely paced, magnificent six-course dinner. We went with the restaurant's selection of three wines for the dinner, though you can choose from a large list. Back to the Château to lounge before the fire with some fine port, and so to bed.

I hope you won't just look at the rates and turn the page. Long after you've forgotten how much it cost, you'll remember dining and staying at this castle by the elderberries.

How to get there: Drive north on Highway 5 toward Sacramento. Take Highway 99 to Fresno. Exit at Highway 41 through Fresno and continue on another 40 minutes to Corsical, 7 miles south of the Château. At inn's sign, turn left at the second lane, through the gates on the right.

Innkeepers: Erna Kubin-Clanin, owner; Kathryn Kincannon, directrice
Address/Telephone: 48688 Victoria Lane (mailing address: P.O. Box 577); (209) 683–6860, fax (209) 683–0800; restaurant reservations (209) 683–6800
Rooms: 9; all with private bath, wood-burning fireplace, balcony, CD stereo system. TV and telephone available upon request. One room with handicapped access.
Rates: $250 to $350, double occupancy, European-style breakfast and afternoon tea. $3,500 for Château exclusive (up to 18 persons).
Open: All year.
Facilities and activities: Swimming pool, walking paths, small chapel; restaurant serves a six-course prix fixe menu ($38.50 to $40 without wine) Wednesday through Monday, and Sunday brunch; will arrange weddings and other special celebrations. Nearby: Yosemite National Park, Badger Pass ski area, boating and skiing on Bass Lake.

Villa Royale

PALM SPRINGS, CALIFORNIA 92264

Only a few blocks from slick downtown Palm Springs with glamorous big hotels lining the main drag, a more romantic alternative lies low on the desert plain just waiting to beguile you. Everything conspires at Villa Royale to make you think you're in an old European resort. Winding brick paths connect a series of courtyards with ancient-looking pillars under the red-tile roofs of surrounding rooms. Everywhere there are shade trees and pots of flowers, exotic vines and palms, small gardens and fountains. And on my March visit, the cascading bougainvillaea was dazzling.

From the blazing Palm Springs sun, you step into a lobby/sitting room with a cool tile floor and squashy sofa and chairs. Through this room you exit to the first large courtyard. Colorful and lush, the courtyard's well-maintained look is a result of the high standards of owner Robert Lee. After being gone for a few years, Bob is back and the inn has been undergoing a flurry of new linens and fresh upholstery. Along with a well-trained staff, always ready to help, you'll also find a generous attitude here. You don't get just *one* extra towel for the pool—you get as many as you need—big thick ones.

The variety of accommodations at Villa Royale is only one of its attractions. Whether you take a standard guest room or splurge on a deluxe studio with kitchenette, private patio, and spa, all the colorful ambience of flowers, fountains, and dramatic views of the San Jacinto Mountains is available to everyone. Every room, large or small, is decorated in an individual international style, the result of Bob's frequent buying trips to Europe. Each one has interesting treasures: woven hangings and table covers, wall carvings, bright pottery, sculpture, pillows, and antique furniture. All these things mean the inn's facilities are not well suited to children.

Across the first courtyard is the dining room, with a glass-enclosed casual area where breakfast is served looking out at the pool. The brick floor extends into a more formal interior room with a wonderful feeling. Armchairs with rush seats and cushions surround tables skirted with dark floral cloths to the floor and topped with lighter-color linen. The walls are a rosy adobe, and the soft lighting, beautiful china, and glassware create an atmosphere I would like to get used to. Our dinner in the restaurant was an attractively presented, relaxing experience: tortellini soup, green salad, scampi, and a marvelous fresh mango sherbet with ripe peaches and raspberries.

Visually rich as days are here relaxing in the sunshine surrounded with colorful flowers, wait 'til you see it at night! Dozens of small ornate brass lanterns hanging from trees and vines gleam with tiny lights and cast light and shadows throughout the courtyards. If you aren't enchanted, check your pulse.

How to get there: Proceed through downtown Palm Springs on its main street, North Palm Canyon. When it becomes East Palm Canyon, look for Indian Trail and turn left. Inn is straight ahead.

Innkeeper: Robert Lee
Address/Telephone: 1620 Indian Trail; (619) 327–2314, fax (619) 322–3794
Rooms: 31 suites and rooms; all with private bath, TV, and telephone, some with fireplace, kitchenette, and private spa. Limited wheelchair access.
Rates: $59 for standard guest room to $150 for 2-bedroom villa in summer; $75 to $225 in winter; double occupancy, continental breakfast poolside. Lower rates for longer stays.
Open: All year.
Facilities and activities: Restaurant serves lunch and dinner; full bar. Two swimming pools, spas, courtyards with fountains, outdoor fireplaces. Nearby: golf, tennis, horseback riding, Palm Springs shops, restaurants, aerial tramway ride up Mt. San Jacinto.

Casa Madrona Hotel

SAUSALITO, CALIFORNIA 94965

John Mays is an innkeeper who knows how to create an atmosphere. He's turned this luxurious old mansion perched on a hill above Sausalito into one of the most romantic inns you'll find. Of course, he has a lot going for him with a town almost too winning for words and spectacular views of the yacht harbor.

Casa Madrona is more than a century old. Time had taken its toll on the former residence, hotel, bordello, and boardinghouse when John Mays rescued it in 1978. It nearly slid off the hill during the rains of '82, but renovations already begun saved it from gliding away.

Since then Mays has added an elegant tumble of cottages that cascade down the hill to Sausalito's main street. Each one is different, with dormers, gables, peaked roofs, and hidden decks. Amazingly, the whole gray-blue jumble lives perfectly with the old mansion.

You've seen "individually decorated" rooms before, but these beat all. Mays gave each one of his hillside cottages over to a different Bay Area decorator. The range of their individual styles resulted in rooms with themes from nautical, to equestrian (The Ascot Suite), to a Parisian Artist's Loft. Most have private decks and superb views. And since it *is* fabled, sybaritic Marin, there are luxurious tubs for two (sometimes elevated and open to the room), refrigerators stocked with fruit juice and mineral water, and fresh flowers. (But no peacock feathers.)

If you're indifferent to unique rooms surrounded by lush gardens, exotic bougainvillea and trumpet vine spilling over decks and walkways, perhaps elegant food will ring your bell. A beautiful wine bar and uncluttered dining room in the old house on top of the hill are lighted and decorated to enchant. Only white linen on round tables and fresh flowers compete with the view from the deck of the bay and Sausalito Yacht Harbor . . . that is, until the food is served.

We began with what I thought was a California standard but which has become a part of American cuisine: radicchio and Belgian endive salad with baked chèvre (goat cheese). Perfection. Our waiter was agreeable when I ordered another first course (Asian crab cakes and lobster mayonnaise) instead of an entree. (I love places that encourage you to order by *your* appetite instead of *their* rules.) Others at our table raved about a grilled rare Ahi tuna and a guava-and-macadamia-crusted rack of lamb. The meal could not have been lovelier.

If this inn can't rekindle a dying ember, no place can.

How to get there: Cross the Golden Gate Bridge; take Alexander Street exit to center of town. San Francisco Airport pickup available. Ferry service from San Francisco.

Innkeeper: John Mays
Address/Telephone: 801 Bridgeway; (415) 332–0502 or (800) 288–0502
Rooms: 34; all with private bath, some with fireplace, private deck, water view.
Rates: $105 to $245, double occupancy; cottages, $165 to $185; 3-room suite, $415; continental breakfast and wine-and-cheese social hour.
Open: All year.
Facilities and activities: Dinner, wine and beer bar nightly; lunch Monday through Friday; Sunday brunch. Outdoor Jacuzzi. Elegant wedding and special events facilities. Nearby: Sausalito's shops and galleries, ferryboat rides across the bay, fine dining, hiking, bicycling.
Recommended Country Inns® Travelers' Club Benefit: Stay two nights, get third night free, Monday–Thursday, November–May, subject to availability.

Timberhill Ranch

TIMBERCOVE, CALIFORNIA 95421

When your stress level hits an octave above high C and you can't bear making one more earth-shaking decision . . . when you want to seclude yourself with nature (and a close, close friend) for some spiritual renewal . . . when you demand the best in fine food, service, and amenities . . . then head for Timberhill Ranch.

This classy resort on a very intimate scale is off the beaten track, perched high in the hills above the Sonoma Coast. Once you've checked in at the reception and dining area, you're shuttled to your cottage in a golf cart, and not a telephone or a discouraging word will ruffle your brow until you grudgingly conclude it's time to go home.

That Sonoma has fabulous climate, rugged beauty, unspoiled high meadows, and redwoods is undisputed. What *is* surprising is to find an inn with such luxury blending into these surroundings. All credit must be given to the two innkeeping couples who planned and built 80 percent of the resort themselves. Their vision accounts for keeping the ranch an underdeveloped oasis of tranquility; for only ten cottages, despite eighty acres of land; for building their world-class tennis courts far from the swimming pool, because "when you're lounging quietly by the water you don't want to hear tennis chatter."

The spacious, cedar-scented cottages are situated for maximum privacy. Each has a stocked minibar, a fire laid, a well-appointed tile bath, a handmade quilt on the queen-sized bed, comfortable chairs, good lights, and a radio. In the morning breakfast is delivered to your door to enjoy on your private deck as you look out at a stunning view.

What more? Superb food served beautifully in an intimate dining room with windows overlooking hills and forest—but without reservations, hurry, hassle, or check to interrupt. (Breakfast and dinner are included in the rate.) The six-course dinners (now open to the public by reservation) are what you might expect in one of San Francisco's finest restaurants. Here's a sample of one recent night: chilled artichoke with lemon mayonnaise, beef barley soup, salad with hearts of palm, raspberry sorbet, loin of lamb with red-pepper butter (among five other entree choices), and a dessert selection including puff pastry blackberry torte.

The four owners are hands-on innkeepers, always giving a level of personal attention far removed from a slick resort atmosphere. One told me, "We really like taking care of people and giving them the kind of service and privacy *we* looked for when *we* used to get away." As I watched the reluctant farewell of one couple, the hugs and promises to be back soon, I decided that Timberhill has all the right stuff, including a warm heart.

How to get there: From Highway One north of Fort Ross, turn east on Timber Cove Road. Follow to Sea View Ridge Road. Turn left; follow to Hauser Bridge Road and inn sign on the right.

Innkeepers: Barbara Farrell, Frank Watson, Tarran McDaid, Michael Riordan
Address/Telephone: 35755 Hauser Bridge Road, Cazadero 95421; (707) 847–3258
Rooms: 15 secluded cottages; all with private bath, fireplace, minibar. Handicap access. Smoking restricted to designated areas.
Rates: $350, double occupancy, Friday, Saturday, Sunday; $296, double occupancy, weekdays; breakfast and six-course dinner included.
Open: All year.
Facilities and activities: Lunch. World-class tennis courts, swimming pool, outdoor Jacuzzi, hiking. Nearby: 4 miles to ocean beach; Salt Point State Park, Fort Ross, The Sea Ranch public golf course.

Mt. Ashland Inn

ASHLAND, OREGON 97520

A late April snow was falling the first time I drove up the road to Mt. Ashland, making the passing scenery all the more breathtaking. At 5,500 feet, just 3 miles from the summit, the beautiful Mt. Ashland Inn sits nestled in the Siskiyou Mountains 16 miles south of Ashland, a snug romantic haven of outstanding craftsmanship and hospitality.

The cedar log structure was handcrafted from lumber cut and milled on the surrounding property. But don't picture a woodsy cottage improvised by a couple with some land and a chain saw. Remarkable design and woodworking skills are apparent everywhere your eyes rest—in hand-carved mountain scenes on the doors, the decorative deck railing, log archways, stained-glass windows, and a unique log-slab circular staircase. Most amazing to me were the six hand-made Windsor chairs, each one a smooth, perfect piece of art.

The peeled log walls of a common room draw you in with the warmth of cushy furniture, brilliant oriental rugs, mellowed antiques, and a stone fireplace. Can you imagine how a fire, music playing softly, and wine or hot spiced cider will hit you on a cold afternoon? Right. It means sleepy time in the mountains.

Each of the guest rooms upstairs has a view toward Mt. Shasta or Mt. McLoughlin, or into the beautiful forest. The Sky Lakes Suite on the ground floor has a Jacuzzi for two, a rock wall with trickling waterfall (operated by the guests), a rock patio, a wet bar, and a view of Mt. McLoughlin and Mt. Shasta.

When I looked out the window in the morning, the fir trees were thickly frosted with snow, and I felt like Heidi in Oregon. But pretending I was roughing it in the wilderness just wouldn't fly in the face of all the comforts: big chairs with reading lights by the windows, a comfortable bed topped with a handmade quilt, and the woodsy aroma of cedar filling the air.

Breakfast in the dining room was fresh juice and fruit and a tasty entree of puffy Orange French Toast. Daffodils on the table were picked that morning as they popped through the snow.

If you must stir from this comforting cocoon, a cross-country skiing path that ties into old logging roads is out the back door. Three miles up the road, Mt. Ashland offers fairly demanding downhill skiing. For hikers, the Pacific Crest Trail passes right through the property. The premier attractions in the area are the Ashland theater and excellent restaurants, about a twenty-minute drive from the inn.

A bonus of being up the mountain is that when Ashland is covered in clouds and fog, you're often in a pocket of sunshine here.

How to get there: North on I–5, take Mt. Ashland exit 6; turn right under the highway. At stop sign turn left; parallel highway ½ mile. Turn right on Mt. Ashland Road to ski area. Inn is 6 miles from the highway.

Innkeepers: Chuck and Laurel Biegert
Address/Telephone: 550 Mt. Ashland Road; (503) 482–8707 or (800) 830–8707
Rooms: 5, including 1 suite with Jacuzzi for two, and 1 with gas fireplace; all with private bath, queen- or king-sized bed, and individual thermostat; VCR available. No smoking inn.
Rates: $85 to $130, double occupancy, full breakfast and beverages. Special rates November through April, excluding holidays and weekends.
Open: All year.
Facilities and activities: New high-tech, lightweight snowshoes for guests' use; hiking, sledding, cross-country and downhill skiing. Nearby: river rafting, Ashland Shakespeare Festival February through October, Britt Music Festival June to September in Jacksonville.
Business travel: Located twenty minutes from downtown Ashland. Meeting room for small gatherings, with sitting area and audiovisual equipment.

Tu Tú Tun Lodge

GOLD BEACH, OREGON 97444

Here is a hideout for couple whose romance never glows more brightly than when they're fishing together, but dims when faced with the gritty realities of camping. Consider the motto of Tu Tú Tun Lodge: "Casual elegance in the wilderness on the famous Rogue River."

That's summing it up modestly, for this is a very special blend of sophistication and outdoors-lover's paradise. Top-notch accommodations and superb food are those of a classy resort, but the young owners create a friendly atmosphere that's more like that of a country inn.

Guest rooms are situated in a two-story building adjacent to the lodge. Each has comfortable easy chairs, extra-long beds, a dressing area, and a bath with tub and shower. Special touches that make wilderness life civilized aren't forgotten—fresh flowers, good reading lamps, and up-to-date magazines. Two recently redecorated rooms now have Japanese-style soaking tubs in their outdoor area. The suites can accommodate up to six persons each. No telephone or television intrudes as you watch the changing colors of the Rogue's waters at sunset from your private balcony or patio.

A bell at 6:30 P.M. calls guests to the lodge for cocktails and hors d'oeuvres. Dirk and Laurie introduce everyone, and by the time they seat you for dinner at round tables set for eight, you'll feel you're dining with friends. The set entree dinner they serve is outstanding. It always features regional specialties, frequently grilled over mesquite. Fresh chinook salmon, soup, crisp salad made from locally grown greens, freshly baked bread or rolls, and raspberry sorbet are a typical dinner.

After dinner, guests usually gather around the two fire pits on the terrace overlooking the river to enjoy a drink, inhale the scent of jasmine, and take in the beauty all around. There's much to talk about as you share ideas for the next day's plans. If those plans call for an early-morning rising for fishing, a river trip, or hiking, breakfast and lunch baskets will be ready for you.

One adventure almost every visitor to the lodge tries is the exciting 104-mile white-water round trip up (and down) the river. Jet boats stop at the lodge's dock to pick up passengers in the morning.

The inn's name comes from the Tu Tú Tun Indians, who lived in a village on the very site of the Lodge. *Tunne* meant "people"; *Tu Tú Tunne* were "people close to the river."

How to get there: Driving north on Highway 101, pass through Gold Beach, cross bridge, and watch for signs on right to Rogue River Tavern. Turn right and drive 4 miles to tavern; follow signs another 3 miles to lodge on the right.

Innkeepers: Dirk and Laurie Van Zante
Address/Telephone: 96550 North Bank Rogue; (503) 247–6664
Rooms: 16, including 2 suites each accommodating 6; all with private bath. Wheelchair access.
Rates: $115 to $155 for river-view rooms, $159 to $169 for suites, $189 for garden cottage, double occupancy, meals extra. $10 each additional person. Daily rate for two including hors d'oeuvres, dinner and breakfast: $190 to $200.
Open: April 27 to October 27. Two suites with kitchens available all year.
Facilities and activities: Breakfast, lunch, dinner for guests or by reservation, full bar. Swimming pool, 4-hole putting green; jet-boat white-water Rogue River trips; salmon and steelhead fishing, seasoned guides available. Nearby: scenic flights over Siskiyou Mountains, hiking, beachcombing, scenic drives, gambling in Gold Beach.

Heron Haus

PORTLAND, OREGON 97210

If an exciting city figures into your plans for a romantic tryst, Portland is a wonderful choice. But instead of an impersonal downtown hotel, consider a very civilized nesting spot like Heron House.

This is a gorgeous house! Its impact comes not from flashy, ostentatious appointments but from the combined impression of its gleaming wood floors, fine furniture, beautiful art and rugs, and hillside setting with stunning views of Mt. Rainier, Mt. St. Helens, and Mt. Hood.

Owner/innkeeper Julie Keppeler has drawn from her former life in Hawaii, her knowledge of Northwest Indians, and her innate good taste in transforming this 1904 Tudor house into a perfect urban inn. The labor of all those many months of work getting back to the original parquet floors, varnishing woodwork, and stripping wallpaper is invisible today. The house has such a solid, tastefully mellow feeling that you can perceive it as always having looked this way.

An abundance of common rooms are here for guests to enjoy: an enclosed east-view sunroom overlooking the pool, the morning room, a mahogany library and study, and a television room. Guests are encouraged to make themselves at home and roam through the house.

Guest rooms—all with Hawaiian names—are on the second and third floors and are especially spacious. Decorated in blues, lavender, and rose, they feel light and airy. All the rooms have queen- or king-sized beds, and all have ample sitting and work space.

It is ironic that the casual elegance of this house, with its atmosphere of gracious living, is every bit as convenient for the business traveler as a downtown hotel, and it's certainly more pleasant. Its close proximity to the heart of Portland, the beautiful library, good lights, and telephone and desk in your room provide no excuse for avoiding your work while you're in Portland. But there *is* an excuse. You're here for romance—so put down that phone!

Julie's dining room is another light-filled, handsome room. She does a sit-down breakfast service here between 8:00 and 10:00 A.M. In addition to fresh fruit, coffee, and teas, she offers cinnamon, raisin, and pumpkin pastries, date nut and orange rolls.

Heron Haus sits in the hills of northwest Portland in a neighborhood of some of Portland's oldest and finest homes. Directly below the house, an orange grove bordered by laurel, holly, and mature rhododendrons provides privacy.

It's an interesting area to walk in. Julie says that some of the best eating places in Portland are close by as well as a lively mixture of small businesses. Marvelous views of downtown Portland (and what a spectacular city it is) and its bridges over the Willamette River are just part of the perks that come with staying at this classy inn.

How to get there: From Highway 405 through Portland, take Everett Street exit to Glisan, a one-way street. Turn right at 24th Street, go 3 blocks to Johnson Street, and bear right onto Westover Road. At top of ½-block incline, you are facing the inn's driveway; proceed all the way up to parking area.

Innkeeper: Julie Keppeler
Address/Telephone: 2545 N.W. Westover Road; (503) 274–1846
Rooms: 5; all with private bath, telephone, alarm/radio, air conditioning, and sitting area, 1 with spa; television available. No smoking inn.
Rates: $85 to $250, double occupancy, generous continental breakfast.
Open: All year.
Facilities and activities: Swimming pool, panoramic views of city and mountains. Nearby: just above Portland's Nob Hill shops, boutiques, restaurants.
Business travel: Located minutes from Portland city center. Private telephones, free local and credit card calls; fax available; work space and desk in all rooms. Will accommodate small meetings. Corporate rates available.

Gilbert Inn

SEASIDE, OREGON 97138

Poets and dreamers are always struggling to express the magic of Oregon's exquisite coast; lovers are only required to enjoy it. That you'll be inspired is almost a guarantee. One special place to experience it is at an exceptionally attractive coastal lodging called Gilbert Inn.

This Queen Anne Victorian was built by Alexander Gilbert in 1892. It must have been the most beautiful house in town then, but today, after the lavish attentions of innkeepers Carole and Dick Rees, it is the very picture of a seaside inn—a yellow-and-white stunner with turret, porches, flagpole, gardens, and white picket fence. The parlor you enter signals the refreshing style of these innkeepers. They have a century-old house but have opted for traditional comfort and contemporary good taste rather than quaint clutter. The big fireplace in the center of the room and the natural fir tongue-and-groove ceilings and walls throughout the house contribute a cozy warmth and appealing period charm. But the dazzling green rug and fresh floral coverings on sofas and chairs are fashionable and lively.

Each of the eight guest rooms and two suites is distinct and decorated so engagingly that I couldn't choose one over another. The thick carpeting, down comforters, linens, and pillows are all of fine quality. Again, Carole has decorated captivating, pretty rooms but without clutter. The Turret Room is popular with its tall four-poster bed, old fir ceilings and walls, and the turret window. The Garret constitutes the entire third floor and has a queen and two twin beds, a sitting area and an ocean peek through a dormer window.

Four new accommodations in the garden offer unusual privacy and flexibility. Each one has a full kitchen, two bedrooms (one with a queen-size bed, the other with two twins), full bathroom, living and dining rooms. Each has its own outside entrance and private patios and gardens. These garden units are a real bargain when you're traveling with children or another couple.

Breakfast is served on a restored side porch that looks out on a flower garden. Pink walls, white iron tables and chairs, pink-and-white oriental rugs, and lots of green plants make the setting one of the prettiest places you'll ever linger over breakfast. I wonder how the Reeses ever get their guests to move on. Breakfast menus include a wide variety of Rees specialties, but one recipe is an especially big hit—French toast with a filling of cream cheese and walnuts, baked and served with an apricot sauce.

But Seaside is a popular and historic town and there are things to see. Many of the town's attractions are within walking distance of the inn. The Turnaround, at the end of Broadway (the main street), is the official end of the Lewis and Clark Trail. This is a spot to watch the sun set over the Pacific.

The standards of quality and comfort to be enjoyed at Gilbert Inn make it one of the best bargains I found on the Oregon Coast.

How to get there: Driving north, exit Highway 101 at the City Center on Holiday Drive. Continue to a flashing red light, Avenue A; turn left and proceed to the beach. Inn is on the left corner at A and Beach. Driving south, exit 101 at North Broadway. Proceed 2 blocks past Broadway to Avenue B. Turn right to the ocean. Inn is on the left.

Innkeepers: Dick and Carole Rees
Address/Telephone: 341 Beach Drive; (503) 738–9770
Rooms: 10, including 2 suites; all with private bath and TV. No smoking inn.
Rates: $79 to $95, double occupancy, full breakfast. Garden units $95 double occupancy, $114 for four, breakfast not included.
Open: All year except January.
Facilities and activities: Nearby: 1 block to the beach, 1 block to main street shops, restaurants, other attractions; Quatat Marine Park, Seaside Museum, Tillamook Head Trail, Fort Stevens State Park, Cannon Beach.

Run of the River

LEAVENWORTH, WASHINGTON 98826

It's safe to say that before you leave Run of the River you'll be planning a return visit. Situated on two acres in an alpine meadow in the Cascade Mountains, this log inn is a hidden jewel. For a romantic hideaway, for nature lovers, for the world-weary, this is a beautiful, safe haven with all the comforts you could desire.

The six bedrooms are uniquely private and quiet. While each is distinct, all the rooms have the warmth of log walls, tall cathedral pine ceilings, hand-hewn log furniture, luxurious baths, and private decks.

They differ in their appointments of colorful Northwest Indian objects, excellent-quality bed linens, and handsome furniture pieces. Three rooms have lofts, snug places to take a snooze or read away a quiet afternoon. But it's the private deck that is each room's most important appointment; it puts you in a front-row seat for one of nature's "tens" on the gorgeous scale.

The inn sits in a meadow sliced through by the Icicle River and surrounded by the magnificent Cascade Mountains. A small island in the river is a wildlife refuge, and if you sit quietly, you'll see the movement and hear the subtle sound of nature all around you—a host of migrating waterfowl, Canada geese, bald eagles, osprey, and the kingfisher, fluttering above the water to dive in and nab a fish. In summer at twilight, deer drink from the river, and there is even an occasional black bear.

Every season has its special rewards here, but innkeepers Monty and Karen say they look forward most to winter. Covered with fresh white snow, meadow and river frozen, Cascades white-tipped, the inn and the entire valley are a spectacular sight. This is when young, enthusiastic innkeepers (like M. and K.) go into action. They know a dozen great cross-country ski trails, which ones are worth buying a pass for, which are free. They'll book you on an old-fashioned sleigh ride or a snowmobile safari. They'll provide the carrots and charcoal if you want to build a snowman in the meadow, and they'll have a fire, the hot tub, and hot coffee ready when you come inside.

A large common room with an attractive kitchen in one corner is the heart of the inn. A big, full breakfast is served here at a long pine table. Windows across the front of the room look out at the meadow and river. You could very cozily spend the day right here.

I haven't told you the delights of spring, summer, and fall at the inn or detailed the Bavarian Village of Leavenworth's attractions, but here's the main lesson: Run of the River is quite special, with two especially caring—and fun—innkeepers.

Slow down . . . listen . . . watch . . . breathe in and out . . . feel the air. This just might be heaven on earth.

How to get there: Traveling south on Highway 2 through Stevens Pass or driving north from Wenatchee, exit at East Leavenworth Road. Drive exactly 1 mile and turn down gravel driveway to the inn.

Innkeepers: Monty and Karen Turner
Address/Telephone: 9308 East Leavenworth Road (mailing address: P. O. Box 285); (509) 548–7171 or (800) 288–6491
Rooms: 6, including 2 suites; all with private bath, spacious deck, and cable TV, 3 with Jacuzzi tub, some with loft. No smoking in inn or on grounds.
Rates: $95 to $150, double occupancy, full breakfast and afternoon refreshments. Two-night minimum stay on weekends and holidays.
Open: All year.
Facilities and activities: Hot tub, mountain bikes available March through November; magnificent views of river and wildlife from decks; will arrange horse-drawn sleigh rides, horseback rides, cross-country ski lessons, rafting, day hikes. Nearby: bird refuge; hiking or cycling along river; cross-country and downhill skiing; snowshoeing; Bavarian Village with Leavenworth's restaurants, unique shops.

Edenwild Inn
LOPEZ ISLAND, WASHINGTON 98261

When your request for a reservation is answered with a map of an island, a ferry schedule, and the assurance that ferry landing, seaplane, and airport pickup are available, I say you're on your way to an adventure. The Edenwild Inn on Lopez Island is such a place. Just getting there is a romantic adventure.

The island slopes gently up from the ferry landing to reveal rural nature at its most picturesque. Pasture, fields, and farms are interspersed with dense woodland, and the shoreline is notched with bays and coves.

The recently built inn is about 4½ miles from the ferry landing. A broad porch dotted with chairs wraps around three sides of the large house, giving it an inviting, traditional look. Dozens of antique rose bushes and a green lawn brighten a brick patio and pergola to the parking area. Inside is a spacious, casually elegant country house with pale oak floors and fresh bouquets. Bright fabrics cover sofas and chairs grouped before the fireplace. An old upright piano sits here, and the work of some wonderful local artists is displayed here and all through the inn. Breakfast and other meals are served in the adjoining dining room.

Each one of the seven bedrooms appeals to me. It could be because they are new and fresh, or perhaps it is the comfortable built-in beds, or the terrific looking black-and-white tile bathrooms, or the views—Fisherman's Bay, garden, or San Juan Channel. From Room 5 we thought our view of the main garden and the channel the best in the house . . . until we watched a magnificent sunset that beat them both.

In addition to a full, family-style breakfast for house guests, Susan offers wintertime island visitors (November through April) her version of a soup kitchen. Her collection of great soup recipes is the source for lunches of a bowl or cup of homemade soup, freshly baked bread from an island bakery, and desserts. Susan is also having fun during the winter months with Saturday-night ethnic dinners—anything from Chinese to Cajun. The only thing certain is that you'll need a reservation. This energetic innkeeper and her staff will see that you eat well, have a good time, and leave totally rejuvenated.

An unexpected bit of excitement occurred as we were packing the car to leave. An awfully attractive man helped put our bags in the trunk and then blushed modestly when we recognized his well-known face. When he's at the inn, this first-rate actor is strictly Susan's husband.

If you're young and have more energy than money, you should consider buying a "walk-on" ticket (much cheaper than taking a car.) Bring your bicycle and backpack, or you can arrange for an inn pickup. This is a wonderful island for bicycling.

How to get there: From the Lopez Island Ferry Landing, proceed 4½ miles to Lopez Village Road. Turn right.

Innkeeper: Susan Aran
Address/Telephone: Lopez Road (mailing address: P. O. Box 271); (360) 468–3238
Rooms: 8; all with private bath, some with fireplace; garden and water views. Handicapped facilities. No smoking inn. Children especially welcome.
Rates: $100 to $140, double occupancy, full breakfast and afternoon aperitif. Winter rates November through March: all rooms $75.
Open: All year.
Facilities and activities: Facilities for small weddings and small conferences. During the summer, gourmet take-out food to eat on outdoor patio or in dining room; during the winter, lunch and Saturday-night ethnic dinners by reservation. Nearby: Lopez Village shops, hiking, bicycling. Ferry landing, seaplane, or airport pickup available.

Turtleback Farm

ORCAS ISLAND, WASHINGTON 98245

When an escape from the fast track is high on your list of romantic priorities, a picturesque inn on one of the San Juan Islands is an ideal choice.

Set back from a country road, Turtleback Farm looks like an attractive, well-kept old farmhouse, a big green two-story clapboard building. But it's been featured in numerous articles, and, despite a remote location, it is usually booked months in advance. This may well be the gem lodging of Orcas Island.

The reasons are clear once you settle in. This is a first-rate, impeccably maintained inn. It delivers the quiet country charm that so captivates inngoers but with all the comforts you could ask for.

The inn was once an abandoned farmhouse being used to store hay, now restored from the ground up. There are seven guest rooms, a parlor, a dining room, and a tree-shaded deck that runs the length of the house. This is a wonderful place to sit on a warm day and enjoy looking out at acres of meadow with mountains beyond. We're talking idyllic, tranquil setting.

Even if the weather turns dismal, the comforts of this house will keep you charmed. The decor is tasteful and nonfussy, with muted colors and mellow wood trim and floors, and open-beam ceilings. Each guest room has a modern bath appointed with antique fixtures, claw-footed tub, pull-chain toilet, and wall shower. The pedestal sinks came from the Empress Hotel in Victoria. There's a cozy parlor where you can curl up and read before a fire. (The custom here is, "If you find a book you can't put down, take it with you and just return it when you finish.")

The dining room is still another place to enjoy the view and have a cup of tea or a glass of sherry. An outstanding breakfast is served here, course by course at individual tables on bone china. The menus change, but a typical morning would see juices, local berries, granola, an omelet with ham, and English muffin. Seconds are always offered. Breakfast is served between 8:00 and 9:00 A.M., but the innkeepers are always ready to accommodate an early ferry schedule.

What do you do on an eighty-acre farm if you're fresh from the city? If you're smart, you settle yourself on the deck with a blade of grass between your teeth, a big hat tipped down over your nose, and think things over—very, very slowly. Then there are the exhausting demands of critter watchin'. There are ducks and blue heron, sheep, chickens, a rambunctious brown ram named Oscar, and visiting Canada geese. If you're a picnic fan, the paths leading to private little spots will be irresistible. The Fletchers make every effort to acquaint you with all that the island offers. They'll make arrangements for you to charter a boat, fish at the nearby park, rent a moped, play golf, or whatever sounds good to you.

How to get there: From Orcas Island ferry landing, proceed straight ahead on Horseshoe Highway to first left turn; follow to Crow Valley Road. Turn right and continue to the inn, 6 miles from ferry landing. Fly-in: Eastsound Airport.

Innkeepers: Bill and Susan Fletcher
Address/Telephone: Crow Valley Road (mailing address: Route 1, Box 650, Eastsound); (360) 376–4914 or (800) 376–4914
Rooms: 7; all with private bath and individual heat control. Wheelchair access. No smoking inn.
Rates: $80 to $110, winter; $80 to $160, April 1 to November 1; double occupancy, full breakfast and afternoon beverage.
Open: All year.
Facilities and activities: Farm animals, pond. Nearby: hiking trails in Moran State Park; bicycle and moped rentals; swim, picnic at Lake Cascade; fishing, kayaking, sailing; good restaurants.

Indexes

Alphabetical Index to Inns

Adams Edgeworth Inn (TN) 140
Adobe & Pines Inn (NM) 214
Agate Cove Inn (CA) 310
American Club, The (WI) 184
Amos Shinkle Town House (KY) 118
Ansonborough Inn (SC) 138
Antrim 1844 (MD) 60
Applewood, An Estate Inn (CA) 304
Barrow House (LA) 124
Bay Breeze Guest House (AL) 100
Bee and Thistle Inn (CT) 8
Bird and Bottle Inn, The (NY) 10
Bisbee Grand Hotel (AZ) 196
Blackwell House Bed & Breakfast, The (ID) . . . 262
Blue Lantern Inn (CA) 296
Bradley Inn at Pemaquid Point, The (ME) 20
Browning Plantation, The (TX) 218
Cambridge Inn (NE) 174
Cameo Rose Bed and Breakfast, (WI) 180
Canoe Bay (WI) 182
Casa de Patron (NM) 210
Casa Europa (NM) 216
Casa Madrona Hotel (CA) 318
Castle Marne (CO) 250
Chalet Suzanne (FL) 110
Charlotte Inn, The (MA) 24
Charnwood Hill Inn (TX) 236
Checkerberry Inn, The (IN) 150
Cheyenne Cañon Inn (CO) 246
Clifton: The Country Inn (VA) 86
Copper Beech Inn (CT) 6
Copper King Mansion Bed & Breakfast (MT) . . 268
Creekwood Inn, The (IN) 152
Crested Butte Club Victorian Hotel
& Spa (CO) 248
Davy Jackson Inn (WY) 282
Edenwild Inn (WA) 332
Estate by the Elderberries, The (CA) 314
Evergreen Inn, The and 1109 South Main
Restaurant (SC) 136
Father Ryan House Bed and Breakfast
Inn, The (MS) 126
Gaige House (CA) 302
Gastonian, The (GA) 114
Gilbert Inn (OR) 328
Gilded Thistle (TX) 226
Glasbern (PA) 84
Glendorn (PA) 80
Glen-Ella Springs (GA) 112
Gold Hill Hotel (NV) 274
Grand Hotel (MI) 164
Gregory's McFarland House (ID) 264
Gruene Mansion (TX) 230
Harbor House (CA) 298
Heartstone Inn and Cottages (AR) 104
Heron Haus (OR) 326
Hickory Nut Gap Inn (NC) 130
Hillbrook Inn (WV) 94

Historic Virginian Hotel, The (WY) 286
Home Hill Inn (NH) 36
Hotel Carter (CA) 300
Hotel St. Germain (TX) 220
Imperial Hotel (CA) 292
Inn above Onion Creek, The (TX) 238
Inn at Brandywine Falls, The (OH) 178
Inn at Buckeystown, The (MD) 58
Inn at Chagrin Falls, The (OH) 176
Inn at Chester, The (CT) 4
Inn at Montchanin Village, The (DE) 52
Inn at Ormsby Hill, The (VT) 44
Inn at the Citadel (AZ) 200
Inn at Thorn Hill, The (NH) 34
Inn at Twin Linden, The (PA) 82
Inn on Winter's Hill, The (ME) 18
Izaak Walton Inn (MT) 270
John Hancock Inn, The (NH) 32
Kimberly Country Estate (MI) 162
La Colombe d'Or (TX) 228
La Corsette Maison Inn (IA) 156
Lakehouse Inn (NY) 78
Lake Placid Lodge (NY) 74
Langdon House (NC) 132
Las Campañas de Taos (NM) 208
Lilac Inn (VT) 40
Little St. Simons Island (GA) 116
Lovelander Bed & Breakfast Inn, The (CO) ... 258
Lumber Baron Inn, The (CO) 252
Madrona Manor (CA) 306
Mainstay, The (NJ) 62
Malaga Inn (AL) 102
Mayflower Inn, The (CT) 12
Meadow Creek Bed & Breakfast Inn (CO) 260
Meadows Inn, The (AZ) 198
Merry Sherwood PLantation (MD) 56
Morgan-Samuels B&B Inn (NY) 66
Mr. Mole Bed and Breakfast (MD) 54
Mt. Ashland Inn (OR) 322
Mulberry Manor (TX) 234
Notchland Inn, The (NH) 30
Oaks Victorian Inn, The (VA) 88
Oak Tree Inn (AR) 106
Ogé House, The (TX) 232
Old Chatham Sheepherding Company Inn (NY) 76
Old Drovers Inn (NY) 68
Orchard Hill Country Inn (CA) 308
Page House Inn, The (VA) 90
Paz de Nogal (NM) 212
Pentagöet Inn, The (ME) 14
Pinecrest Bed & Breakfast Inn (UT) 278
Pine Garth Inn (MI) 166
Pine Ridge Inn (MI) 160
Prospect Hill (VA) 92
Queen Anne Bed & Breakfast (CO) 254
Rabbit Hill Inn (VT) 42
Rainsford Inn (WY) 280
Red Castle Inn, The (CA) 312
River Song Inn (CO) 256
Rose Bed and Breakfast (WI) 180
Rose Inn (NY) 72
Rosemont Inn, The (MI) 158
Rosewood Inn (MN) 168
Run of the River (WA) 330
Saddle Rock Ranch (AZ) 202
Sanders-Helena's Bed & Breakfast, The (MT) 272
Sardy House (CO) 244
Saybrook Point Inn & Spa (CT) 10
1735 House, The (FL) 108
Shepherd Place (KY) 120
Squiers Manor (IA) 154
St. Charles House (MO) 172
St. Croix River Inn (WI) 188
Suncatcher, The (AZ) 204

Sunset Heights Inn (TX) 222
Terry Ranch (AZ) 206
Tezcuco Plantation (LA) 122
Thorwood Inn (MN) 170
Timberhill Ranch (CA) 320
Turtleback Farm (WA) 334
Tu Tú Tun Lodge (OR) 324
Twin Farms (VT) 38
Ventana Inn (CA) 294
Veranda Country Inn (TX) 224
Villa Royale (CA) 316
Victorian Treasure Bed and Breakfast (WI) 186
Village Country Inn, The (VT) 46
Von-Bryan Inn (TN) 142
Voss Inn, The (MT) 266
Washington School Inn (UT) 276
Wequassett Inn (MA) 22
Weymouth Hall (MS) 128
Wheatleigh (MA) 26
Wheaton, The (IL) 148
White Barn Inn (ME) 16
White Lace Inn (WI) 190
Wildflower Inn, The (WY) 284
Windsong (NC) 134
Woolverton Inn, The (NJ) 64
Yankee Clipper Inn (MA) 28

Inns on or near Lakes or Rivers

Blackwell House Bed & Breakfast, The (ID) . . . 262
Canoe Bay (WI) 182
Cheyenne Cañon Inn (CO) 246
Clifton: The Country Inn (VA) 86
Creekwood Inn, The (MI) 152
Davy Jackson Inn (WY) 282
Grand Hotel (MI) 164
Gregory's McFarland House (ID) 264
Gruene Mansion (TX) 230
Hillbrook Inn (WV) 94
Hotel St. Germain (TX) 220
Inn above Onion Creek (TX) 238
Inn at Brandywine Falls, The (OH) 178
Inn at Chagrin Falls, The (OH) 176
John Hancock Inn, The (NH) 32
Kimberly Country Estate (MI) 162
Lakehouse Inn (NY) 78
Lake Placid Lodge (NY) 74
Meadows, The (AZ) 198
Oak Tree Inn (AR) 106
Page House Inn, The (VA 90
Paz de Nogal (NM) 212
Pinecrest Bed & Breakfast Inn (UT) 278
Pine Garth Inn (MI) 166
Rosemont Inn, The (MI) 158
Run of the River (WA) 330
Terry Ranch (AZ) 206
Turtleback Farm (WA) 334
Twin Farms (VT) 38
Washington School Inn, The (UT) 276
Wheatleigh (MA) 26

Inns at or near the Seashore

Agate Cove Inn (CA) 310
The Ansonborough (SC) 138
Applewood, An Estate Inn (CA) 304
Bay Breeze Guest House (AL) 100
Bee and Thistle Inn (CT) 8
Blue Lantern (CA) 296
Bradley Inn (ME) 20
Casa Madrona Hotel (CA) 318
Charlotte Inn, The (MA) 24
Edenwild Inn (WA) 332
Father Ryan House Bed and Breakfast Inn, The (MS) 126
Gilbert Inn (OR) 328
Gilded Thistle, The (TX) 226
Harbor House (CA) 298
Hotel Carter (CA) 300
Langdon House (NC) 132
Little St. Simons Island (GA) 116
Mainstay, The (NJ) 62
Merry Sherwood Plantation (MD) 56
Page House Inn, The (VA) 90
Pentagöet Inn, The (ME) 14
Saybrook Point Inn & Spa (CT) 10
1735 House, The (FL) 108
Timberhill Ranch (CA) 320
Turtleback (WA) 334
Tu Tú Tun Lodge (OR) 324
Ventana (CA) 294
Wequassett Inn (MA) 22
White Barn Inn (ME) 16
Yankee Clipper Inn (MA) 28

Inns with, or with Access to, a Swimming Pool

American Club, The (WI) 184
Antrim 1844 (MD) 60
Applewood, An Estate Inn (CA) 304
Browning Plantation, The (TX) 218
Chalet Suzanne (FL) 110
Crested Butte Club (CO) 248
Estate by the Elderberries, The (CA) 314
Father Ryan House Bed and Breakfast Inn (MS) 126
Gaige House (CA) 302
Glasbern (PA) 84
Glendorn (PA) 80
Glen-Ella Springs (GA) 112
Grand Hotel (MI) 164
Heron House (OR) 326
Home Hill Inn (NH) 36
Inn at Thorn Hill, The (NH) 34
Inn on Winter's Hill, The (ME) 18
Kimberly Country Estate (MI) 162
Las Campañas de Taos (NM) 208
Little St. Simons Island (GA) 116
Lovelander Bed & Breakfast Inn, The (CO) .. 258
Madrona Manor (CA) 306
Prospect Hill (VA) 92
Rosemont Inn, The (MI) 158
Sardy House (CO) 244
Saybrook Point Inn & Spa (CT) 10
Suncatcher, The (AZ) 204
Sunset Heights Inn (TX) 222
Timberhill Ranch (CA) 320
Tu Tú Tun Lodge (OR) 324
Ventana Inn (CA) 294

Villa Royale (CA) 316
Village County Inn, The (VT) 46
Windsong (NC) 134
Yankee Clipper Inn (MA) 28

Inns with Downhill or Cross-Country Skiing Nearby

American Club, The (WI) 184
Blackwell House Bed & Breakfast, The (ID) . . 262
Canoe Bay (WI) 182
Casa de Patron (NM) 210
Casa Europa (NM) 216
Castle Marne (CO) 250
Checkerberry Inn, The (IN) 150
Cheyenne Cañon Inn (CO) 246
Copper King Mansion Bed & Breakfast (MT) 268
Creekwood Inn, The (IN) 152
Crested Butte Club (CO) 248
Davy Jackson Inn (WY) 282
Estate by the Elderberries, The (CA) 314
Glasbern (PA) 84
Glendorn (PA) 80
Gold Hill Hotel (NV) 274
Gregory's McFarland House (ID) 264
Historic Virginian Hotel, The (WY) 286
Inn at Brandywine Falls, The (OH) 178
Inn at Ormsby Hill, The (VT) 44
Inn at Thorn Hill, The (NH) 34
Inn on Winter's Hill, The (ME) 18
Izaak Walton Inn (MT) 270
John Hancock Inn, The (NH) 32
Kimberly Country Estate (MI) 162
La Corsette Maison Inn (IA) 156
Lake Placid Lodge (NY) 74
Lovelander Bed & Breakfast Inn, The (CO) . . 258
Meadow Creek Bed & Breakfast Inn (CO) . . . 260
Meadows Inn (AZ) 198
Mt. Ashland Inn (OR) 322
Notchland Inn, The (NH) 30
Paz de Nogal (NM) 212
Pinecrest Bed & Breakfast Inn (UT) 278
Pine Garth Inn (MI) 166
Pine Ridge Inn (MI) 160
Queen Anne Inn (CO) 254
Rabbit Hill Inn (VT) 42
Red Castle Inn, The (CA) 312
River Song Inn (CO) 256
Rose Bed and Breakfast (WI) 180
Rose Inn (NY) 72
Rosemont Inn, The (MI) 158
Rosewood Inn (MN) 168
Run of the River (WA) 330
Sanders-Helena's Bed & Breakfast, The (MT) 272
Sardy House (CO) 244
St. Croix River Inn (WI) 188
Thorwood Inn (MN) 170
Twin Farms (VT) 38
Victorian Treasure Bed and Breakfast 186
Voss Inn, The (MT) 266
Washington School Inn, The (UT) 276
Wheatleigh (MA) 26
White Lace Inn (WI) 190
Wildflower Inn, The (WY) 284

Inns with, or with Access to, Golf or Tennis Facilities

Adams Edgeworth Inn (TN) 140
Agate Cove Inn (CA) 310
Antrim 1844 (MD) 60
Applewood, An Estate Inn (CA) 304
Blackwell House Bed & Breakfast (ID) 262
Canoe Bay (WI) 182
Castle Marne (CO) 250
Chalet Suzanne (FL) 110
Checkerberry Inn, The (IN) 150
Cheyenne Cañon Inn (CO) 246
Clifton: The Country Inn (VA) 86
Crested Butte Club (CO) 248
Davy Jackson Inn (WY) 282
Glen-Ella Springs (GA) 112
Grand Hotel (MI) 164
Gregory's McFarland House (ID) 264
Harbor House (CA) 298
Inn at the Citadel (AZ) 200
Inn at Ormsby Hill (The (VT) 44
Inn on Winter's Hill, The (ME) 18
Kimberly Country Estate (MI) 162
La Corsette Maison Inn (IA) 156
Lake Placid Lodge (NY) 74
Lovelander Bed & Breakfast Inn (CO) 258
Lumber Baron Inn, The (CO) 252
Madrona Manor (CA) 306
Mayflower Inn, The (CT) 12
Meadow Creek Bed & Breakfast Inn (CO) . . . 260
Merry Sherwood Plantation (MD) 56
Morgan-Samuels B&B Inn (NY) 66
Old Chatham Sheepherding Company Inn (NY) 76
Old Drovers Inn (NY) 68
Paz de Nogal (NM) 212
Pinecrest Bed & Breakfast (UT) 278
Prospect Hill (VA) 92
Queen Anne Bed & Breakfast Inn (CO) 254
River Song Inn (CO) 256
Sardy House (CO) 244
Terry Ranch (AZ) 206
Timberhill Ranch (CA) 320
Turtleback Farm (WA) 334
Tu Tú Tun Lodge (OR) 324
Twin Farms (VT) 38
Villa Royale (CA) 316
Washington School Inn, The (UT) 276
Wheatleigh (MA) 26
White Lace Inn (WI) 190
Wildflower Inn, The (WY) 284
Windsong (NC) 134

Inns with a Sauna, Whirlpool, or Hot Tub

American Club (WI) 184
Antrim 1844 (MD) 60
Casa Europa (NM) 216
Castle Marne (CO 250
Cheyenne Cañon Inn (CO) 246
Crested Butte Club Victorian Hotel & Spa (CO) 248
Davy Jackson Inn (WY) 282
Glasbern (PA) 84
Grand Hotel (MI) 164

Heartstone Inn and Cottages (AR) 104
Hickory Nut Gap Inn (NC) 130
Hillbrook Inn (WV) 94
Hotel St. Germain (TX) 220
Inn above Onion Creek (TX) 238
Inn at the Citadel (NM) 200
Inn at Montchanin Village, The (DE) 52
Inn at Twin Linden, The (PA) 82
Lakehouse Inn (NY) 78
Lake Placid Lodge (NY) 74
Las Campañas de Taos (NM) 208
Lovelander Bed & Breakfast Inn, The (CO) .. 258
Lumber Baron Inn (CO) 252
Mainstay, The (NJ) 62
Meadow Creek Bed & Breakfast (CO) 260
Morgan-Samuels B&B Inn (NY) 66
Mulberry Manor (TX) 234
Oak Tree Inn (AR) 106
Oaks Victorian Inn, The (VA) 88
Old Chatham Sheepherding Company Inn (NY) 76
Page House Inn, The (VA) 90
Paz de Nogal (NM) 212
Pinecrest Bed & BReakfast (UT) 278
Prospect Hill (VA) 92
Rainsford Inn (NY) 280
River Song Inn (CO) 256
Rose Inn (NY) 72
Rosemont Inn, The (MI) 158
Sardy House (CO) 244
Suncathcer (AZ) 204
Sunset Heights (TX) 222
Von-Bryan Inn (TN) 142
Washington School Inn (UT) 276
Wildflower Inn, The (WY) 284
Woolverton Inn, The (NJ) 64

Inns with a Full-Service Dining Room or Dinners Available by Special Arrangement

American Club, The (WI) 184
Antrim 1844 (MD) 60
Applewood, An Estate Inn (CA) 304
Bird & Bottle Inn, The (NY) **10**
Casa de Patron (NM) 210
Casa Madrona (CA) 318
Castle Marne (CO) 250
Clifton: The Country Inn (VA) 86
Edenwild Inn (WA) 332
Estate by the Elderberries (CA) 314
Evergreen Inn and 1109 South Main Restaurant (SC) 136
Glasbern (PA) 84
Glendorn (PA) 80
Gold Hill Hotel (NV) 274
Grand Hotel (MI) 164
Harbor House (CA) 298
Hillbrook Inn (WV) 94
Historic Virginian Hotel, The (WY) 286
Hotel Carter (CA) 300
Imperial Hotel (CA) 292
Inn above Onion Creek (TX) 238
Inn at Buckeystown, The (MD) 58
Inn at the Citadel (AZ) 200
Inn at Chagrin Falls (OH) 176
Inn at Montchanin Village, The (DE) 52
Izaak Walton Inn (MT) 270
Lake Placid Lodge (NY) 74
Las Campañas de Taos (NM) 208
Lovelander Bed & Breakfast Inn, The (CO) .. 258
Madrona Manor (CA) 306
Malaga Inn (AL) 102

Meadow Creek Bed & Breakfast Inn (CO) 260
Meadows Inn (AZ) 198
Old Chatham Sheepherding Company Inn (NY) 76
Old Drovers Inn (NY) 68
Paz de Nogal (NM) 212
Prospect Hill (VA) 92
Red Castle Inn (CA) 312
River Song Inn (CO) 256
Rose Inn (NY) 72
Sardy House (CO) 244
Timberville Ranch (CA) 320
Tu Tú Tun Lodge (OR) 324
Ventana (CA) 294
Villa Royale (CA) 316

Inns with Bicycles, Canoes, or Other Sports Equipment

American Club, The (WI) 184
Antrim 1844 (MD) 60
Canoe Bay (WI) 182
Father Ryan House Bed and Breakfast Inn (MS) 126
Glendorn (PA) 80
Grand Hotel (MI) 164
Langdon House (NC) 132
Lakehouse Inn (NY) 78
Lake PLacid Lodge (NY) 74
Little St. Simons Island (GA) 116
Suncatcher (AZ) 204

Inns Offering Travelers' Club Benefits

Adobe & Pines Inn (NM) 214
Applewood, An Estate Inn (CA) 304
Barrow House (LA) 124
Bird and Bottle Inn, The (NY) 10
Bisbee Grand Hotel (AZ) 196
Blue Lantern Inn (CA) 296
Canoe Bay (WI) 182
Casa de Patron (NM) 210
Casa Europa (NM) 216
Casa Madrona Hotel (CA) 318
Castle Marne (CO) 250
Checkerberry Inn 150
Cheyenne Cañon Inn (CO) 246
Copper Beech Inn (CT) 6
Davy Jackson Inn (WY) 282
Heartstone Inn and Cottages (AR) 104
Hillbrook Inn (WV) 94
Inn at Chester, The (CT) 4
Lilac Inn, The (VT) 40
Little St. Simons Island (GA) 116
Lumber Baron Inn, The (CO) 252
Madrona Manor (CA) 306
Mainstay, The (NJ) 62
Meadows Inn, The (AZ) 198
Oak Tree Inn (AR) 106
Orchard Hill Country Inn (CA) 308
Paz de Nogal (NM) 212
Pinecrest Bed & Breakfast Inn (UT) 278
Pine Garth Inn (MI) 166
Rose Inn (NY) 72
Saddle Rock Ranch (AZ) 202
1735 House, The (FL) 108
Squiers Manor 154
Sunset Heights Inn (TX) 222
Victorian Treasure Bed and Breakfast (WI) .. 186
Village Country Inn, The (VT) 46
Von Bryan Inn (TN) 142
Voss Inn, The (MT) 266
White Lace Inn (WI) 190
Windsong (NC) 134
Woolverton Inn, The (NJ) 64
Yankee Clipper Inn (MA) 28